Scalable Data Streaming with Amazon Kinesis

Design and secure highly available, cost-effective
data streaming applications with Amazon Kinesis

Tarik Makota

Brian Maguire

Danny Gagne

Rajeev Chakrabarti

BIRMINGHAM—MUMBAI

Scalable Data Streaming with Amazon Kinesis

Copyright © 2021 Packt Publishing

Group Product Manager: Kunal Parikh

Publishing Product Manager: Devika Battike

Senior Editor: Mohammed Yusuf Imaratwale

Content Development Editors: Sean Lobo and Tazeen Shaikh

Technical Editor: Devanshi Deepak Ayare

Copy Editor: Safis Editing

Project Coordinator: Aparna Ravikumar Nair

Proofreader: Safis Editing

Indexer: Tejal Daruwale Soni

Production Designer: Shankar Kalbhor

First published: March 2021

Production reference: 1300321

Published by Packt Publishing Ltd.
Livery Place
35 Livery Street
Birmingham
B3 2PB, UK.

ISBN 978-1-80056-540-1

www.packt.com

Contributors

About the authors

Tarik Makota hails from a small town in Bosnia. He is a principal solutions architect with AWS, a builder, a writer, and the self-proclaimed best fly fisherman at AWS. Never a perfect student, he managed to earn an MSc in software development and management from RIT. When he is not "doing the cloud" or writing, Tarik spends most of his time fly fishing to pursue slippery trout. He feeds his addiction by spending summers in Montana. Tarik lives in New Jersey with his family, Mersiha, Hana, and two exceptionally perfect dogs.

Brian Maguire is a solutions architect at AWS, where he is focused on helping customers build solutions in the cloud. He is a technologist, writer, teacher, and student who loves learning. Brian lives in New Hope, Pennsylvania, with his family, Lorna, Ciara, Chris, and several cats.

Danny Gagne is a solutions architect at AWS. He has extensive experience in the design and implementation of large-scale, high-performance analysis systems. He lives in New York City.

Rajeev Chakrabarti is a principal developer advocate with the Amazon Kinesis and the Amazon MSK team. He has worked for many years in the big data and data streaming space. Before joining the Amazon Kinesis team, he was a streaming specialist solutions architect helping customers build streaming pipelines. He lives in New Jersey with his family, Shaifalee and Anushka.

About the reviewers

Ritesh Gupta works as a software development manager with AWS, leading the control plane and data plane teams on the Kinesis Data Streams service. He has over 20 years of experience in leading and delivering geographically distributed web-scale applications and highly available distributed systems supporting millions of transactions per second; he has 10 years of experience in managing engineers and managers. Prior to Amazon, he worked at Microsoft, EA Games, Dell, and a few successful start-ups. His technical expertise cuts across building web-scale applications, enterprise software, and big data. I thank my wife, Jyothi, and daughter, Udita, for putting up with the late-night learning sessions that have allowed me to be where I am.

Randy Ridgley is an experienced technology generalist working with organizations in the media and entertainment, casino gaming, and public sector fields that are looking to adopt cloud technologies. He started his journey into software development at a young age, building BASIC programs on the Commodore 64. In his professional career, he started by building Windows applications, eventually graduating to Linux with multiple programming languages. Currently, you can find Randy spending most of his time building end-to-end real-time streaming solutions on AWS using serverless technologies and IoT.

Table of Contents

2
Messaging and Data Streaming in AWS

3
The SmartCity Bike-Sharing Service

Section 2: Deep Dive into Kinesis

4
Kinesis Data Streams

5
Kinesis Firehose

Section 3: Integrations

8

Kinesis Integrations

Other Books You May Enjoy

Index

Preface

Amazon Kinesis is a collection of secure, serverless, durable, and highly available purpose-built data streaming services. These data streaming services provide APIs and client SDKs to enable you to produce and consume data at scale.

Scalable Data Streaming with Amazon Kinesis begins with a quick overview of the core concepts of data streams along with the essentials of the AWS Kinesis landscape. You'll then explore the requirements of the use cases shown throughout the book to help you get started, and cover the key pain points encountered in the data stream life cycle. As you advance, you'll get to grips with the architectural components of Kinesis, understand how they are configured to build data pipelines, and delve into the applications that connect to them for consumption and processing. You'll also build a Kinesis data pipeline from scratch and learn how to implement and apply practical solutions. Moving on, you'll learn how to configure Kinesis on a cloud platform. Finally, you'll learn how other AWS services can be integrated into Kinesis. These services include Redshift, Dynamo Database, AWS S3, Elasticsearch, and third-party applications such as Splunk.

By the end of this AWS book, you'll be able to build and deploy your own Kinesis data pipelines with **Kinesis Data Streams (KDS)**, **Kinesis Firehose (KFH)**, **Kinesis Video Streams (KVS)**, and **Kinesis Data Analytics (KDA)**.

Who this book is for

This book is for solutions architects, developers, system administrators, data engineers, and data scientists looking to evaluate and choose the most performant, secure, scalable, and cost-effective data streaming technology to overcome their data ingestion and processing challenges on AWS. Prior knowledge of cloud architectures on AWS, data streaming technologies, and architectures is expected.

What this book covers

Chapter 1, What Are Data Streams?, covers core streaming concepts so that you will have a detailed understanding of their application in distributed systems.

Chapter 2, Messaging and Data Streaming in AWS, takes a brief look at the ecosystem of AWS services in the messaging space. After reading this chapter, you will have a good understanding of the various services, be able to differentiate them, and understand the strengths of each service.

Chapter 3, The SmartCity Bike-Sharing Service, reviews the existing bike-sharing application and how the city plans to modernize it. This chapter will provide the background information for the examples used throughout the book.

Chapter 4, Kinesis Data Streams, teaches concepts and capabilities, common deployment patterns, monitoring and scaling, and how to secure KDS. We will step through a data streaming solution that will ingest, process, and feed data from multiple SmartCity data systems.

Chapter 5, Kinesis Firehose, teaches the concepts, common deployment patterns, monitoring and scaling, and security in KFH.

Chapter 6, Kinesis Data Analytics, covers the concepts and capabilities, approaches for common deployment patterns, monitoring and scaling, and security in KDA. You will learn how real-time streaming data can be queried like a database with SQL or code.

Chapter 7, Amazon Kinesis Video Streams, explores the concepts, monitoring and scaling, security, and deployment patterns for real-time communication and data ingestion. We will step through a solution that will provide real-time access to a video stream and ingest video data for the SmartCity data system.

Chapter 8, Kinesis Integrations, reviews how to integrate Kinesis with several Amazon services, such as Amazon Redshift, Amazon DynamoDB, AWS Glue, Amazon Aurora, Amazon Athena, and other third-party services such as Splunk. We will integrate a wide variety of services to create a serverless data lake.

To get the most out of this book

All of the examples in the chapters in this book are run using an AWS account to access services such as Amazon Kinesis, DynamoDB, and Amazon S3. Readers will need a Windows, Mac, or Linux computer with an internet connection. Many of the examples in the book use a command-line terminal such as PuTTY, macOS Terminal, GNOME Terminal, or iTerm2 to run commands and change configuration. The examples written in Python are written for the Python 3 interpreter and may not work with Python 2. For the examples written for the Java platform, readers are encouraged to use Java version 11 and AWS Java SDK version 1.11. We make extensive use of the AWS CLI v2 and will also use Docker for some examples. In addition to software, a webcam or IP camera and Android device will be needed to fully execute some of the examples.

If you are using the digital version of this book, we advise you to type the code yourself or access the code via the GitHub repository (link available in the next section). Doing so will help you avoid any potential errors related to the copying and pasting of code.

Download the example code files

You can download the example code files for this book from GitHub at `https://github.com/PacktPublishing/Streaming-Data-Solutions-with-Amazon-Kinesis`. In case there's an update to the code, it will be updated on the existing GitHub repository.

We also have other code bundles from our rich catalog of books and videos available at `https://github.com/PacktPublishing/`. Check them out!

Download the color images

We also provide a PDF file that has color images of the screenshots/diagrams used in this book. You can download it here: `https://static.packt-cdn.com/downloads/9781800565401_ColorImages.pdf`.

Conventions used

There are a number of text conventions used throughout this book.

Code in text: Indicates code words in text, database table names, folder names, filenames, file extensions, pathnames, dummy URLs, user input, and Twitter handles. Here is an example: "In this command, we'll send the `test2.mkv` file we downloaded to the KVS stream."

A block of code is set as follows:

```
aws glue create-database --database-input
"{\"Name\":\"smartcitybikes\"}"
aws glue create-table --database-name smartcitybikes --table-
input file://SmartCityGlueTable.json
```

When we wish to draw your attention to a particular part of a code block, the relevant lines or items are set in bold:

```
mediaSource.start();
```

Any command-line input or output is written as follows:

```
aws rekognition start-stream-processor --name kvsprocessor
```

Bold: Indicates a new term, an important word, or words that you see onscreen. For example, words in menus or dialog boxes appear in the text like this. Here is an example: "Once you have entered the appropriate information, all that's left is to click **Create signaling channel**."

> **Tips or important notes**
> Appear like this.

Get in touch

Feedback from our readers is always welcome.

General feedback: If you have questions about any aspect of this book, mention the book title in the subject of your message and email us at customercare@packtpub.com.

Errata: Although we have taken every care to ensure the accuracy of our content, mistakes do happen. If you have found a mistake in this book, we would be grateful if you would report this to us. Please visit www.packtpub.com/support/errata, selecting your book, clicking on the Errata Submission Form link, and entering the details.

Piracy: If you come across any illegal copies of our works in any form on the Internet, we would be grateful if you would provide us with the location address or website name. Please contact us at copyright@packt.com with a link to the material.

If you are interested in becoming an author: If there is a topic that you have expertise in and you are interested in either writing or contributing to a book, please visit authors.packtpub.com.

Reviews

Please leave a review. Once you have read and used this book, why not leave a review on the site that you purchased it from? Potential readers can then see and use your unbiased opinion to make purchase decisions, we at Packt can understand what you think about our products, and our authors can see your feedback on their book. Thank you!

For more information about Packt, please visit packt.com.

Section 1: Introduction to Data Streaming and Amazon Kinesis

In this section, you will be introduced to the concept of data streams and how they are used to create scalable data solutions.

This section comprises the following chapters:

1
What Are Data Streams?

A data stream is a system where data continuously flows from multiple sources, just like water flows through a stream. The data is often produced and collected simultaneously in a continuous flow of many small files or records. Data streams are utilized by a wide range of business, medical, government, social media, and mobile applications. These applications include financial applications for the stock market and e-commerce ordering systems that collect orders and cover fulfillment of delivery.

In the entertainment space, live data is produced by sensing devices embedded in player equipment, video game players generate large amounts of data at a massive scale, and there are new social media posts thousands of times per second. Governments also leverage streaming data and geospatial services to monitor land, wildlife, and other activities.

Data volume and velocity are increasing at faster rates, creating new challenges in data processing and analytics. This book will detail these challenges and demonstrate how Amazon Kinesis can be used to address them. We will begin by discussing key concepts related to messaging in a technology-agnostic form to provide a solid foundation for building your Kinesis knowledge.

Incorporating data streams into your application architecture will allow you to deliver high-performance solutions that are secure, scalable, and fast. In this chapter, we will cover core streaming concepts so that you will have a detailed understanding of their application to distributed systems. You will learn what a data stream is, how to leverage data streams to scale, and examine a number of high-level use cases.

This chapter covers the following topics:

- Introducing data streams
- Challenges associated with distributed systems
- Overview of messaging concepts
- Examples of data streaming

Introducing data streams

Data streams are a way of storing a sequence of messages. They enable us to design systems where we think about state as a series of events instead of only entities and values, or rows and columns in a database. This shift in mindset and technology enables real-time analytics to extract the value from data by acting on it before it is stale. They also enable organizations to design and develop resilient software based on microservice architectures by helping them to decouple systems. We will begin with an overview of streaming data sources, why real-time data analysis is valuable, and how they can be used architecturally to decouple systems. We will then review the core challenges associated with distributed systems, and conclude with an overview of key messaging concepts and some high-level examples. Messages can contain a wide variety of information and come from different sources, so let's look at the primary sources and data formats.

Sources of data

The proliferation of data steadily increases from sources such as social media, IoT devices, web clickstreams, application logs, and video cameras. This data poses challenges to most systems, since it is typically **high-velocity**, **intermittent**, and **bursty**, making it difficult to adequately provision and design downstream systems. Payloads are generally small, except when containing audio or video data, and come in a variety of formats.

In this book, we will be focusing on three data formats. These formats include the following:

- **JavaScript Object Notation (JSON)**
- **Log files**
- **Time-encoded binary files** such as video

JSON streams

JSON has become the dominant format for message serialization over the past 10 years. It is a lightweight data interchange format that is easy for humans to read and write and is based on the JavaScript object syntax. It has two data structures – **hash tables** and **lists**. A **hash table** consists of key-value pairs, {"key":"value"}, where the keys must be unique. A list is a set of values in a specific order, ["value 1", "value 2"]. The following code sample shows a sample IoT JSON message:

```
{
    "deviceid" : "device001",
    "eventTime": -192778200,
    "temp" : 68.4,
    "humidity" : 77.3,
    "coords" : {
        "latitude" : 32.779039,
        "longitude" : -96.808660
    }
}
```

Log file streams

Log files come in a variety of formats. Common ones include **Apache Commons Logging**, **Apache Combined Log**, **Apache Error Log**, and **RFC3164 Syslog**. They are plain text, and usually each line, delineated by a newline ('\n') character, is a separate log entry. In the following sample log, we see an HTTP GET request where the IP address is 10.13.37.01, the datetime of the request, the HTTP verb, the URL fragment, the HTTP version, the response code, and the size of the result.

The sample log line in Apache Commons Logging format is as follows:

```
10.13.37.01 - - [03/Sep/2017:12:00:01 +0830] "GET /mailman/
listinfo/test HTTP/1.1" 200 2457
```

Time-encoded binary streams

Time-encoded binary streams consist of a time series of records where each record is related to the adjacent records (prior and subsequent records). These can be used for a wide variety of sensor data, from audio streams and RADAR signals to video streams. Throughout this book, the primary focus will be video streams and their applications.

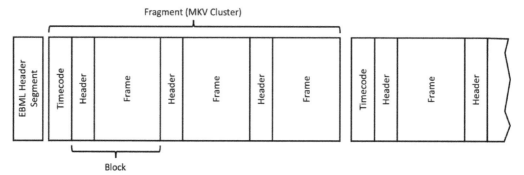

Figure 1.1 – Time-encoded video data

As shown in *Figure 1.1*, video streams are composed of fragments, where each fragment is a self-contained sequence of media frames. There are no dependencies between fragments. We will discuss video streams in more detail in *Chapter 7, Kinesis Video Streams*. Now that we've covered the types of data that we'll be processing, let's take a step back to understand the value of real-time data in analytics.

The value of real-time data in analytics

Analysis is done to support decision making by individuals, organizations, or computer programs. Traditionally, data analysis has been done on batches of data, usually in long-running jobs that occur overnight and that happen periodically at predetermined times: nightly, weekly, quarterly, and so on. This not only limits the scope of actions available to decisions makers, but it is also only providing them with a representation of the past environment. Information is now available seconds after it is produced, so we need to design systems that provide decision makers with the freshest data available to make timely decisions.

The **OODA – Observe, Orient, Decide, Act** – loop is a decision-making, conceptual framework that describes how decisions are made when reacting to an event. By breaking it down into these four components, we can optimize each to reduce the overall cycle time. The key idea is that if we make better decisions quicker than our opponent, we can outmaneuver them and win. By moving from batch to real-time analytics, we are reducing the observed portion of this cycle.

> **John Boyd**
>
> John Boyd was a USAF colonel and military strategist. He developed the OODA loop to better understand pilot combat operations. It has since been expanded and is used at a more strategic level by the military, sports teams, and businesses.

By reducing the OODA loop cycle time, new actions become available. They can be taken while events are unfolding and not merely responding to them after the event has occurred. These time-critical decisions can range from responding to security log anomalies to providing customer recommendations based on a user's recently viewed items. These actions are extremely valuable because they allow us to quickly respond to changing events and are only possible because we can process the data in near real time. The following diagram, inspired by the Perishable Insights report by Mike Gualtieri, shows how time to action correlates to the data's perishability. Each insight has a corresponding action that can only be taken if the data is processed quickly enough – before the insight perishes:

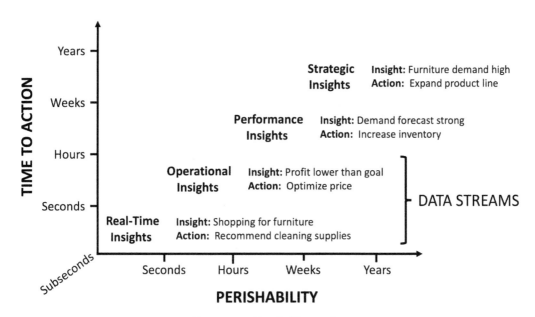

Figure 1.2 – Perishable insights

The preceding diagram uses shopping as an example to highlight the key distinction between time-critical and historical analysis. Combining historical data and recent data is extremely valuable since it allows deeper insights and can be used to detect patterns and anomalies. The goal of stream analysis is to reduce the amount of time between an event occurring and the appropriate response.

Decoupling systems

A distributed system is composed of multiple networked servers that work together by sending messages between each other. They allow applications to be built that require more compute, storage, or resiliency than is available on a single instance. Some common distributed systems are the World Wide Web, distributed databases, and scientific computing clusters. Distributed systems are often fractal. For example, the three-tier web application, perhaps the most common architecture you will see in the wild, is often constructed of distributed databases, log analysis systems, and payment providers.

The need for distributed systems has increased dramatically over the past 10 years. There are three primary drivers for this: data scale, computational requirements, and organization design and coordination. At first, these systems were brittle and challenging to manage, but over time, certain key patterns emerged that have enabled them to scale by reducing complexity.

The first key in managing complexity was adopting standardized interfaces and common data formats and encodings. This allowed the development of microservice-based architectures where different teams could manage functionality and provide it as a service to the rest of the organization. This reduced the amount of coordination among teams and allowed them to iterate and release at their own appropriate speed, thereby acknowledging and leveraging Conway's Law.

> Conway's Law
>
> In 1967, Melvin Conway stated: "Any organization that designs a system (defined broadly) will produce a design whose structure is a copy of the organization's communication structure." This is based on the observation that people need to communicate in order to design and develop systems. When this is applied to microservices, it allows the groups to own their services directly and explicitly model the organization/communication/software architecture correspondence.

The second was to separate the program into different fault domains by moving to a loosely coupled architecture. This is often achieved by having one system send another system a message. However, messages being sent from one fault domain to another made it difficult to reason and understand the complex failure modes of these systems. By introducing asynchronous message brokers, we can define clear boundaries between different fault domains, making it possible to reason about them. The message queue acts as an invariant in the system. It provides a clean interface where it can send messages and retrieve them. If another system is unavailable, the message broker will be able to cache the messages, called a backlog, and that system is responsible for handling them when it resumes service.

There are still many challenges to the design, deployment, and orchestration of these decoupled systems. However, the introduction of modern highly available message brokers has been key in reducing their complexity.

Now that we've seen how asynchronous messaging can separate fault domains, let's learn how they fit into distributed systems.

Challenges associated with distributed systems

The fundamental challenge of distributed systems is intra-system communication. When possible, a messaging system can provide a core decoupling function, allowing intermittent and transient failures not to cascade or cross fault boundaries. These systems must be highly available, scalable, and durable. The following core concepts are essential to understand and reason about these systems: transactions per second, scaling, latency, and high availability. They allow us to understand the system's key dynamics so that resources can be provisioned to support the workload.

Transactions per second

The most important metric for all messaging systems is **Transactions Per Second** (TPS). This metric is not as simple as it may seem initially, as the maximum TPS is constrained by either a discrete number of transactions or the maximum size of data that can be processed. This max TPS is called **capacity**. In general, messaging systems have different capacity for the inbound side and the outbound side, with the outbound side normally having a greater capacity to support multiple consumers and prevent large message backlogs.

Backpressure refers to a system state in which the producer TPS is higher than the consumer TPS. The input is coming in faster than it can be processed. There are multiple strategies for handling backpressure. The easiest is to reduce the number of messages being sent, for example, having a temperature sensor send data once a minute instead of once a second. The second is to scale the compute for the consumers to increase the consumer TPS. If the flow of messages is intermittent or bursty, a buffer can temporarily hold the messages and allow the consumers to catch up. Buffers are often used in conjunction with scaling to store messages while compute is scaled up. The last method is to drop messages. Depending on the message type, this can be unacceptable – you don't want to drop customer orders – but, in the case of sensor data, **sampling**, can be used to process a fixed percentage of data, for example, 5% of data.

Scaling

Messaging systems need to present an access point that hides the complexity of the internal system. In general, messaging systems consist of multiple independent channels and shards. A shard is an independent unit of capacity. This internal complexity cannot be completely hidden from users since the way data is distributed to the different shards needs to be understood by both senders and receivers. Scaling is used to increase the capacity of the messaging system. One way to think about scaling is to consider cables supporting a bridge. If it has 5 strands, it can support 50 tons, and with 50 strands it can support 500 tons. Thus, one unit of scaling for bridges would be the number of cable strands.

As a system scales, its ability to maintain the global order of records becomes limited. In general, order will only be maintained at a sub-global group level. This is an important design consideration that must be covered when designing real-time solutions. If global order is needed, there are fundamental limits on the system's maximum throughput, and if the throughput required is higher, the system will have to be rearchitected.

Etymology of the shard

In 1997, the game Ultima Online was released. In order to reduce latency and handle scale, there were multiple servers around the world that a player could log in to. Each server functioned independently and existed as its own universe in a multi-verse. This was explained in-game by the wizard Mondain capturing the world of Sosaria in the Gem of Immortality. This gem was then shattered by the Avatar into multiple shards. The player then selected which shard they wanted to play in. The term *shard*, or *sharding*, is another way to talk about the horizontal partitioning of data, that is, spreading data across multiple servers.

Latency

Latency is the amount of time between a cause and effect in a system. In the context of a messaging system, there are multiple measures of latency that are important in understanding its behavior. In general, it is the time between when a message enters the system and when the message leaves the system. For example, it can be thought of as the time between pressing the brakes in a car and the vehicle stopping. Some workloads, for example, real-time audio/video communication, are especially latency-sensitive and care must be taken to minimize this across all aspects of the system.

The two primary measures of latency in a messaging system are **propagation delay** and **age of message**.

The propagation delay is the amount of time from when a message is written to the message broker to when it is read by the consumer application. In most cases, propagation delay is a reflection of how often producers or consumers are polling the message broker. Network effects on the producer's connection to the message system and the acknowledgment of putting a message are known as **producer latency**, and correspondingly, the time it takes for a request to complete on the consumer side is **consumer latency**.

The last measure of latency that is extremely important is understanding how long a message has been in the system before it is retrieved, that is, the **age of the message**. If the average age of messages is increasing, that indicates a backlog and means that messages are being added faster than they are being retrieved.

Fault tolerance/high availability

Messaging systems are foundational to modern distributed systems and need to be designed in such a way to be highly available.

> *"Everything fails all the time."*
>
> – *Werner Vogel, Amazon CTO*

The preceding quote hints at the difficulty of building highly available systems. To avoid single points of failure, **redundancy** is required, and messages, once acknowledged, need to be **durably** stored. Even though messaging systems present a simple interface, to achieve this level of performance, they are actually comprised of many systems configured as a cluster.

Now that we have the vocabulary to talk about inter-system communication, let's introduce the components of messaging systems.

Overview of messaging concepts

In this section, we will review the concept of message brokers in a high-level, implementation-agnostic manner. First, we will go over the core components of all messaging systems and then we will review some key terminology and concepts related to their use.

Overview of core messaging components

There are four components in all messaging systems: **producers**, **consumers**, **streams**, and **messages**. The following diagram shows a logical breakdown of producers sending messages to a stream, the stream buffering them, and consumers receiving them:

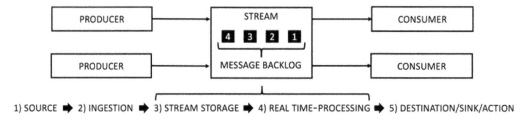

Figure 1.3 – High-level view of messaging

Despite this design's relative simplicity, there is a substantial amount of configuration and optimization that is possible. Now, let's dive a little deeper into each component.

Streams

The stream is the system that stores the messages or records sent by the producers and retrieved by the consumers. They can be ordered in a **First In First Out** (**FIFO**) model. Messages in the stream that have been received, but not yet retrieved, are referred to as a **backlog**.

The **retention period** is the length of time that the records are accessible after they are added to the stream. This is the maximum size the backlog can be, and it is also the maximum time a new, slow, or intermittent consumer can access the records.

Messages (records)

A message consists of a payload and header information. The header information consists of information set by the producer, and it includes a unique identifier assigned by the message broker when it is inserted into the stream. In general, messages are relatively small, in the order of kilobytes, and messaging systems generally have a maximum payload size.

Producers

The producer is an application that is the source of data that will go into the message or record. It connects to the message broker and puts the data into the stream. There can often be multiple producers sending data to the same message broker.

Consumers

The consumer is an application that receives the messages that are sent by the producer. It connects to the message broker and retrieves the data from the stream. The responsibility for keeping track of the last read message, so that the consumer can retrieve the next message, can be handled either by the message broker (RabbitMQ or SQS) or by the consumer (Kinesis or Kafka). There can be multiple consumers for a message broker.

Real-time analytics

When thinking about real-time analytics, it can be useful to expand it from the producer, stream, consumer model to a five-stage model (*Figure 1.3*): 1) source of data; 2) data ingestion mechanisms; 3) stream storage; 4) real-time stream processing; and 5) destination, data sink, or action. This model helps us elevate our thinking from the structural communication level to the data processing level. For instance, filtering can be applied at every stage to reduce compute downstream.

The source of data refers to where the data is coming from. For example, it could be mobile devices, web clickstreams, log analytics, IoT devices, or smart devices. Once you have the source, the data needs to be ingested into the stream. This requires a solution that can capture data coming from hundreds of thousands of devices, in a scalable and reliable manner, into a stream for analysis. You then need a platform that can reliably and durably store the data while simultaneously reading from any point in the stream. This refers to the stream storage platform. The stored data is then processed by real-time applications to generate actionable insights, perform actions, and execute real-time **extract-transform-load** (**ETL**) operations that deliver the stream of data to an end destination, such as a data lake.

Next, let's see how systems can be designed in a resilient manner.

Messaging concepts

While relatively simple, the implementation of the four components can be nuanced. In all networked systems, failure is complicated. Every network call can have issues, and the systems need to be resilient to handle them. In the following sub-sections, we will review a few key concepts related to resilient systems and also a few advanced stream processing features.

Here are eight fallacies associated with distributed computing. In 1994, Peter Deutsch identified the fact that everyone who builds distributed systems initially gets into trouble by making the assumptions listed here:

- The network is reliable.

- Latency is zero.

- Bandwidth is infinite.

- The network is secure.

- The topology doesn't change.

- There is one administrator.

- The cost of transport is zero.

- The network is homogeneous (added by James Gosling in 1997).

> **Note**
>
> All systems should be designed with those fallacies in mind, and with special attention to the unreliability of the network. Systems that don't properly handle these issues will exhibit complicated and confusing behavior as well as error modes that are challenging to debug.

Timeouts

Timeouts allow for efficient allocation of resources and help prevent cascading failures. If an individual process has an error, it can fail to return a value and hang. In this case, the client may continue to wait indefinitely for a response. Timeouts help prevent server resource exhaustion by ending the connection after a maximum amount of time has passed. This allows the server to free up limited resources, for example, memory, connections, and ports, and use them to handle new requests. The client can **retry** the request again.

Retries

Many errors are ephemeral, and merely retrying the exact same request again will succeed. In order for retries to be safe, the system handling them must be **idempotent**, meaning that it is designed in such a way that the same input will cause the same side effects. At a more systemic level, to prevent a server from being inundated with retry requests, each client should implement back-off and jitter.

Back-off is the process of increasing the time between subsequent retries. Jitter is the process of adding a bit of random delay to retries. Together, these two mechanisms spread out message requests over time so that the server is able to handle the number of requests.

When a producer has to retry due to a timeout, it will send the request again. There is the possibility that a duplicate record could be created. If a record should only be processed once, it is important that the payload of the record has a unique ID that the final system can use to remove duplicates. When a consumer fails, it can fetch the same records again. Consumer retries tend to happen more often than producer retries. It is up to the final application to handle the message payload data properly and in an idempotent manner.

Backlogs

A backlog is the number of messages that the stream contains that have yet to be received by a consumer. Backlogs occur when the number of messages a producer sends into a stream is higher than the number of messages received by a consumer. This often happens when the system consuming the messages has an error and the messages keep being added to the stream. This can quickly go from a small backlog to a large backlog. Large backlogs increase the overall system latency by a large amount as the backlog must be processed before the recently arriving messages are processed. This typically results in a bimodal distribution of message latencies, where the latency is low when the system is working correctly and high when the system is having errors.

Large backlogs are a hidden risk that need to be considered when designing asynchronous applications because they can increase the recovery time following an outage – that is, instead of merely restarting the system and it being down for a brief period of time, the system has to work through the large backlog before it can function properly again.

Dead letter queues

Dead letter queues store messages that cannot be processed correctly by the message broker for some reason or another. It could be that it is an invalid message, it is too big, or, for some reason, it fails a certain number of retry attempts. It is important to periodically review dead letter queues because they represent errors in the system.

Replay

Replay is the ability to read, or replay, the same records in the same order multiple times. This means that a new consumer can be added and re-read messages that have already been consumed. Replay is limited to data in the stream. Data is **aged out** of the stream after it has existed for a specified period of time, for example, 1 hour, 1 day, or 7 days. This **retention period** affects the amount of storage required to support the stream.

Record processing

When processing records, there are multiple approaches depending on the type of data in the payload and the type of analysis required. In the simplest of systems, each record is processed one at a time, that is, **record by record**. A more complicated approach is to aggregate records by a **sliding time window**, where records are accessed by the consumer over a period of time, for instance, calculating the highest, lowest, and the average message value over the last 10 seconds.

Filtering

Filtering allows consumers to receive only the messages that they are interested in. This reduces the amount of data that is needed to be processed and transmitted, which helps the system scale. Messages can be filtered at multiple stages: source, ingestion, stream storage, stream processing, and in the consumer stage. In general, it is best to filter messages as early in the five-stage model as possible as it reduces compute and storage requirements in all subsequent stages. Filtering is determined by the message contents, the source, or the destination. For instance, the producer can send different types of messages to different streams.

Now that we've covered the core concepts, let's see them applied in some example use cases.

Examples of data streaming

Data streams are essential for supporting a wide variety of workloads. This section will go into detail on how data streams can be used for near real-time monitoring of applications through log aggregation, support bursty IoT workloads, be fast to insert recommendations into web applications, and enable machine learning on video. The following diagram shows the data flow of these workloads:

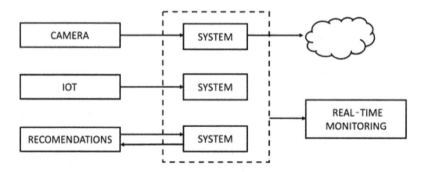

Figure 1.4 – Examples of data stream applications

While these workloads have different performance requirements and scale, the fundamental architecture is the same – producing and consuming messages. Now, let's look at an example of real-time monitoring.

Application log processing

Near real-time monitoring of applications and systems can be used to identify usage patterns, troubleshoot operation events, detect and monitor security incidents, and ensure compliance. Log events are generated on multiple systems and are pushed to a centralized system for analysis. Messaging systems enable this by decoupling the log processing and the analysis systems. In general, for log analysis, there are two different systems consuming the messages: one for near real-time analysis and one for larger historical batch analysis. The near real-time analysis system, often Elasticsearch, contains only fresh data as specified by a data retention policy, and might only hold an hour, a day, or a week's worth of information. The historical system is often an Apache Spark cluster processing data in a data lake (data stored in S3).

Log events are generated in real time and are pushed to the messaging system. The two consumers access the data and perform ETL operations on the data to convert it into the appropriate format for further analysis. For instance, an Apache Commons Logging format can be converted to JSON for insertion into Elasticsearch. The message broker simplifies the system by providing a clear boundary between the log collection and log analysis systems. Since it's designed in a highly available manner, it can cache events if the log analysis system goes down.

There are many sources of log events; two common ones are **CloudWatch** Logs and agents that can be installed on a machine, for example, Kinesis Agent. CloudWatch is an AWS service that collects logs, metrics, and events from AWS resources and user applications. The logs are sent to streams based on subscriptions and subscription filters that define patterns to determine which log events should be sent. The events are Base64-encoded and compressed with **gzip**. Agents monitor sets of files and stream events normally delineated by a new line (\n) character.

By bringing all the logs together in near real time, proactive measures can be taken. For example, imagine an attacker is trying to use an automated tool, for example, SQLMAP, to perform a SQL injection attack via an HTTP query string. A query string is a set of key-value pairs separated from the base URL by a question mark (?) character, and each key-value pair is separated by the ampersand (&) character. For example, in the following URL, there are two keys, key1 and key2, and their corresponding values, value1 and value2:

```
https://example.com/mypage?key1=value1&key2=value2
```

The first thing that will be detected is a lot of query strings that are different, originating from a single IP address. Once the IP address is identified, it can be blocked to prevent further attacks. The analysis system can be used to determine all requests made by the client and detect whether they were able to exploit any vulnerabilities.

Internet of Things

IoT devices present unique challenges as they are often only connected to the internet intermittently to save bandwidth and conserve energy. This intermittent connectivity, combined with a large number of devices, can lead to extremely bursty workloads. For instance, a fleet of IoT devices with temperature sensors might send data back every hour. The messaging system provides a buffer that allows downstream systems to be provisioned for the average velocity of data and not the peak loads.

Real-time recommendations

Clickstream events are generated at extremely high volume and velocity as users navigate and use web applications and mobile applications. Clickstream analysis can be used for A/B testing, understanding user engagement, detecting system issues, and in this example, recommendations.

Simple recommendations can be pre-computed based on historic usage patterns, for instance, people who watched this movie also liked these movies. However, this fails to capture the user's intent – that is, personalized recommendations depending on the user's behavior in the given session. This requires clickstream data to be captured in real time, analyzed, and recommendations made, all in the time it takes for a page to load. In other words, the system needs to work in milliseconds. These performance constraints require highly scalable messaging systems to achieve extremely low latency so that page load performance is not degraded.

Video streams

Video streams can be used for both real-time workloads (chat, peer to peer) or batch (surveillance, machine learning). In the batch case, multiple cameras can be streaming the video to the messaging system and machine learning can be applied to detect faces. These faces can then be identified and checked against a set of known individuals. Any face that doesn't match a known individual can trigger an alert and send the relevant portion of the video to the appropriate person. Messaging frameworks simplify the architecture by providing a highly scalable system to handle large volumes of data from multiple devices. Much like in the IoT case, they also provide a buffer to provide time for downstream resources to be provisioned in response to demand as new devices connect.

Summary

In this chapter, we discussed the need for streams, the types of data they can handle, the core concepts of messaging services, and some examples of how messaging can be applied to support challenging use cases, such as near real-time monitoring and video processing. You should now have a detailed understanding of distributed systems as a solution for scale, what a data stream is, and its properties.

In the next section, we will take what we've learned here and review the messaging services available on Amazon Web Services and introduce Kinesis.

Further reading

- *How Do Committees Invent?,* by Melvin E. Conway: http://www.melconway. com/Home/Committees_Paper.html

- *Certain to Win: The Strategy of John Boyd, Applied to Business,* by Chet Richards

- *Fallacies of Distributed Computing Explained,* by Arnon Rotem-Gal-Oz:

  http://citeseerx.ist.psu.edu/viewdoc/
  summary?doi=10.1.1.90.7285

2
Messaging and Data Streaming in AWS

AWS has an extensive array of services in the messaging space and is constantly adding more services and features to its repertoire. Some of these services are purpose-built and proprietary to Amazon, such as **Amazon SQS**, **Amazon SNS**, and the **Amazon Kinesis** umbrella of services. Several are open source projects being offered as managed services such as **Amazon MQ** and **Amazon MSK**.

In this chapter, we will take a brief look at the ecosystem of AWS services in the messaging space. After reading this chapter, you should have a good understanding of the various services, be able to differentiate between them, and understand the strengths of each service and how best to apply them to different architectures depending on the use case. The similarities and differences between each of these messaging services are also summarized in a table at the end of the chapter. The list of services covered in this chapter is as follows:

- Amazon **Kinesis Data Streams (KDS)**
- Amazon **Kinesis Data Firehose (KDF)**
- Amazon **Kinesis Data Analytics for SQL (KDA SQL)**
- Amazon **Kinesis Video Streams (KVS)**

- Amazon **Simple Queue Service (SQS)**

- Amazon **Simple Notification Service (SNS)**

- Amazon **MQ for Apache Active MQ**

- IoT Core

- Amazon EventBridge

- Amazon **Managed Streaming for Apache Kafka (MSK)**

Before we get started on the services, let's take a brief look at some AWS concepts that are common across services.

AWS services are API-driven, and all functionality is exposed via REST APIs. Amazon SDKs offered in multiple programming languages such as Java, Python, JavaScript, Node.js, and others simplify the use of the services by providing higher-level abstractions and a library consistent across languages that can handle many boilerplate tasks, such as credential management, retries, and data serialization. In addition to the API, the control plane functionality is also available through the AWS **command-line interface (CLI)** and the AWS console.

AWS service APIs use secure HTTP (HTTPS) to provide encryption in transit through TLS (`https://en.wikipedia.org/wiki/Transport_Layer_Security`). In addition, most services provide encryption at rest using a **customer master key (CMK)** from **AWS Key Management Service (KMS)** utilizing envelope encryption. Envelope encryption is a mechanism where an entity is encrypted using a plaintext data key and the data key, in turn, is encrypted using a master key.

AWS KMS

AWS KMS is a fully managed cryptographic key management service that provides highly available key storage, auditing, and management, allowing you to encrypt and decrypt your data stored across AWS services.

AWS **Identity and Access Management (IAM)** is used to provide authentication and authorization. Authentication for programmatic access (via AWS SDKs) is provided through a Signature Version 4 signing process using keys associated with IAM users, or by using temporary credentials by assuming roles.

Let's take a look at some of the streaming and messaging services in AWS, starting with the Kinesis umbrella of services.

Amazon Kinesis Data Streams (KDS)

Amazon KDS was launched in November 2013 and was the first service in the Amazon Kinesis umbrella of services. It is a fully managed, serverless platform for streaming data at any scale. It provides a highly durable, scalable, and elastic service for real-time data streaming that requires no provisioning of any infrastructure and enables users to get started with just a few clicks on the AWS console.

Amazon KDS falls into stage 3 of the 5 stages of enabling stream analytics described in *Chapter 1, What Are Data Streams?*. There are a number of core requirements of a stream storage platform. They include the following:

- **Data durability**: Data, once sent to and received by a stream storage system, needs to be durably stored; there should be no data loss.

- **High parallelism**: Provide high throughput and low latency in data retrieval or low overall propagation delay.

- **Read from any point in the stream**: The ability to rewind to different points in a stream for a defined retention period.

- **Support one-to-many read**: Support multiple consumers reading the same set of messages at the same time.

Amazon KDS embodies these core tenets of a stream storage platform.

There are thousands of organizations using **Amazon KDS** for myriad use cases. The scale ranges from only few kilobytes to gigabytes per second from thousands of data sources. In addition, within AWS, it is considered to be a tier-0 service since there are other services that are dependent on it. It is used as the backbone for services such as AWS metering, Amazon S3 events, and Amazon CloudWatch Logs. KDS is also used by other Amazon companies, such as Amazon.com for their online catalog and Amazon Go for video analytics.

Amazon KDS has APIs for both the control plane and the data plane. On the control plane, the APIs allow creating streams, deleting streams, describing streams, listing streams, setting up stream consumers, changing stream capacity and properties, enabling and disabling monitoring, and enabling and disabling encryption. On the data plane, the APIs allow inserting records (both one at a time and as batches) and getting records from streams. We will go through most of these capabilities in this book.

Figure 2.1 illustrates the shards in a data stream and the ecosystem of different types of producers and consumers available that work with Amazon KDS:

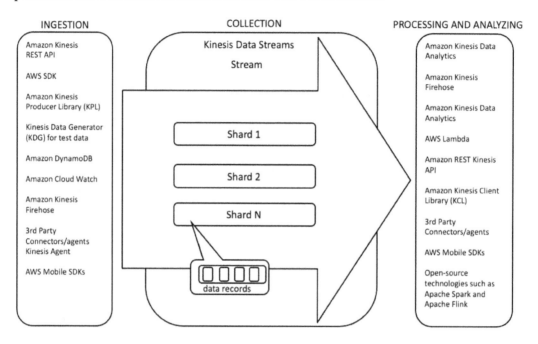

Figure 2.1 – KDS ecosystem of producers and consumers

A stream in Amazon KDS is composed of one or more shards. A shard is a unit of capacity and also a unit of parallelism. There are fixed capacity constraints for each shard and the number of shards in a stream defines the capacity and throughput for a stream both on the ingress side and the egress side. On the ingestion or ingress side, each shard can support a throughput of 1 MB per second or 1,000 records per second. On the egress side, for standard consumers (there are two supported types of consumers – standard, which utilizes the pull model, and **Enhanced Fan Out** (**EFO**), which utilizes the push model; the service pushes records to consumers), each shard supports 2 MiBs per sec (or double the ingress throughput) and five transactions per second (a transaction is a `GetRecords` API call to get records from a KDS stream). In addition, the maximum size of an individual record is 1 MB before base-64 encoding.

To calculate how many shards are needed for a stream, workload information around ingress and egress throughputs and the number of consumers is needed. There are calculators available from AWS and other third parties that make this task easier. Armed with information on the number of shards required for the workload, a new KDS stream can be created in seconds. Once created, applications can start sending and receiving records from the KDS stream immediately. There is no administration needed at all apart from monitoring the capacity usage of the shards and adding and removing shards as needed.

It is very easy to scale up the capacity of the stream by adding additional shards, as well as to scale down by removing shards, thus cost-effectively managing capacity by tracking the capacity requirements of the workload. Scale-up happens by splitting shards and scale-down by merging shards, and they can be performed online while the stream is actively receiving records and consumers are consuming records, with no downtime. Mechanisms exist to orchestrate the scaling automatically by tracking stream or shard metrics using a Lambda function.

For durability, once a record is received by Amazon KDS, it is durably stored across multiple Availability Zones, before sending a response back to the producer. The service provides a default retention period of 24 hours once a message is successfully received but it can be increased up to 8,760 hours, or 365, days at an additional cost. The service provides an SLA (`https://aws.amazon.com/kinesis/sla/`) of 99.9%.

Encryption, authentication, and authorization

Both the control plane and the data plane are integrated with AWS IAM and support authentication via AWS Signature Version 4 and identity-based IAM policies for authorization. At this time, resource-based IAM policies are not supported.

The service also offers encryption at rest by encrypting messages as soon as they're received, before writing to the storage layer and decrypted after reading from the storage layer and before returning it to the consumer. It uses a CMK from KMS, which can be either user-managed or service-managed.

Producing and consuming records

Amazon KDS provides a simple API for producing and consuming records that is wrapped in AWS SDKs offered in multiple programming languages, but there still exists considerable work in actually writing high-performance, scalable, highly available producers and consumers that provide an array of consumer and producer metrics for monitoring performance. In order to ease those tasks, Amazon KDS provides a producer library called the **Kinesis Producer Library** (**KPL**) and a consumer library called **Kinesis Client Library** (**KCL**), which are offered under the Apache 2.0 license and are open source. The KPL and KCL are both written in Java. The KPL has a C++ core with a Java wrapper. The KCL does provide support for other languages through a multi-lang daemon. These libraries can be used to accelerate creating high-quality producers and consumers and are used by many other third-party products to integrate with Amazon KDS, such as the Logstash kinesis plugin and the Fluent plugin for Amazon Kinesis. In addition, connectors exist for popular data processing frameworks such as Apache Spark and Apache Flink.

Data delivery guarantees

Amazon KDS supports at-least-once delivery. The consumers need to be either idempotent, which means processing the same message multiple times does not change the outcome, or capable of deduping the message.

Integration with other AWS services

Amazon KDS is tightly integrated with a number of AWS services and is able to directly ingest records from them. One important integration is with AWS Lambda, wherein a Lambda function can be invoked with a payload of records retrieved from Amazon KDS either periodically (with standard consumers) or whenever records are available (with EFO consumers).

Monitoring

For monitoring, Amazon KDS is integrated with **Amazon CloudWatch**, and metrics at both the stream level (enabled by default) and the shard level (referred to as enhanced shard-level metrics; this needs to be enabled and costs extra) are available.

Next, we take a look at a closely related service that simplifies the ingestion and delivery of streaming data to a number of destinations.

Amazon Kinesis Data Firehose (KDF)

Amazon KDF was launched in October 2015. It is a fully managed, serverless service for ingesting streaming data and delivering to destinations in AWS, third-party services such as Splunk, or even generic HTTP endpoints. In terms of the five core stages of enabling real-time analytics, Amazon KDF straddles stream storage and real-time stream processing. Some of the core capabilities of Amazon KDF are as follows:

- Ingesting data at high volumes

- Ingesting high-throughput streaming data from myriad data sources

- Buffering and aggregating data

- Transforming and processing data inline

- Sending data to one of a number of destinations

- Handling errors and retries while sending

- Storing ingested data in the service for 24 hours, to enable retries and handle situations when destinations are unavailable

When Amazon KDS first launched, the majority of organizations used the service to ingest streaming data and store it in **Amazon S3** or load it in **Amazon Redshift**. Amazon Redshift is a fully managed, highly parallel data warehousing service for analytical processing and analytical querying. With KDS, customers were spending a lot of time and energy on writing custom applications to store the data in S3 and Redshift. AWS recognized this need across a large segment of customers and built Amazon KDF to support the most popular destinations, thereby reducing customer effort and providing an easier experience for landing persistent data in near real time. If there appears to be some overlap between the Amazon KDS and Amazon KDF services, it is because Amazon KDF was designed to ease the burden of doing some common stream storage and processing tasks.

In general, since Amazon KDF buffers data; in any scenarios where latency is important, Amazon KDS should be considered instead. Similarly, even though Amazon KDF provides the ability to perform some degree of inline **Extract, Transform, and Load (ETL)**, if the requirement is to do heavy transformations, custom stream processing, or stateful (processing events depend on previous events) processing, Amazon KDS is a better fit. However, if the use case requires stateless, low-touch ingestion and delivery of streaming data with some inline transformations, encryption, batching, and compression to supported destinations, Amazon KDF is the best choice.

Just like Amazon KDS, Amazon KDF is an API-driven service and has APIs for both the control plane and the data plane. In the control plane, it has APIs for creating and deleting delivery streams, listing and describing delivery streams, starting and stopping encryption at rest, and updating the destination for the delivery stream (changing the target destination to deliver records to). On the data plane, it has APIs to send records to the service both one at a time and in batches.

Figure 2.2 illustrates producers sending data to Amazon KDF and the delivery destinations it supports:

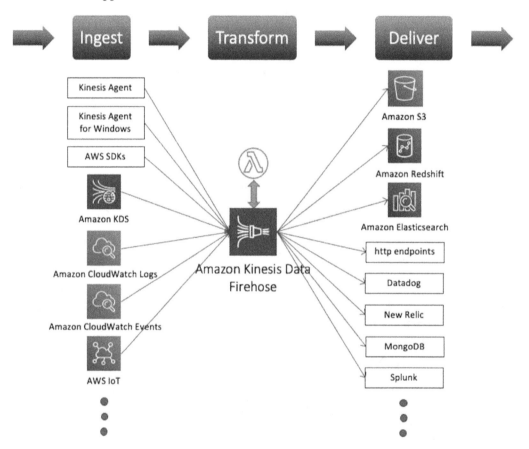

Figure 2.2 – Producers and delivery destinations for Amazon KDF

A delivery stream is the core construct of Amazon KDF and defines the entity streaming records are sent to. Unlike Amazon KDS, however, there is no need to define the capacity of the delivery stream. The service supports two ways of sending data:

- Direct PUT

- Using Amazon KDS stream as a source

For Direct PUT, the service provides the `PutRecord` and `PutRecordBatch` APIs to send records one by one and in batches, respectively. In this case, the default delivery stream capacity is based on the choice of AWS region. For US East (N. Virginia), US West (Oregon), and Europe (Ireland), it is 5,000 records/second, 2,000 requests/second, and 5 MiB/second. For many other regions, it is 1,000 records/second, 1,000 requests/second, and 1 MiB/second. The important thing to note here is that these are soft limits and if the throughput for a particular use case is higher than the specified limits, a limit increase support ticket needs to be submitted and the service raises the limit for the delivery stream. In addition, the service is able to auto-scale up to the delivery stream capacity limit. If an Amazon KDS stream is used as a source, the delivery stream capacity is the capacity of the source Amazon KDS stream and the service can auto-scale up to that limit.

For durability, Amazon KDF redundantly stores data across multiple Availability Zones and provides an SLA (`https://aws.amazon.com/kinesis/sla/`) of 99.9%. It stores records in the service for 24 hours in case it is unable to send records to the destination.

Encryption, authentication, and authorization

For authentication and authorization, both the control plane and the data plane are integrated with AWS IAM and support Signature V4 for authentication and identity-based IAM policies for authorization. At this time, resource-based IAM policies are not supported.

The service also provides encryption at rest using AWS KMS CMK, which could be either user-managed or service-managed. However, how encryption at rest is provided differs based on whether the source is Amazon KDS or Direct PUT. If an Amazon KDS stream is the source, Amazon KDF does not store the data; instead, it depends on the records being encrypted at rest in the Amazon KDS stream. When it reads records from the stream, Amazon KDS decrypts the data before Amazon KDF receives it and then Amazon KDF buffers the records in memory for the timeframe specified in the configuration and delivers the records to the destination without storing them at rest in the service. If Direct PUT is used, Amazon KDF provides APIs to start and stop encryption or configuration parameters when creating a delivery stream with an AWS KMS CMK to encrypt the data at rest.

Monitoring

For monitoring, Amazon KDF is integrated with both **CloudWatch metrics** and **CloudWatch Logs**. There are metrics collected and made available for data ingestion, data delivery, individual APIs, data transformation, data format conversion, server-side encryption at rest, and Amazon KDF usage. Also, if enabled, when inline data transformation is used within Amazon KDF using a Lambda function, Amazon KDF logs errors when Lambda invocation fails. In addition, if there are errors delivering to the specified destination, Amazon KDF logs the errors to CloudWatch Logs as well.

Producers

As mentioned, in addition to having an Amazon KDS stream as a data source, Amazon KDF provides APIs to send data to a delivery stream that are wrapped in AWS SDKs offered in multiple programming languages as well as in the AWS CLI. Producer applications can be written using the SDKs to send data to a delivery stream. In addition, there are a number of other methods and integrations that allow the easy ingestion of data into a delivery stream. These include Kinesis Agent (Linux-based), Kinesis Agent for windows and integrations with other AWS services including Amazon **CloudWatch Logs**, **Amazon CloudWatch Events**, **AWS IoT**, **AWS Web Application Firewall** (**WAF**), and **Amazon MSK**.

Delivery destinations

Once ingested, Amazon KDF offers the ability to buffer and aggregate records before delivery to a configured destination. Only one destination is supported per delivery stream and the buffering options provided vary by destination. At this time, the supported destinations include **Amazon S3**, **Amazon Redshift**, **Amazon Elasticsearch Service**, generic HTTP endpoints, and service providers such as **Datadog**, **New Relic**, **Splunk**, and **MongoDB**. The service handles delivery failures and retries and message backups to **Amazon S3** on failures for subsequent processing, but the semantics vary by destination. Amazon KDF supports at-least-once data delivery semantics.

Transformations

Amazon KDF provides the ability to do multiple transformations inline after data ingestion and before delivery. This includes the ability to do data transformations by invoking a Lambda function (called a Lambda transform), and multiple Lambda function blueprints are provided to do common transformations such as **Apache Log** to JSON and **CSV**, **Syslog** to **JSON**, and **CSV** and **General Firehose Processing**.

Figure 2.3 illustrates data transformation in KDF using a Lambda transform:

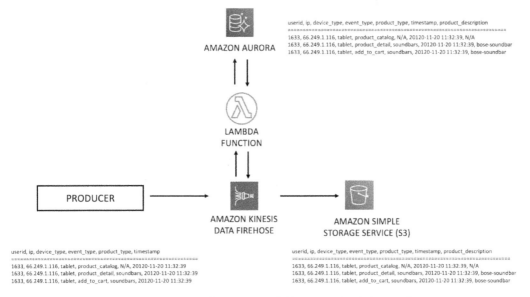

userid, ip, device_type, event_type, product_type, timestamp, product_description
==
1633, 66.249.1.116, tablet, product_catalog, N/A, 20120-11-20 11:32:39, N/A
1633, 66.249.1.116, tablet, product_detail, soundbars, 20120-11-20 11:32:39, bose-soundbar
1633, 66.249.1.116, tablet, add_to_cart, soundbars, 20120-11-20 11:32:39, bose-soundbar

AMAZON AURORA

LAMBDA FUNCTION

PRODUCER

AMAZON KINESIS DATA FIREHOSE

AMAZON SIMPLE STORAGE SERVICE (S3)

userid, ip, device_type, event_type, product_type, timestamp
==
1633, 66.249.1.116, tablet, product_catalog, N/A, 20120-11-20 11:32:39
1633, 66.249.1.116, tablet, product_detail, soundbars, 20120-11-20 11:32:39
1633, 66.249.1.116, tablet, add_to_cart, soundbars, 20120-11-20 11:32:39

userid, ip, device_type, event_type, product_type, timestamp, product_description
==
1633, 66.249.1.116, tablet, product_catalog, N/A, 20120-11-20 11:32:39, N/A
1633, 66.249.1.116, tablet, product_detail, soundbars, 20120-11-20 11:32:39, bose-soundbar
1633, 66.249.1.116, tablet, add_to_cart, soundbars, 20120-11-20 11:32:39, bose-soundbar

Figure 2.3 – Data transformation in KDF using a Lambda transform

In addition, the service also provides the ability to do data format conversion in which the format of the incoming records can be converted from JSON to **Apache Parquet** or **Apache ORC**, before sending the data to **Amazon S3** (Amazon S3 is the only destination supported). Data transformation using Lambda functions and data format conversions can be combined in a pipeline inside the Amazon KDF service for various use cases, such as converting the data format of records in **comma-separated values** (**CSV**) format to Apache Parquet. In this case, a Lambda transform can be used to first convert the CSV format to JSON before using data format conversion to convert the record to Apache Parquet and store it in Amazon S3. For the Amazon S3 destination, an additional facility using expressions is provided to customize the Amazon S3 object keys for objects delivered to Amazon S3. This feature can be used to store data in partitions using Apache Hive naming conventions, which requires partition names to be defined in key=value format, for example, year=2021.

Now let's look at a service that provides fully managed, serverless, real-time data processing.

Amazon Kinesis Data Analytics (KDA)

Amazon KDA was launched in August 2016. KDA is a fully managed, serverless service for continuously processing real-time streaming data. When it launched in August 2016, it supported the SQL engine, allowing users to query continuously streaming data and get insights from the data in real time without learning a new API or a new programming language. KDA supports ANSI SQL standard with extensions. Later, in November 2018, Amazon KDA launched the second supported underlying real-time processing engine in Apache Flink. It is now called Amazon Kinesis Data Analytics for Apache Flink. As the name suggests, it offers the popular, open source, highly parallel, and low-latency distributed processing framework for stateful computations Apache Flink as a fully managed serverless service. In terms of the five core stages of enabling real-time analytics, Amazon KDA falls in the real-time stream processing stage.

Amazon KDA for SQL

Before getting into how the SQL engine in Amazon KDA works, let's first take a look at how SQL works with streaming data. In general, drawing a parallel with batch data, where SQL is used to query a table with data, the query is bounded by data present in the table at the time the query is executed. Any aggregations or calculations performed by the SQL query uses that bounded dataset, which is finite, and the query results are deterministic. However, with streaming data, it is akin to having an in-memory table with the data just flowing through the table with no bounds. So, if a SQL query is to be executed against the table, what dataset is it going to work against? How are aggregations going to be computed and calculations performed? So, in order to run a deterministic SQL query against the table, the data needs to be bounded. These bounds are created by windowing. Windows are bound based on time or number of messages or some other metric. The most common forms of windows use time. Later chapters will go into the details of windowing.

In Amazon KDA for SQL, the in-memory tables are called in-application streams. If a table receives data directly from the source, it is called an in-application input stream.

Figure 2.4 illustrates the processing pipeline using Amazon KDA for SQL:

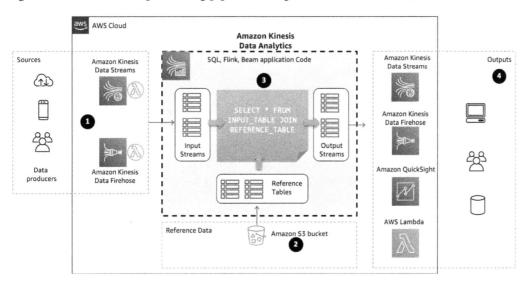

Figure 2.4 – Processing pipeline using Amazon KDA for SQL

The core component of Amazon KDA for SQL is an application that encapsulates all functionality and has a configuration associated with it. There are control plane APIs available to create and manage applications, and these APIs are wrapped in SDKs offered in multiple programming languages and available through the AWS console and AWS CLI. The application consists of the following:

- Input, shown as **1** in *Figure 2.8*, which is the source of streaming data and can either be an Amazon KDS stream or an Amazon KDF delivery stream (there are no APIs to directly send data to an Amazon KDA for SQL application).

- Application code, shown as **3** in *Figure 2.8*, which is written in SQL and can be either a single SQL statement or a string of SQL statements feeding results to intermediate in-application streams that are read by subsequent SQL statements and fed to an output destination.

- Output, shown as **4** in *Figure 2.8*, which comprises in-application output streams that send data to configured destinations that can either be an Amazon KDS stream, an Amazon KDF delivery stream, or an AWS Lambda function. The application configuration specifies each of these and the AWS console provides the interface to create and update the application code and displays sample data as it flows and gets transformed by the application.

- Reference data, shown as **2** in *Figure 2.8*, which is data that provides additional information about the incoming event, such as address information for an event that contains location information. It is stored in an S3 object and loaded by KDA to an in-memory table to facilitate streaming joins.

The SQL language supports **ANSI 11** with some data streaming extensions. The SQL application code can utilize a variety of functions to analyze the data, including aggregate, analytic, boolean, conversion, data/time, numeric, log parsing, sorting, statistical, streaming SQL, string, search, and machine learning functions. These functions can be used in-line with the SQL statements and make it very easy to do complex analysis by encapsulating the complexity in the functions. In addition, user-defined functions can be created in SQL to encapsulate logic not available as a standard function. It is recommended that several small SQL statements with results flowing into intermediate in-application streams be used instead of large, complex SQL statements, as that approach makes it easier to troubleshoot application code. In addition to the input source, the application code supports a reference (or lookup) data source (one only), with the source being an object in S3 that is loaded into an in-application stream in the application and allows joins with other in-application streams.

Amazon KDA uses a **Kinesis Processing Unit** (**KPU**) as a unit of capacity to provision capacity and resources needed for an application. A KPU roughly translates to 1 vCPU and 4 GB of memory. The service is able to elastically scale the application in response to the throughput of data coming in from the source and the complexity of the application code.

Encryption, authentication, and authorization

Amazon KDA SQL provides encryption in transit between supported data sources and the application as well as between the internal components of Amazon KDA and Amazon KDA and Amazon KDF. In addition, the service encrypts the application code and the reference data at rest using an internal key.

The control plane APIs of the service are integrated with AWS IAM and support authentication using Signature V4 and authorization with identity-based IAM policies.

Monitoring

For monitoring, Amazon KDA for SQL is integrated with Amazon CloudWatch and provides a number of metrics in the **AWS/KinesisAnalytics** namespace.

Data delivery guarantees

Amazon KDA for SQL supports at-least-once data delivery semantics. Now let's look at the more recent engine offered as part of the Amazon KDA service.

Amazon Kinesis Data Analytics for Apache Flink (KDA Flink)

In addition to using SQL, a developer can create Apache Flink applications and deploy them as KDA applications. This feature was added to KDA during re:Invent 2018. The key advantage of using KDA to run your Flink applications is that you don't need to worry about infrastructure. KDA will provision the underlying resources needed to run your application and provides the ability to automatically scale those resources on your behalf. It's a turnkey solution for your Apache Flink applications. The high-level steps for deploying your KDA application include creating and building it locally, packaging it (in a JAR file), and uploading the code. To start your Flink application, once you have created the JAR file, you have two options to upload it to KDA. You can use the Amazon KDA `kinesisanalytics:CreateApplication` API or go through the the Amazon KDA console. KDA manages the underlying infrastructure, from scaling through security.

While removing the overhead of handling the infrastructure, you do retain a lot of Flink capabilities; however, you lose some of the flexibility. KDA will control the state backend and manage it on your behalf. KDA uses **RocksDB** and S3 is used as a distributed state backend; Flink savepoints (called snapshots in **KDA Flink**) get persisted on S3. You can use externalized parameters called **runtime properties** to modify or change the behavior of your application. KDA will also manage the application life cycle on your behalf. If an update of your Flink application fails, KDA will retry the application update. When updating your job, KDA will create a snapshot unless it is turned off in the configuration. The application is then stopped and updated by KDA. KDA is capable of maintaining up to a thousand snapshots that you can then restore from. KDA maintains your application metadata in a DynamoDB database internally.

Amazon KDA is a serverless service and abstracts the underlying instances from you and you don't get to choose the instance type that your KDA application runs on. Your application will run on underlying instances controlled and managed by KDA. KDA will allocate appropriate instance size from its fleet based on parallelism that you configure for your application. In addition to selecting instances for your Flink application, KDA will determine whether your application will be run on memory-optimized or CPU-optimized instances. KDA determines this based on metrics your application produces, so if your application consumes lots of CPU, KDA will move it to an appropriate compute-optimized instance such as the C instance family.

KDA allocates capacity to your application in terms of **Kinesis Processing Units (KPUs)**. 1 KPU is roughly equivalent to 1 vCPU and 4 GB of memory and includes 50 GB of disk. When it comes to scaling your application, KDA automatically scales up and scales down the underlying infrastructure on your behalf. You can turn this behavior off if you wish to do so. If you don't want automatic scaling, you can specify parallelism, as well as parallelism per KPU. Parallelism is a setting that determines how many Flink computation processes should operate on data in parallel. As KDA detects an increase in CPU, it will scale up your application. A drop in CPU usage triggers a scale down. When you turn on autoscaling, KDA will not, however, reduce your application's *CurrentParellelism* value to below the setting for your application's *Parallelism* value. You can still set a maximum *Parallelism* value and KDA autoscaling will honor it. If you want full control, you can turn off autoscaling and set your application's parallelism. If you have steady load and you know what resources your application sources and sinks need, you can set parallelism yourself. KDA will then scale your application according to the parallelism boundaries that you have set.

Access and interaction with the KDA deployed Flink app is done through the KDA native AWS API. The downside of this is that you lose some of the flexibility of using the Flink REST API to manage jobs. However, the advantage is that you get out-of-the-box integration with AWS IAM. In addition, KDA encrypts all the data at rest and transit using an internal key. To ensure that your application is running in the case of failures in AWS Availability Zones, KDA seamlessly fails your application over to another Availability Zone. This removes the need for you to worry about disaster recovery within the AWS Region. KDA monitors your Flink application as well as the underlying infrastructure for any failures or issues such as bad drive, **out of memory (OOM)**, and so on. KDA restarts your application and publishes events into CloudWatch Logs or metrics to notify you. You can use these to perform any processing that you may need to do when the job is restarted.

The Apache Flink framework contains connectors for accessing data from a variety of sources. For information about connectors available in the Apache Flink framework, see `https://ci.apache.org/projects/flink/flink-docs-stable/dev/connectors/`.

Amazon Kinesis Video Streams (KVS)

Amazon KVS was released on November 29th, 2017. KVS is a fully managed, serverless service for ingesting video and other time-encoded data such as audio, **Light Detection and Ranging** (**LIDAR**), and **Radio Detection and Ranging** (**RADAR**) signals. KVS abstracts away many of the core challenges of building video systems, enabling developers to focus on the application instead of the complex video infrastructure required to handle low-latency video at scale.

Video cameras can stream live video into KVS with only a few seconds' buffer delay. The video can then be consumed with both real-time and batch-oriented processes. KVS also supports **Web Real-Time Communication** (**Web-RTC**) to enable peer-to-peer two-way video/audio communication. This is a low-latency peering technique designed for real-time human-to-human interaction features such as video chat.

With KVS, a video is a series of images, and each one of these images is called a **frame**. Frames are grouped together when compressing video. Frames usually have very little visual difference, so only the incremental changes need to be stored in subsequent frames. In KVS, the fundamental data structure is the **fragment**. It is a sequence of frames that have no dependencies on frames in any other fragment. Each fragment is assigned a unique fragment number (an increasing number), a producer-side timestamp (absolute or relative to the start time of the recording), and a server-side timestamp. KVS data is consumed in streams of chunks, where a **chunk** contains the fragment, media metadata, and KVS-specific metadata.

The KVS producer and stream parser libraries are based on the **Matroska Multimedia Container** (**MKV**) video format. This format can package an unlimited amount of video, audio, and other data. The name Matroska is derived from the Russian word matryoshka, which is the name of the wooden Russian nesting dolls. The KVS producer libraries can support any time-serialized format, but the H.264 codec is required to be viewed in the AWS Management Console.

There are three main use cases that KVS supports: live video streaming and recorded stream playback, real-time two-way streaming, and computer vision-based applications. Live video streaming is built on **HTTP Live Streaming** (**HLS**). HLS is an industry standard that supports both on-demand and live streaming. HLS provides an HTTP endpoint that multiple open source players can connect and display video on a mobile device or browser-based web page. Lower latency is required to support bi-directional interactive communication instead of broadcast streaming. KVS achieves lower latency through support for WebRTC. It provides libraries that enable clients to directly connect to each other in a peer-to-peer manner. However, due to firewall rules or certain **Network Address Translation** (**NAT**) configurations, it is not always possible to connect directly in this manner. In this case, the KVS libraries then provide a fallback to a Kinesis **Traversal Using Relays around NAT** (**TURN**) server. The TURN server is a simple relay that receives the data from one client and sends it to the other.

One of the most compelling use cases for KVS is building computer vision/machine learning applications that analyze video data. The video can be either processed in real time or in batches by a wide variety of machine learning services. These AWS services range from high-level services such as Amazon Recognition and Amazon Transcribe to custom models built using TensorFlow, MxNet, or PyTorch. Through these services, developers can identify and label potentially unsafe or inappropriate content for moderation, perform facial recognition, and identify key objects in the video.

Kinesis video streams enable the development of video-based applications that can scale and remove many of the challenges involved in video consumption and processing.

Amazon Simple Queue Service (SQS)

Amazon SQS was launched in July 2006 and was one of the earliest services to launch on Amazon Web Services. With more than 14 years in service, Amazon SQS has delivered messaging services to some of the busiest e-commerce companies in the world. Amazon SQS is a fully managed, serverless service that is highly scalable and easy to get started with and use. It is one of the primary AWS native services providing message queue functionality in AWS and has been used by numerous companies for myriad use cases.

Amazon SQS offers a publisher/subscriber pattern with consumers pulling the messages from a queue. It offers queues without the need to set up message brokers. Authentication and authorization to SQS queues are managed with Amazon **Identity and Access Management** (**IAM**) and fine-grained IAM policies. These policies can be used to control who has access to an Amazon SQS queue. This allows you to manage who has the ability to send and receive messages from Amazon SQS.

Amazon SQS is a highly reliable and available service. The service leverages redundant server infrastructure spread across multiple Availability Zones in an AWS Region. This diversification protects against server and network failure, providing an uptime SLA (`https://aws.amazon.com/messaging/sla/`) of 99.9%.

> **Availability Zone**
>
> An AWS **Availability Zone** (**AZ**) is a logical group of one or more data centers in an AWS Region. A Region is a geographical area where AWS data centers are clustered together. The AZs are isolated from each other with redundant networking and power to provide high availability and fault tolerance. They are connected with low-cost, high-bandwidth, high-throughput, and low-latency networking, allowing the operation of applications and databases with high availability, fault tolerance, and scalability.

Figure 2.5 illustrates the integration between an Amazon SQS queue and **AWS Lambda**. Here a Lambda trigger can be created that automatically polls the SQS queue for messages and invokes the provided Lambda function to process the messages:

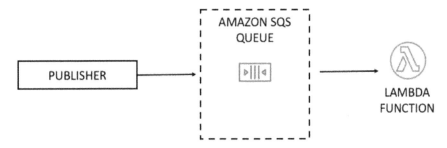

Figure 2.5 – Integration between an Amazon SQS queue and AWS Lambda

Amazon SQS offers two types of queues – **Standard** and **First-In-First-Out** (**FIFO**).

Standard queues offer nearly unlimited throughput, including the number of API calls per second per API action for `SendMessage`, `ReceiveMessage`, or `DeleteMessage`. Amazon SQS provides **at-least-once** message delivery, which means that a message will be delivered once but can be delivered more than once. This is due to the distributed architecture of Amazon SQS and Amazon SQS storing a copy of the message on multiple servers. It could happen, albeit rarely, that during the process of receiving and deleting a message, one of the servers that a copy resides on is unavailable, which can cause the same message to be delivered more than once. Consumers are, therefore, required to be designed to be idempotent (processing the same message multiple times does not change the outcome) or capable of deduping the message. Finally, it offers *ordering* as a best effort, which means that even though an effort is made to deliver messages to consumers in the order it was received by Amazon SQS, occasionally, they can arrive out of order.

FIFO queues offer **exactly-once** processing, which guarantees that the message is delivered once and only once. FIFO delivery guarantees that messages are delivered strictly in the order they were received in. FIFO queues have reduced throughput quotas over standard queues. Amazon SQS FIFO queues offer 300 API calls per second per API action, which when combined with batching (the maximum batching level is 10 messages per API call) supports a maximum throughput of 3,000 messages per second. In December 2020, Amazon SQS launched a preview of high-throughput FIFO queues that offers 3,000 messages per second per API call.

Both queue types support message payloads up to 256 KB in size, and with the Amazon SQS Extended Client Library for Java (`https://github.com/awslabs/amazon-sqs-java-extended-client-lib`), larger messages can be sent by first storing the messages in Amazon S3 and then sending a reference to the message payload in Amazon S3 to Amazon SQS. Furthermore, both queues support batching up to 10 messages, long polling, message retention up to 14 days, visibility timeouts for message locking, **dead letter queues** (**DLQs**), and **server-side encryption** (**SSE**) with keys using Amazon Key Management Service.

Now that we have had an overview of Amazon SQS and understand that it uses the pull model, let's look at another extensively used AWS messaging service that uses the push model: Amazon Simple Notification Service.

Amazon Simple Notification Service (SNS)

Amazon SNS was launched in 2010 and it is a fully managed serverless service offering the publisher/subscriber pattern with a push mechanism for sending messages to subscribers. Similar to Amazon SQS, Amazon SNS provides a highly scalable, available, and elastic service that can be used for decoupled architectures.

Amazon SNS uses the concept of topics. Topics are logical entities used to denote a specific category, subject, or type of event. The topic forms an "access point" of the service. Subscribers can subscribe to one or more topics of interest and get messages, and publishers send messages to their topics of interest. Amazon SNS identifies the list of subscribers for a particular topic and then delivers the messages sent to those topics to the corresponding list of subscribers. Unlike SQS message queues, where messages are received by one consumer, SNS messages are delivered to all subscribers in a process called *fan-out*. The topic owner can also specify which notification protocols are supported. Supported protocols include `http`, `https`, `email`, `email-json`, `sms`, `sqs`, `application`, and `Lambda`. Subscribers either subscribe to a topic and then go through a subscription confirmation process or are subscribed by the topic owner. Subscribers, when subscribing, need to provide the protocol and the corresponding endpoint to receive notifications.

The topic owner can define permissions in two ways: through Amazon SNS by using resource-based permissions (attached to topics that define the identities and the actions those identities are authorized to perform on the topic) and identity-based permissions (attached to identities that define the resources and the actions that are authorized on those resources). In either case, permissions are specified using IAM policies.

Figure 2.6 illustrates Amazon SNS and the subscription endpoints that it supports:

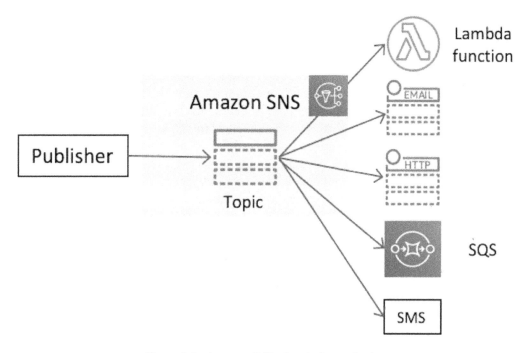

Figure 2.6 – Amazon SNS subscription endpoints

One important distinction between Amazon SNS and Amazon SQS is that Amazon SNS does not provide message retention. When a publisher sends a message to a topic, Amazon SNS immediately tries to deliver the message to all subscribers of the topic. If message delivery fails or the subscriber is not available, Amazon SNS goes through a four-phase delivery retry policy that is pre-defined for each protocol. Only the HTTP(S) retry policy can be modified. Once the delivery retry policy is exhausted, Amazon SNS discards the message. In order to prevent message loss, it is recommended that a DLQ is attached to the subscription (DLQs are attached to the subscription and not to the topic). Storing undelivered messages in a DLQ enables you to re-process the messages at a later time if they are still relevant.

Amazon SNS supports optional message attributes when the message structure is a string, but they're not supported with JSON messages. Though separate from the message payload, these message attributes, when defined, are sent along with the messages. These attributes can help the subscriber process the message and implement simple logic without having to process the message payload; for instance, the subscriber could ignore messages with a certain attribute or forward them to another service. Amazon SNS validates the attribute values for adherence to the data types specified for the message attributes and can filter the messages based on attribute values.

Amazon SNS provides a very useful feature called message filtering. Filtering makes it very efficient for consumers to receive only the messages they're interested in instead of all messages sent to the subscribed topic. This is achieved by the subscriber assigning a *filter policy* to the topic subscription. The filter policy is a simple JSON policy where the subscriber specifies the message attributes and the values that the subscriber is interested in. Amazon SNS performs the task of comparing the incoming topic message attributes to the filter policy attributes and sends the message to the subscriber if any attribute matches or skips the subscriber if there are no matches. Since the service performs this function, filtering and routing functions are offloaded from both publishers and subscribers. This also has the beneficial effect of allowing topic consolidation.

Amazon SNS by default supports message sizes up to 256 KB. For message sizes above that, up to 2 GB, the Amazon SNS Extended Client Library for Java (`https://github.com/awslabs/amazon-sns-java-extended-client-lib/`) can be used, which uses Amazon S3 to store the message payloads and sends a reference to the message payload to the Amazon SNS topic. Corresponding de-referencing libraries are available when the subscriber is either an Amazon SQS queue (with the Amazon SQS Extended Client Library for Java: `https://github.com/awslabs/amazon-sqs-java-extended-client-lib`) or AWS Lambda (with the Payload Offloading Java Common Library for AWS: `https://github.com/awslabs/payload-offloading-java-common-lib-for-aws`), which provide the ability to use the reference in the message to retrieve the payload from Amazon S3.

The messaging patterns enabled by Amazon SNS can be broadly categorized into two categories:

- Application-to-application messaging
- Application-to-person messaging

Let's take a look at each of them in detail.

Application-to-application messaging

With application-to-application messaging, the asynchronous communication is between two applications. One application is the publisher to a topic and other applications are subscribers to that topic. Amazon SNS supports HTTP(S) endpoints, Amazon SQS queues, AWS Lambda functions, and AWS Event Fork Pipelines as subscribers. When there is more than one subscriber to the same topic, the messaging pattern is referred to as **fan-out**.

Application-to-person messaging

In application-to-person messaging, the asynchronous communication is between an application and a user. The user can be a mobile application, mobile phone number, SMS, or email address. The primary purpose of this type of messaging is user notification, but the notification can also be used in a mobile application to take automated action on the client side.

Amazon SNS integrations with other AWS services

Amazon SNS is tightly integrated with a number of AWS services. One important integration is with **Amazon CloudWatch**, a service for monitoring applications and infrastructure. **Amazon CloudWatch** provides the ability to create alarms based on configurable thresholds and then natively utilize a configured Amazon SNS topic to send notifications. Amazon SNS sends notifications to configured email subscribers, AWS Lambda functions, or Amazon SQS queues to direct actions that should be performed when the alarm is triggered. For instance, a high CPU usage alarm can send an email to the system administrators notifying them of the issue, while at the same time triggering a Lambda function to automatically provision more capacity. These notifications can also fan out through Amazon SNS, so other AWS services and third-party services can receive the message. A commonly used pattern for application and operation automation is to have SNS send messages to an SQS queue that is then drained by other applications, including Lambda functions, to take the appropriate action. This pattern allows the messages to be processed at the rate of the downstream systems.

Encryption at rest

In Amazon SNS, messages are encrypted as they are received using a CMK from **AWS Key Management Service** (**KMS**). The encrypted messages are then stored across multiple AZs and decrypted right before they're delivered to subscribers.

Amazon SNS is a fundamental service that is essential for notification and message exchange in most AWS cloud-based architectures.

Next, let's take a look at Amazon MQ and how it helps with lift-and-shift approaches for moving messaging workloads easily into the cloud.

Amazon MQ for Apache ActiveMQ

Amazon MQ is a managed message broker service for Apache ActiveMQ and RabbitMQ that launched in 2017. Apache ActiveMQ is a popular Java-based open source message broker that supports multiple protocols providing a choice of a wide range of programming languages and protocol options for clients. The supported APIs and protocols include **JMS**, **NMS**, **AMQP**, **STOMP**, **MQTT**, and **WebSocket**. RabbitMQ is an open source, very popular lightweight message broker that supports many protocols, including AMQP 0-9-1 and extensions, AMQP 1.0, STOMP, MQTT, AMQP 1.0, WebSocket, and JMS via a plugin. Amazon MQ is a managed service that provides high availability, infrastructure management, broker setup, software updates, and operations and management of the brokers. Amazon MQ provides access to the industry-standard APIs, the ActiveMQ console, and the RabbitMQ web console. One of the main advantages of Amazon MQ is the ability to easily move to a managed service when using any message broker utilizing one of the aforementioned protocols. When migrating to Amazon MQ, there is no need to change the clients or applications interfacing with the message brokers. The primary purpose of this service is to support such migrations.

Amazon MQ for Apache Active MQ offers two types of broker configurations from a storage standpoint:

- High durability
- High throughput and low latency

In the high-durability configuration (the default), the service uses **Amazon Elastic File System** (**EFS**) for broker storage. Amazon EFS is a cloud-based **network file system** (**NFS**) that is elastic, scalable, fully managed, and highly durable as it is spread across multiple AZs. It is possible to mount it on multiple broker nodes, so the broker nodes can read and modify the same files on shared storage, allowing active/standby broker configurations for high availability and failover.

In the high-throughput and low-latency configuration, the service uses Amazon **Elastic Block Store** (**EBS**) for broker storage. While Amazon EBS maintains multiple copies of the storage volume in the same AZ, the storage is not spread across multiple Availability Zones. Correspondingly, it cannot be used for active/standby broker configurations.

Amazon MQ for Apache Active MQ provides the ability to set up brokers in multiple configurations. Let's take a look at them.

Single-instance brokers

Single-instance brokers, as the name suggests, have a single broker in a single Availability Zone using either Amazon EFS or Amazon EBS for storage. This configuration does not provide any high availability or failover.

Active/standby brokers

Active/standby brokers utilize two separate brokers in two different Availability Zones using **Amazon EFS** for storage. Clients can connect to either of the brokers but typically only one broker is active at a time. Amazon MQ provides a separate ActiveMQ web console URL for each broker but only one is active at a time. Correspondingly, the service provides separate endpoint URLs for each wire protocol for each broker with only one being active at a time. ActiveMQ Failover Transport can be used by clients to connect to the wire protocol endpoints of either broker and transparently handle connection failures and broker failovers.

Network of brokers

A network of brokers consists of multiple active brokers, single-instance or active/standby, configured in a variety of topologies such as hub and spoke, concentrator, mesh, and tree. It provides both high availability and scalability and the ability to fail over almost instantly in the case of broker failure. The service provides integration with AWS IAM for control plane API authentication and authorization, via identity-based policies (resource-based policies are currently not supported). In addition, encryption at rest is supported with AWS KMS and a CMK, both user-managed and service-managed (when a user-managed CMK is not provided).

All communication between brokers is encrypted using TLS V 1.2 and clients can access the brokers over TLS using protocols AMQP, MQTT, MQTT over WebSocket, OpenWire, STOMP, and STOMP over WebSocket. For message authentication and authorization both native ActiveMQ authentication and LDAP authentication and authorization are supported.

Next, let's take a quick look at the deployment options for Amazon MQ for Rabbit MQ.

Single-instance standalone

This deployment mode is primarily intended for development or low-latency workloads that want to avoid replication There is a single broker, in a single Availability Zone that can be either publicly accessible over the internet or deployed in a VPC with access only within the VPC.

Cluster deployment

This deployment mode is intended for production workloads and utilizes three brokers spread across three Availability Zones fronted by a **network load balancer** (**NLB**) to provide a single access point for APIs and the RabbitMQ web console. To ensure high availability, classic mirroring is employed. In addition, both private brokers as well as publicly accessible brokers are supported.

Next, we look at a service that is at the heart of the IoT services offered by AWS.

IoT Core

AWS IoT Core is a family of managed services that allows IoT-connected devices to interact with each other as well as with other cloud applications and services. You can use a variety of protocols with AWS IoT Core. MQTT is the primary protocol used as it is optimized for publish/subscribe messaging between various remote devices with scarce resources and when network bandwidth is nominal.

This book will not cover IoT in depth; however, the purpose and key functionality apply to streaming data solutions with IoT use cases.

Device software

FreeRTOS is an open source operating system for microcontrollers. FreeRTOS is similar to the **Raspberry Pi Raspian** operating system. FreeRTOS is intended for embedded software (software that controls devices and hardware) development for microcontrollers. FreeRTOS provides you with building blocks to create software for microcontrollers and implement multitasking. Whereas Raspian is an operating system intended for end users just to install and run, FreeRTOS is a baseline operating system for developers to build on top of. You can think of Raspian as a meal at the restaurant and FreeRTOS as being a set of ingredients that you put together and cook to create a meal.

AWS Greengrass brings IoT capabilities to the edge. As IoT devices generate large amounts of data, Greengrass provides the ability to filter that data. Rather than filtering data once it arrives in the cloud, Greengrass lets you filter it on the device and only send the data that you want. The AWS Greengrass functionality is similar to that performed by "check-in" agents at the airport. Instead of letting everybody go to the gate, check-in agents filter passengers in the pre-gate area inside the terminal.

Control services

AWS IoT Device Management enables the management of large device fleets from a single management console. If you think of your car's dashboard, that's similar to IoT Device Management: you can monitor your devices just like you monitor how much fuel you have in your car or the temperature of the engine. It also allows you to access the remote devices in a secure manner and perform maintenance tasks such as upgrades and setting changes.

AWS IoT Device Defender is to devices what AWS Config is to the cloud. Device Defender examines device configurations against expected security parameters. If it detects deviations or tampering with device settings that aren't within the boundaries of your expected baseline, it sends an alert.

AWS IoT 1-Click is for extending the functionality of simple devices, such as switches or buttons. Actual devices such as IoT Button (`https://aws.amazon.com/iotbutton/`) would send signals to AWS IoT 1-Click, which in turn executes an AWS Lambda function to perform your desired functionality.

Analytics services

AWS IoT Analytics is a service that provides insights from the IoT data that the devices in an IoT fleet produce. AWS IoT Analytics is a fully managed service that allows the devices' data to be queried and analyzed using machine learning.

IoT Events provides a convenient way to take actions based on events produced by device fleets. IoT Events can act across multiple data points such as weight, temperature, or speed and invoke actions. The service is simple to use as it follows the if-else-then notion. Once you determine that an event has occurred, for example, a temperature is above 32F, it can trigger actions from a predefined set. Some of the actions include saving to DynamoDB, sending messages to Kinesis, or invoking AWS Lambda.

AWS IoT SiteWise is intended for industrial large-scale monitoring of facilities such as manufacturing plants or warehouses storing goods. For example, SiteWise can be set up in a car manufacturing plant to capture equipment data and allow you to assess how your equipment is performing and troubleshoot problems without needing to have physical access to the devices.

AWS IoT Things Graph is kind of like a glue to connect various vendor devices or different device types. It is a simplified orchestration engine to allow vendor devices to communicate with each other by building common models of communication, leveraging a no-code visualization tool. A useful analogy to understand the function of Things Graph is the "translation" services provided during United Nations meetings and summits. There are multiple countries and languages that participate in UN meetings and they all need to coordinate with each other. Since not all of them speak the same language (they all use different protocols, in IoT terms), the translation service ensures that everyone understands each other. IoT Things Graph does exactly the same by allowing you to visually connect different devices into cohesive applications.

Now, let's look at Amazon Managed Streaming for Apache Kafka.

Amazon Managed Streaming for Apache Kafka (MSK)

Amazon MSK is a fully managed service for **Apache Kafka**. Launched in May 2019, Amazon MSK removed the difficult setup and management tasks for Apache Kafka. Apache Kafka is a popular open source, distributed, high-throughput, and low-latency streaming platform that is used by thousands of companies and is extremely popular. It is available under the Apache 2.0 license.

Amazon MSK allows you to focus on building applications and simply use Apache Kafka for stream storage.

Let's dive deeper into Apache Kafka and Amazon MSK in the following sections.

Apache Kafka

Apache Kafka is a distributed system that is typically installed as a cluster on multiple machines, EC2 instances (in AWS), or containers. The core component of a cluster is the broker. Multiple brokers form a cluster working together to provide high availability and durability. The brokers depend on **Apache ZooKeeper** for cluster management and coordination, although the Apache Kafka community is progressively moving toward removing this dependency.

The brokers host topics, which are logical entities representing a category to which events with similar event types are sent. Producers send messages to topics of interest and consumers subscribe to topics of interest. Underlying each topic is a commit log, which is at the heart of Apache Kafka. It is an append-only, ordered sequence of records with each incoming record appended to the end of the log. Each message in the log gets a unique offset. When consumers read from a topic, they are read from the commit log and can start from any point (offset) in the commit log. Consumers can read the earliest (the start of the log) or the latest (end of the log). The commit log for a topic is distributed across multiple brokers based on the number of partitions defined for the topic. Partitions provide scalability and parallelism in Apache Kafka. As partitions for a topic are added, the overall throughput for the topic increases. Correspondingly, consumers can read from multiple partitions in parallel to drain the queue faster. Each partition gets its own commit log, which is a physical file on disk, and the offsets in each partition log file start from 0 and can be the same across multiple partitions.

Figure 2.7 shows a high-level architecture of an Apache Kafka cluster with three broker nodes, a three-node ZooKeeper ensemble, a producer sending records to all three brokers of the cluster, and a consumer group with three consumers load balancing incoming records from the three brokers:

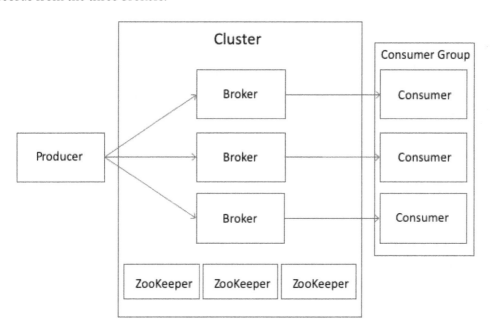

Figure 2.7 – High-level architecture of an Apache Kafka cluster

In order to achieve durability and high availability, Apache Kafka provides the ability to replicate messages to multiple brokers by setting the replication factor at the cluster level or the topic level. When set to more than one, Kafka creates the specified number of copies of the partition log for the topic(s). Each copy is called a replica. If the replication factor for a topic is set to three, there will be a total of three replicas for every partition for that topic distributed across the available brokers. One of the replicas is the partition leader and the others are followers. The leader serves write and read requests while the followers fetch records from the leader and keep their partition logs in sync (as of Apache Kafka 2.4.0, KIP-392 (`https://cwiki.apache.org/confluence/display/KAFKA/KIP-392%3A+Allow+consumers+to+fetch+from+closest+replica`) allows consumers to fetch from the closest replica, whereby followers serve read requests). The partition logs for all follower replicas look identical to the leader, except for the possibility of some unreplicated messages. This provides the ability to fail over to a surviving replica if the partition leader becomes unavailable. This happens through a process called leader election and is automatic.

Producers send messages to topics. The messages are key/value pairs with headers. Messages may or may not have keys. If keys are not present, then the producer API uses a default partitioner that round robins the message to all available partitions. If the key is present, then the default behavior is to create a hash of the key to determine the partition and send it to that partition. It is also possible to specify a custom partitioner in the producer to implement a custom partitioning strategy.

On the consumer side, Kafka supports both the **publish-subscribe** model as well as the **queuing** model. On the publish-subscribe side, Kafka can have many independent consumers consuming from the same topic, all getting the same set of messages and having the ability to read from different offsets in the commit log. On the queuing side, consumers are usually deployed in a **consumer group** consisting of multiple consumers started with the same **group.id** consumer property. They work together in concert and read from all partitions of a topic in parallel, but there is always a 1:1 mapping between a topic partition and a consumer instance in the consumer group.

A consumer instance can read from multiple partitions depending on the number of partitions and the number of consumer instances, but one partition can be read by one and only one consumer instance at a time, thus maintaining queuing semantics where only one consumer gets a message. The consumer group model utilizes the Kafka group protocol to coordinate among consumer instances and can identify failed consumer instances, whereupon the consumer group goes through a "rebalance" and the consumer instances get a new set of partitions to read from.

In order to do that, consumer instances need to know where the failed consumer instances left off. By default, Kafka consumers commit the offsets they have read and processed to an internal topic called `__consumer_offsets`, which is read by the consumer instances after rebalancing to start reading their assigned partitions from the committed offsets.

One of the great advantages of Kafka, and one that provides a great deal of performance, is the binary protocol used by Kafka over TCP. The binary data format for producers, on-disk storage at brokers, and consumers is the same and requires no conversion. This allows Kafka to use zero-copy, in which the data is not copied from the kernel space to application space.

Amazon MSK

Many Kafka users find it challenging to set up a distributed, fault-tolerant Kafka cluster and manage, scale, and operate it in production. It requires a lot of expertise on the DevOps and support side and a lot of time and effort spent on infrastructure, to provision and replace servers as needed, patch and upgrade servers, perform disk maintenance, and set up monitoring and alerting. In addition, Apache Kafka has a dependency on **Apache ZooKeeper**, which most people do not want to be in the business of maintaining.

With Amazon MSK, it is possible to set up a Kafka cluster with a few clicks on the AWS console or using the **AWS CLI** or **AWS SDKs** in the supported programming languages. The brokers and the ZooKeeper nodes are set up in a service-managed **Virtual Private Cloud** (**VPC**), which provides an isolated, dedicated virtual network in an AWS account. The service VPC is a dedicated, independent VPC for every cluster and also has a dedicated ZooKeeper ensemble for every cluster. The Kafka producers, consumers, and other tools can access the Amazon MSK Apache Kafka cluster using virtual network interfaces (**Elastic Network Interfaces – ENIs**) in the user account VPCs. Amazon MSK uses the open source Apache Kafka software and is therefore compatible with all Apache Kafka ecosystem tools and third-party tools that work with open source Apache Kafka, such as **Kafka Connect**, **Kafka streams**, **Schema Registry**, and **REST Proxy**. The only caveat is that tools that upload a custom jar to the Apache Kafka brokers do not work as Amazon MSK does not allow custom jar uploads. Amazon MSK identifies broker problems and failures and replaces the brokers as necessary, but it maintains the same IP addresses and broker DNS endpoints and re-attaches the same disk volumes (unless the disk volumes have issues) to maintain healthy clusters with minimal application downtime. The service offers an SLA (`https://aws.amazon.com/msk/sla/`) of 99.9%.

Figure 2.8 illustrates how connectivity works between the VPC and the broker and ZooKeeper nodes in the service-managed VPC:

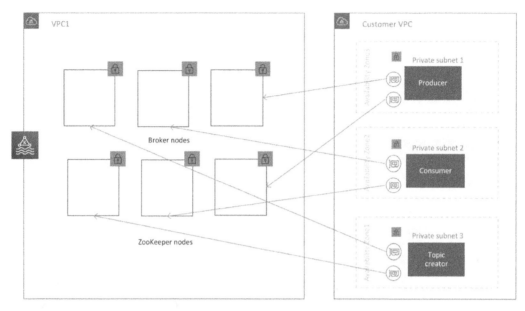

Figure 2.8 – Connectivity between your VPC and Amazon MSK

The control plane of Amazon MSK provides the ability to create and delete clusters, create and delete configurations (configurations are mechanisms to provide supported server properties to Amazon MSK to influence broker and cluster behavior), list and describe cluster properties, add additional brokers, increase broker storage, and perform a number of other actions.

When creating an Amazon MSK cluster, the number and type of **Amazon EC2** instances to be used for the Apache Kafka brokers need to be specified. The brokers are spread across multiple AZs for high availability, fault tolerance, and data durability. Two topologies are supported: **two AZs** and **three AZs**. The three-AZ setup is recommended for most production setups.

Encryption, authentication, and authorization

The control plane is integrated with AWS IAM and supports authentication via AWS Signature Version 4, which uses a keyed **Hash Message Authentication Code** (**HMAC**) for authentication and Identity-based IAM policies for authorization. At this time, resource-based IAM policies are not supported. The data plane uses the Apache Kafka APIs (the Producer API, Consumer API, and the AdminClient API) and utilizes supported authentication mechanisms for Apache Kafka.

At the time of writing, TLS certificate-based mutual authentication, using certificates from **AWS Certificate Manager Private Certificate Authority**, and **SASL/SCRAM** authentication with integration with **AWS Secrets Manager** are supported. TLS encryption in transit between clients and brokers and in-cluster between brokers is also supported. In addition, Apache Kafka authorization using **Access Control Lists** (**ACLs**) at all resource levels is supported with both authentication mechanisms. AWS VPC security groups and network ACLs can also be used to control access to the Amazon MSK cluster in addition to the authentication and authorization mechanisms provided by Apache Kafka. It is recommended that the ZooKeeper nodes be secured by using a separate security group from the one used for the Apache Kafka broker nodes and only exposed to a specific security group utilized by an administrative client. While there is full access provided to the ZooKeeper nodes as port 2181 is open and the ZooKeeper ensemble can be used for custom applications outside of Amazon MSK, it is recommended not to do so as it is a fully managed service.

Amazon MSK provides encryption at rest by utilizing symmetric keys from **AWS KMS** and supports both service-managed CMKs and customer-managed CMKs. Customer-managed CMKs should be used where possible, as they provide the advantage of controlling which principals have access to the keys, the ability to audit key usage via AWS CloudTrail, and the ability to perform key rotations. Amazon MSK uses **Amazon EBS** volumes for storage and utilizes EBS encryption using envelope encryption.

Logging and monitoring

For monitoring, Amazon MSK has integrations with **AWS CloudWatch** for both metrics and brokers logs. The broker logs can also be sent directly to Amazon S3 or to **Amazon Kinesis Data**. The **JMX metrics** for the brokers is also exported using a Prometheus JMX exporter and can be scraped using a **Prometheus server** or other third-party software such as Datadog.

With the popularity of Apache Kafka in the industry, Amazon MSK provides a compelling managed service for Apache Kafka.

Next, let's take a brief look at a serverless event bus offered by AWS.

Amazon EventBridge

Amazon EventBridge is an implementation of the event-driven architecture pattern that AWS launched in July 2019. EventBridge is a serverless event bus service that allows you to build event-driven architectures in your applications and integrate with partners. The key advantage that EventBridge offers is the ability to remove the need for point-to-point integrations, so you can become more flexible and agile as you connect to other applications. Since it's a fully managed service, there are no servers for you to manage, and you pay only for usage, with no minimum fees or upfront commitments. The service is metered by events published, schema discovery usage, and event replay:

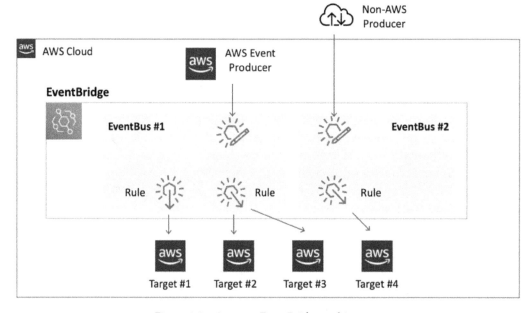

Figure 2.9 – Amazon EventBridge architecture

EventBridge has event buses, events, rules, and targets. The service provides an out-of-the-box event bus called "default." The event bus is the starting point to using EventBridge; it is the central hub that receives and distributes events. You can create up to 100 event buses per AWS account. An event is an indication of a change in an application, system, server, and so on. For example, an event can represent a change in an AWS service, such as an EC2 instance state change from running to shutting down, or an event from an application indicating that a customer placed an order with an item needing to be shipped. In addition to "live" events, EventBridge also allows you to schedule events just like you would do with a cron job or an application scheduler. Rules perform the filtering and routing of the events to particular targets. Rules can send an event to multiple targets and can modify the event itself by adding data or transforming event data. An event bus has a quota of up to 300 rules, with each rule pattern having up to 2,048 characters. Targets are the receiving endpoints for an event bus. Popular targets are AWS Lambda functions, SNS and SQS, and Kinesis. There is a limit of up to five targets per rule. In *Chapter 8, Kinesis Integrations*, we will show you how you can use EventBridge and Kinesis to implement rule-based routing.

The EventBridge Schema Registry is useful for the creation of the code bindings based on events structure. Schema Registry uses the OpenAPI and JSON Schema Draft4 standards to discover and manage these event schemas. Schema Registry can automatically generate a schema by providing the JSON of the event or allowing EventBridge to infer schemas based on the events in the event bus. Once a schema is created, you can generate code bindings for several languages, such as Java, Python, and TypeScript.

When it comes to security, Amazon EventBridge uses IAM to control access to other AWS services and resources. For data in transit, you can use TLS 1.2 or later to communicate with the event bus. When EventBridge passes data to other services, it is encrypted using TLS. Data at rest is fully encrypted using 256-bit Advanced Encryption Standard (AES-256). You can use an AWS-owned CMK, which is provided at no additional charge. The compliance certifications for Amazon EventBridge include SOC, PCI, FedRAMP, HIPAA, and several others; a full list can be found at the AWS Services in Scope by Compliance Program (https://aws.amazon.com/compliance/services-in-scope/). You can use EventBridge to send events between your AWS accounts. You can do this with your own AWS organization or accounts belonging to other organizations by controlling whether an account can send or receive events. When using the AWS Organizations feature, you can grant access at the organization level.

Service comparison summary

Figure 2.10 shows a comparison of the services under the Kinesis umbrella across various aspects relevant to streaming and messaging:

	Amazon Kinesis Data Streams	Amazon Kinesis Data Firehose	Amazon Kinesis Data Analytics for KDA SQL	Amazon Kinesis Data Analytics for Flink	Amazon Kinesis Video Streams
AWS managed	Yes	Yes	Yes	Yes	Yes
Strengths	Low Latency with replay	Pre-built integrated consumers	Real-time data analytics with ANSI 2011 SQL code	Real-time data analytics Open source compatibility, pre-built operators	Streaming video analysis
Trade Offs	Customized consumers are required	Higher latency/limited destinations	Limited capabilities	Limited Flink configurations and REST APIs	Purpose built for video
Protocols	AWS REST API	AWS REST API	AWS REST API	AWS REST API	AWS REST API, HLS, DASH, Web-RTC
Guaranteed ordering	Yes	No	Yes	Yes	Yes
Delivery (deduping)	At least once	At least once	At least once	Exactly Once	
Data retention period(max)	365 days	24 hours	Limited by KPU total memory	Limited by KPU total storage	365 days
Availability	Three AZ	Three AZ	Three AZ	Three AZ	Three AZ
Scale/throughput	No limit / ~ shards	No limit / automatic	Amazon Kinesis Processing Units (KPU)	Amazon Kinesis Processing Units (KPU)	12.5 MB per second per stream
Multiple consumers	Yes	No	3 destination per application	Yes – up to 50	Yes
Row/object size	1 MB	Destination row/object size	512 KB	Configurable	1 second

Figure 2.10 – Service comparison summary of the Kinesis umbrella of services

Figure 2.11 shows a comparison of the messaging and streaming services other than those under the Kinesis umbrella of services in AWS, across various aspects relevant to streaming and messaging:

	Amazon Managed Streaming for Apache Kafka(MSK)	Amazon Simple Queue Service (Amazon SQS) (Standard)	Amazon SQS (FIFO)	Amazon SNS	IoT Core
AWS managed	Yes	Yes	Yes	Yes	Yes
Strengths	Low latency open source compatibility with replay	Easy setup, deduplication, parallel processing	Easy setup, FIFO	Notification message types	IoT device message data
Trade Offs	Manual scaling	No order guarantee/no replay	Performance	Data retention duration	Data retention
Protocols	TCP	Rest API	Rest API	Rest API, SMTP, SMS, HTTPS	MQTT, AWS Rest API
Guaranteed ordering	Yes	No	Yes	Yes	No
Delivery (deduping)	At least/At most/exactly once	At least once	Exactly once	No (Yes with FIFO)	At least once / at most once
Data retention period	Configurable	14 days	14 days	Retries over days	1 hour
Availability	Configurable	Three AZ	Three AZ	Three AZ	Three AZ
Scale/throughput	25 Soft limit	No limits / automatic	3000 TPS / API action	300 TPS or 10 MB per second, per topic	No limits / automatic
Multiple consumers	Yes	No	No	Yes	No
Row/object size	1MB default Configurable	256 KB	256 KB	256 KB	256 KB

Figure 2.11 – Service comparison summary of other AWS messaging services

The service comparison summaries take into account the most common aspects related to streaming and messaging and are intended to be a quick lookup when making a choice between AWS services for streaming and messaging architectures.

Summary

In this chapter, we reviewed the extensive array of services offered by Amazon Web Services in the messaging and streaming space. We discussed how each of these services is purpose-built to solve specific use cases and achieve application scalability and compatibility. These services have several similarities and differences, as described through the chapter. Now that we have covered all these topics, you should have a good understanding of the different AWS offerings. It should now be easier for you to pick the right service for your needs.

In the next chapters, we will focus specifically on each of the Amazon Kinesis services, with a deep dive into a fictitious use case for SmartCity, USA.

3
The SmartCity Bike-Sharing Service

Throughout the book, a fictional bike-sharing service, **SwipeBike**, will be used as an example to illuminate how Amazon Kinesis can be applied in a variety of different situations. Bike-sharing services provide city commuters with environmentally friendly alternatives to traditional personal vehicles and buses. Cities such as New York City, Paris, London, Hangzhou, and Mumbai have implemented successful bike-sharing programs with significant commuter adoption and reduced city traffic.

The use case is situated in the fictional municipality of SmartCity, USA. SmartCity wants to further improve on the success of its recently deployed bike-sharing program. Since its launch, it has reduced traffic, contributed to significant improvements in the city's air quality, and has increased the citizens' physical health.

SmartCity conducted a year-long feedback survey and determined that riders wanted a "*more real-time and immersive riding experience*," "*safer riding conditions*," and "*improved and more efficient operations at the bike stations*." Throughout the rest of this book, we will see how SmartCity developed several new services to address these new requirements derived from rider feedback.

In this chapter, we will review the data streaming requirements for the fictional bike-sharing use case.

The following topics will be covered in the chapter:

- The mission for sustainable transportation
- SmartCity new mobile features
- The AWS Well-Architected Framework

The mission for sustainable transportation

During an average day in SmartCity, commuters pour in from several surrounding areas, nearly doubling the city's population from 1.6 million to 3.1 million people. For SmartCity to accommodate this population surge, bicycle usage must be optimized during the morning and evening commute. Any systems we design will need to be able to handle these surges in use.

A bicycle-sharing system is a service in which bicycles are made available for shared use on a short-term usage for a small price or even for free. SmartCity visitors can borrow a bike from one station and return it to another destination station. Stations are special bike racks that secure and protect the bike from theft or misuse. The bikes are unlocked by a cloud-based control system when the riders enter their payment information using a registered member swipe card. The rider can later return the bike to another station.

SmartCity is the nation's largest bike-share program, with 14,500 bikes and 950 stations spread throughout the city. Managing a bike-share program at this scale requires collecting and processing massive amounts of data produced by thousands of sensors and millions of users. SmartCity will build and deploy the applications on Amazon Web Services because of its unmatched experience, maturity, reliability, security, and performance.

In the next section, we will review the SmartCity mobile app and the operational dashboard features developed for the SmartCity bike-share program. The data pipeline required to support the following features will be referenced throughout the book. These new SmartCity features will be used as examples for learning how to build scalable data streaming solutions with Amazon Kinesis.

SmartCity new mobile features

SmartCity will be implementing several new real-time data-driven features for the mobile application (*Figure 3.1*). These real-time data features will enable riders to have a safer and more enjoyable experience:

Figure 3.1 – Mockup for the SmartCity mobile application

SmartCity will implement a streaming and analytics platform that will provide service operators, riders, financers, and researchers access to the data and services that enable them to support thousands of riders each day.

SmartCity will need a scalable data pipeline to deliver the volume of data that the millions of riders produce. In the next section, we will review some of the requirements for the data pipeline.

SmartCity data pipeline

SmartCity realized that they need to provide immediate communication on safety and schedule information to keep riders informed about what is going on in the city. The data required to provide these services is stored and managed in several independent data systems throughout the city. These data systems include data from road construction schedulers, crime alerts, and city events announcements. A data pipeline will collect the data streaming from several independent city data systems and make the data available to downstream applications and services such as the mobile app, data lakes, operational dashboards, and social video sharing applications. SmartCity will utilize Amazon **Kinesis Data Streams (KDS)** as the core service to collect and process real-time data so that the data can be efficiently consumed and processed by other services such as Amazon **Kinesis Data Firehose (KDF)**.

In addition, to the traditional end-user experience, the following core components are essential to meeting the requirements:

- A data lake for flexible and centralized analytics

- Facilities so that the rider can access video to see the context of the bike stand

- Dashboard systems for real-time operational analytics

The following architectural diagram (*Figure 3.2*) shows how the data is collected, processed, and made available to users on mobile phones and operational dashboards:

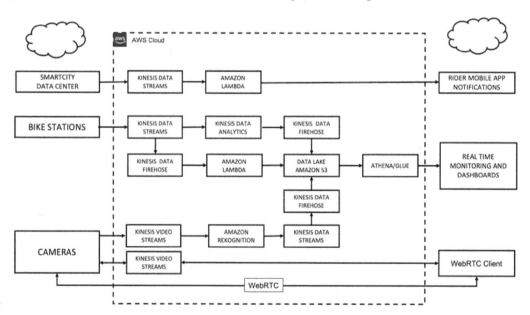

Figure 3.2 – Architecture design for the SmartCity data pipeline

Let's dive a little deeper into the components, starting with the data lake.

SmartCity data lake

SmartCity needs to operationalize all the data consumed and produced by the bike-sharing service. The data needs to be available for long-term planning and forecast analytics, collaborative rider mobile services, machine learning data development, and ongoing research studies. SmartCity will implement a secure, scalable, highly available data lake that will provide a self-service data culture for the software developers, research analytics, and program auditors.

SmartCity will be utilizing **Amazon Kinesis Data Firehose** (**KDF**) as the core service to collect and transform data, so the data can be efficiently analyzed, consumed, and archived into **Simple Storage Service** (**Amazon S3**). KDF will perform much of the heavy lifting required to stream and process data for the data lake.

As discussed in the next section, real-time data metrics will improve the bike-sharing service team's decision-making process with real-time operational dashboards and reports.

SmartCity operations and analytics dashboard

Along with the SmartCity app's new mobile features, the operational teams will need access to data and metrics to help them with budgeting and operation decisions. Adjustments and decisions often need to be made in near real time to accommodate the bikes' on-demand usage. SmartCity needs to adjust the operations leveraging the real-time data, rather than relying on outdated weekly and monthly forecasts.

SmartCity will develop an operations management dashboard to manage the bicycle fleet. The dashboard can display calculated metrics such as these:

- Number of riders at given time intervals
- Average distance traveled per ride
- Alerts and forecasts regarding bike stations that are empty and full
- Environmental metrics such as noise, temperature, and alerts for system closures due to weather

SmartCity will use Amazon **Kinesis Data Analytics** (**KDA**) and **Apache Flink** to analyze the streaming data through near real-time windows. KDA integrates with several AWS services, allowing SmartCity to create a sophisticated management dashboard rapidly.

The SmartCity bike-sharing service also needs to ingest video data. We will review the features and how Amazon **Kinesis Video Streams (KVS)** will be used as the scalable video streaming service for SmartCity.

SmartCity video

In addition to all the data and sensors available for monitoring the SmartCity bike-sharing system, there has been interest in using video as a data source. Video supports two primary use cases, the first allowing the user to get access to a real-time video feed from the bike stand using Web-RTC. The second allows security to use facial recognition to identify when known vandals are in the area. SmartCity and the riders want a safe and predictable experience, and the use of video will help enable that. These two services will use Amazon **Kinesis Video Streams (KVS)** and **AI machine learning** services to collect and process the video.

In the next section, we will review some best practices for designing and architecting data analytics services.

The AWS Well-Architected Framework

SmartCity will utilize best practices for delivering applications on the cloud. Amazon Web Services offers the **AWS Well-Architected Framework** (https://aws.amazon.com/architecture/well-architected) for architecting and improving cloud-based workloads.

The pillars of the AWS Well-Architected Framework include the following:

- *Operational excellence* – Operating the application with insight that enables the improvement of processes, procedures, and how value is delivered
- *Security* – Protecting the systems and data and utilizing services to support security
- *Reliability* – Maintaining consistent performance through the measurement and monitoring of the complete system
- *Efficiency* – Leveraging cloud services that scale the system to demand
- *Cost optimization* – Cost optimizing the system for financial efficiency

The Well-Architected Framework also includes application-specific guidance called **lenses**. The lenses extend the guidance of the AWS Well-Architected Framework to include specific industry and technology domains. For example, SmartCity would utilize the Analytics Lens (`https://docs.aws.amazon.com/wellarchitected/ latest/analytics-lens/general-design-principles.html`) guidance. The Analytics Lens general design principles facilitate good design in the cloud for analytics applications.

The Well-Architected Framework Analytics Lens includes the following:

- Automating the process of ingesting data
- Designing for failures, including duplication
- Maintaining the original source of data
- Visibility of data through its origin to its destination
- Selecting the best storage for the data
- Securing the data pipeline
- Designing for scalability and reliability

Summary

In this chapter, we reviewed the SmartCity bike-sharing program and the features that SwipeBike will be building. These features will be built with AWS and designed in the chapters throughout the book.

In the next chapter, we will learn about KDS and how it can collect near real-time data from many data sources.

Further reading

Please refer to the following for more information:

- NYC Bike Share System Data

    `https://www.citibikenyc.com/system-data`

- AWS Well-Architected Framework

    `https://aws.amazon.com/architecture/well-architected`

- AWS Well-Architected Framework Analytics Lens

    `https://docs.aws.amazon.com/wellarchitected/latest/analytics-lens/general-design-principles.html`

Section 2: Deep Dive into Kinesis

In the next four chapters, you will get a deep dive into the capabilities of each of the four Kinesis managed services. We will talk about the concepts, common deployment patterns, monitoring and scaling, and the security of Kinesis Data Streams, Kinesis Firehose, Kinesis Analytics, and Kinesis Video Streams. We will see how Amazon Kinesis can be used to meet the SmartCity bike-sharing service requirements.

This section comprises the following chapters:

- *Chapter 4, Kinesis Data Streams*
- *Chapter 5, Kinesis Firehose*
- *Chapter 6, Kinesis Data Analytics*
- *Chapter 7, Kinesis Video Streams*

4
Kinesis Data Streams

In the previous chapter, you learned about several purpose-built data streaming and message queueing technologies. When designing a data streaming solution, we select the best purpose-built technology that meets business requirements. When an application needs to offer real-time performance from many different sources, Amazon **KDS** (**KDS**) is often the best choice.

Amazon **KDS** is a managed, massively scalable, durable, and low latency real-time data streaming service used by many of the largest data pipelines in the cloud. With KDS, you can collect large volumes of data per second from many sources, including connected devices, application logs and events, financial transactions, social media, marketing events, and geolocation tracking feeds. KDS enables you to build custom applications that process and analyze data from these sources with the most flexibility. You want to use KDS when you need to deliver near real-time sub-second performance.

When utilizing shards and **partition keys**, KDS offers a strong guarantee for the ordering of records and the ability to read and replay records in the same order from multiple applications. Your applications can also process data from a stream through the parallelization of consumers.

In this chapter, you will learn concepts and capabilities, common deployment patterns, monitoring and scaling, and how to secure KDS. We will step through a data streaming solution that will ingest, process, and feed data from multiple SmartCity data systems.

The following topics will be covered in the chapter:

- Discovering Amazon Kinesis Data Streams
- Creating a stream producer application
- Creating a stream consumer application
- Data pipelines with Amazon Kinesis Data Streams

Technical requirements

There are multiple requirements you need to have ready before you get started with this chapter. The following are those requirements:

- **AWS account setup**: You will need to get an AWS account to run the examples included in this chapter. If you do not have an account already, you can go to `https://aws.amazon.com/getting-started/` to create an account. AWS accounts offer a Free Tier (`https://aws.amazon.com/free`). The AWS Free Tier allows you to use many AWS services for free within specified usage limits. AWS Lambda, AWS Cloud9, AWS CloudWatch, and EC2 are eligible Free Tier services. Please note that Amazon Kinesis Data Streams is **not** currently available as a Free Tier service. Refer to the Kinesis Data Streams pricing for the associated costs: `https://aws.amazon.com/kinesis/data-streams/pricing/`.

- **Using a local development environment**: You will need a working Python 3.x environment. You can install Python 3.x by downloading and running the installer (`https://www.python.org/downloads/`) for your environment's operating system.

- You need to set up the AWS **Software Development Kit (SDK)** for Python (`https://aws.amazon.com/sdk-for-python/`). The AWS SDK for Python includes several tools for developing in AWS with Python and includes libraries such as boto3.

- **Using an AWS Cloud9 development environment**: As an alternative to setting these up in your local development environment, you can create an AWS Cloud9 development environment: `https://docs.aws.amazon.com/cloud9/latest/user-guide/setting-up.html`.

- **AWS Cloud9** is a web-based development environment that makes it easy to develop applications on AWS. AWS Cloud9 supports development languages such as Python, Go, PHP, and JavaScript. The **Integrated Development Environment (IDE)** provides features for building, debugging, and running code. You can use the built-in terminal to clone the example code Git code repository, execute AWS CLI commands, and run the Python code examples.

  You can use the following guide to set up your Python environment on AWS Cloud9 (`https://docs.aws.amazon.com/cloud9/latest/user-guide/sample-python.html`).

- **Code examples**: The code examples in this book are available on GitHub at `https://github.com/PacktPublishing/Streaming-Data-Solutions-with-Amazon-Kinesis`. You will need a Git client to access them (`https://git-scm.com/`).

Discovering Amazon Kinesis Data Streams

Amazon KDS is a service composed of streams, shards, and records. A data stream is a logical container of shards. A data stream continuously ingests data from many data sources. Each stream has one or more shards where records are grouped and stored.

Sharding allows the stream to handle more records, while record order is preserved within each shard. Records are the unit of data in the Kinesis data stream, composed of a sequence number, a partition key, and a data blob. KDS segregates the data records belonging to a stream into multiple shards. When you have multiple shards, you can use a partition key to group data on specific shards. Kinesis uses the partition key to assign records to an individual shard. Records are accessed from the stream with the partition level sequence number. Data can be ingested and processed from many sources, such as the listed applications in the diagram:

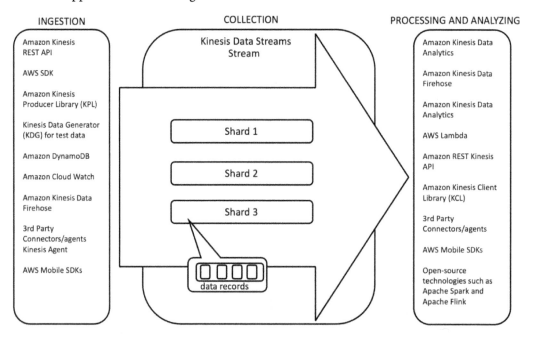

Figure 4.1 – A stream has shards, and a shard has data records

The records are put into the data stream through a producer application using the KDS API, the Amazon **Kinesis Producer Library** (**KPL**), Amazon Kinesis Agent, and other open source projects. The KPL is a code library that abstracts much of the complexity of adding data into a stream. The KPL library is optimized for performance and handling failures, and simplifies integration with producer applications.

In this chapter, we will be using Kinesis Agent as an example of a producer application. The agent will send records from the SmartCity notification service.

Records are gathered from the data stream by a consumer application using the KDS API, the Amazon **Kinesis Client Library** (**KCL**), Lambda functions, or other integrated AWS services. The KCL consumer interface retrieves all records for a given partition key, starting from a given sequence number. The KCL will transparently track the record's sequence number in an Amazon DynamoDB table. The KCL uses the sequence number as a checkpoint, so if the consumer is stopped, it could later restart with the last unprocessed record.

Now that we've seen how data flows through KDS, we will learn how to create KDS streams and put data into the streams to be processed. We will design a KDS data pipeline that enables SmartCity to collect data from several city systems and process the records with low latency to several SmartCity's bike-sharing applications and services.

Creating streams and shards

Let's get started creating a stream with a shard and configure it for performance and cost. As described in the previous section, a stream is a logical container in which data is collected in KDS.

When you create a Kinesis data stream, you only need to set the stream's name and the number of shards. Let's create a stream, by first logging into the AWS console at `https://aws.amazon.com/console/`. Next, let's head over to the KDS service console. Once, logged in to AWS, in the **Search for Services** search box type in `Kinesis` and click the service **Kinesis: Work with Real-Time Streaming Data**. Under **Getting Started**, select the **KDS** option and click **Create Data Stream**. Create a new stream by specifying the stream name and the number of shards, as shown in the following screenshot:

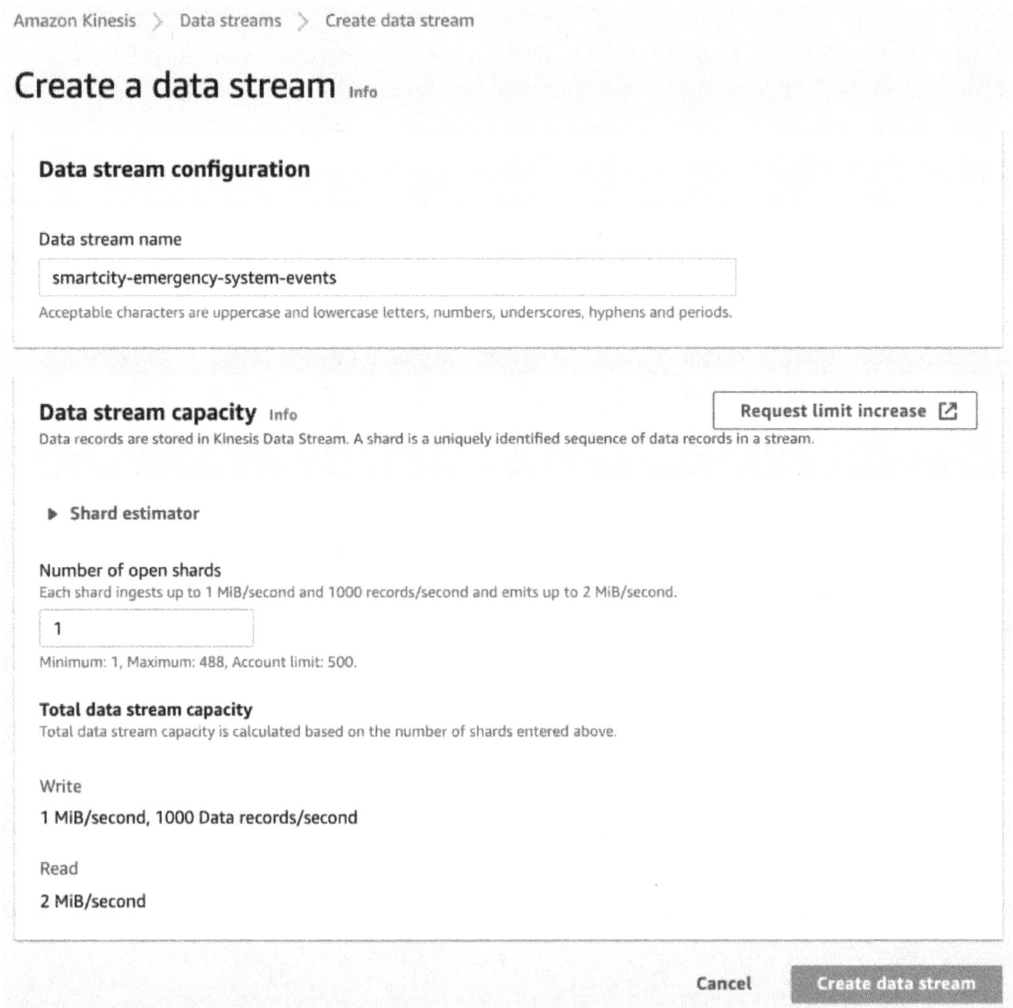

Amazon Kinesis > Data streams > Create data stream

Create a data stream Info

Data stream configuration

Data stream name

```
smartcity-emergency-system-events
```

Acceptable characters are uppercase and lowercase letters, numbers, underscores, hyphens and periods.

Data stream capacity Info

Request limit increase ↗

Data records are stored in Kinesis Data Stream. A shard is a uniquely identified sequence of data records in a stream.

▶ Shard estimator

Number of open shards

Each shard ingests up to 1 MiB/second and 1000 records/second and emits up to 2 MiB/second.

```
1
```

Minimum: 1, Maximum: 488, Account limit: 500.

Total data stream capacity

Total data stream capacity is calculated based on the number of shards entered above.

Write

1 MiB/second, 1000 Data records/second

Read

2 MiB/second

Cancel   **Create data stream**

Figure 4.2 – Choosing a name and selecting the number of shards in the stream

There are no upper limits on the number of streams you can create with a single AWS account. The minimum number of shards you can have in a stream is one shard. Each AWS Region has a soft shard number quota limit that can be increased with an AWS support request.

The number of shards for a stream is one of the primary settings that impacts the scale and cost. Although AWS fully manages the streams and the shards, the number of shards required for a workload to perform is not autoscaled by Kinesis. You need to select the number of shards necessary to scale to your workload's peak performance. The number of shards configured for your stream can be increased or decreased after a stream is created.

When considering the shard count for a workload, you will need to understand your data records' properties and requirements, such as the read and write volume and velocity. A shard provides an ingestion capacity of 1 MB/per second and 1,000 PUT records per second. The consumption capacity is 2 MB/per second and 2,000 GET records per second. The number of shards can be specified when creating the stream and modified when additional capacity is needed.

The following table (*Figure 5.3*) provides some examples of read and write capacity based on shard counts:

Stream Write and Read Capacity	Stream Capacity Examples:
The shard capacity for **producer writes** into the stream is 1MB.	For each shard in the stream, your producer data payload can be 1MB per second and 1,000 PutRecord API requests per second.
	If there is a stream with 5 shards, your stream can support 5 MB per second and 5,000 PUT API requests.
The shard capacity for **consumer reads** from the stream is 2MB.	For each shard in the stream, your consumer data payload can be 2MB per second and 2,000 GetRecord API requests per second.
	If there is a stream with 5 shards, your stream can support 10 MB per second and 10,000 GetRecord API requests.

Figure 4.3 – Read and write capacity examples

When creating a stream, you can use the shard estimator (*Figure 5.4*) to obtain a recommendation for the number of needed shards. The estimator will calculate the estimated number of required shards based on the maximum records written per second, the total number of consumers, and the average record size (in KiB). When you open the shard estimator (*Figure 5.4*), you can set the average and maximum record sizes to get the estimated required shards:

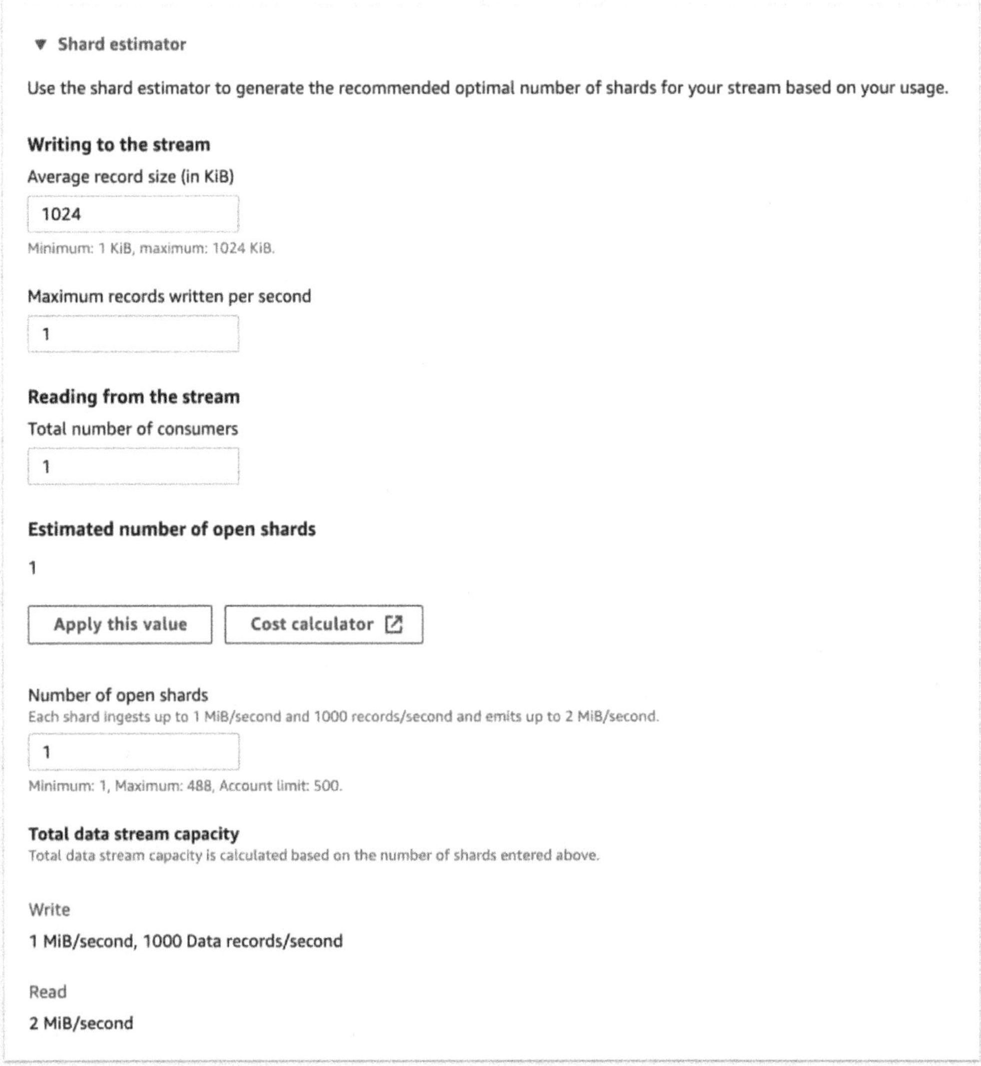

▼ Shard estimator

Use the shard estimator to generate the recommended optimal number of shards for your stream based on your usage.

Writing to the stream
Average record size (in KiB)

1024

Minimum: 1 KiB, maximum: 1024 KiB.

Maximum records written per second

1

Reading from the stream
Total number of consumers

1

Estimated number of open shards

1

Apply this value   Cost calculator ↗

Number of open shards
Each shard ingests up to 1 MiB/second and 1000 records/second and emits up to 2 MiB/second.

1

Minimum: 1, Maximum: 488, Account limit: 500.

Total data stream capacity
Total data stream capacity is calculated based on the number of shards entered above.

Write
1 MiB/second, 1000 Data records/second

Read
2 MiB/second

Figure 4.4 – Estimating the number of required shards when creating a stream

AWS also provides a service cost calculator (`https://calculator.aws/`). It estimates the cost of a stream based on the number of *records, average record size, number of consumer applications, number of* **Enhanced Fan-Out (EFO)** *consumers*, and the *extended data retention period.* The calculator calculates the monthly price of the stream and consumers based on the specified requirements:

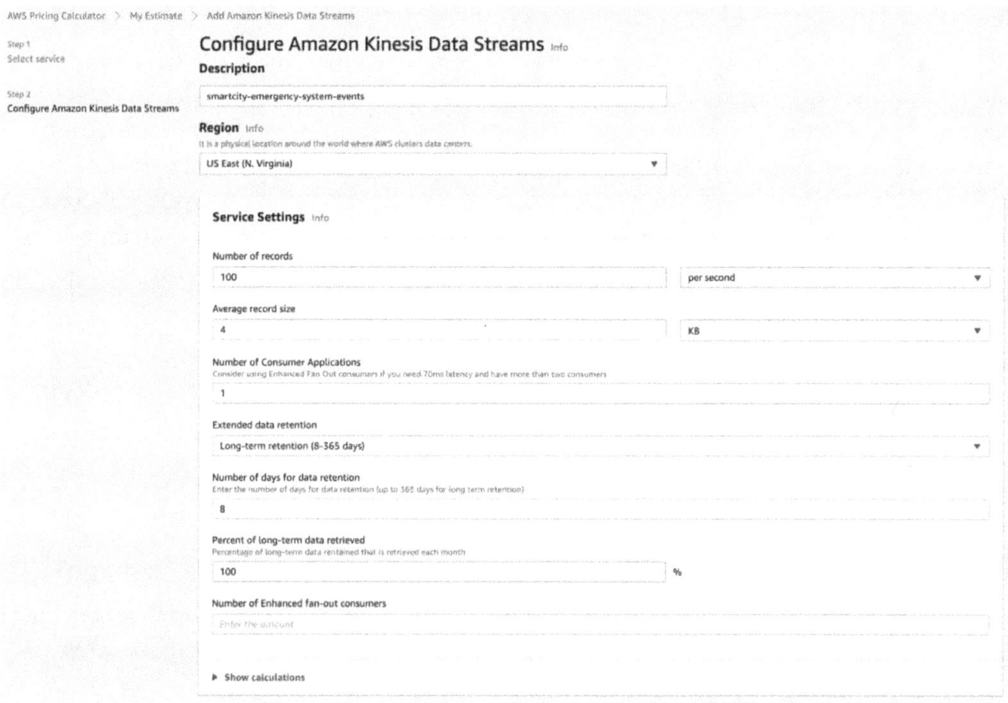

Figure 4.5 – AWS calculator (https://calculator.aws) for Amazon Kinesis Data Streams

Based on the determined scale of records, shards, and consumers, the calculator will break down the exact costs and calculations associated with each metered component of the stream.

You can monitor the shard-level metrics discussed later in the chapter to determine whether you need to add or remove shards from the stream. Shards can be dynamically added or removed through resharding. The actual sharding process within a stream, such as the splitting and merging of data, is fully managed by Amazon KDS: `https://docs.aws.amazon.com/streams/latest/dev/kinesis-using-sdk-java-resharding.html`.

> **Note**
> Scaling in increments of 25% of the current capacity helps the scaling process operation to complete faster. This approach is not required, but it helps reduce the number of times the shards need to split or merge. The Amazon Kinesis Scaling Utility, discussed later in the chapter, helps manage the shard splitting and merging through an autoscaling approach.

The default data retention duration for a stream is 24 hours. Once you write data into the stream, it is available to consumers for the specified retention duration. As data cannot be deleted from a stream, the data retention length is how data is eventually deleted from the stream. Data retention can be extended for up to 1 year for an additional cost. By extending the retention period, you can leave data in the stream for other workload tasks such as machine learning. For example, a machine learning model could be built and remodeled from a dedicated consumer that continuously trains with 1 years' worth of retained data.

Now that we have a stream and understand how the number of shards determines the capacity, we will create a producer that will write records into the stream. We will learn the different methods for writing records and how to optimize the performance and scale of ingesting data.

Creating a stream producer application

A producer is an application that adds data records into the data stream. There are several options to ingest data, including REST APIs, SDKs, agents, and tools that help you create a stream producer for your application.

Amazon Kinesis application technology options include the following:

- The Amazon Kinesis API and AWS Python SDK
- The Amazon KPL
- The **Kinesis Data Generator** (**KDG**) for test data
- Third-party connectors/agents
- Kinesis Agent
- AWS Mobile SDKs

Let's start by looking at how we can write data into the stream using the Amazon KDS REST APIs. We will walk through an API request and its response. This section will also demonstrate how we can use Kinesis Agent and the AWS Python SDK to write custom producer applications. As shown in the following diagram, the REST API, Kinesis Agent, and the Python SDK are a few of the many options for data ingestion:

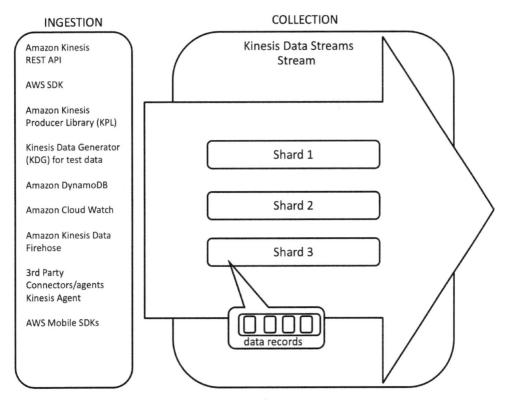

Figure 4.6 – Producer options

Using the PutRecord and PutRecords APIs

The available SDKs, agents, and tools simplify the steps to use the Amazon Kinesis Data Stream's **PutRecord** and **PutRecord** APIs. With the **PutRecord** API, a producer can write a single record into the stream. With the **PutRecords** API, a producer can write a batch of records into the stream.

When you use the `PutRecord` API, the payload requires a `blob` data type parameter called `Data`. The `Data` parameter is **Base64-encoded**, and the total size of the data (your data before base64-encoding) must not exceed the maximum record size (1 MiB). Let's look at the JSON data structure for the `PutRecord` API:

```
{
    "Data": blob,
    "ExplicitHashKey": "string",
    "PartitionKey": "string",
    "SequenceNumberForOrdering": "string",
    "StreamName": "string"
}
```

As example data, we will use a sample JSON record from SmartCity's emergency notification system. The emergency notification system provides SmartCity weather, crime, traffic, and other essential notifications through a REST API. We will collect and write these JSON data messages into a stream. Let's first look at how the message can be sent to the PutRecord API using the REST API HTTP POST, and then later using the AWS Python library.

> **Note**
>
> To get more city notification data in the format as used in the examples, you can use the New York City OpenData project OEM Emergency Notification API: `https://data.cityofnewyork.us/Public-Safety/OEM-Emergency-Notifications/8vv7-7wx3`.
>
> The Notification API provides information about emergency events and essential city services. The REST API endpoint is available at `https://data.cityofnewyork.us/resource/8vv7-7wx3.JSON`.

The following is an example JSON record from the SmartCity services system. This data includes the `record_id`, `date_time`, `notificationtype`, `notification_title`, and `email_body` message content:

```
[{
        "record_id": "18742",
        "date_and_time": "2002-07-03T15:53:00.000",
        "notificationtype": "Weather",
        "notification_title": "Coastal Flood Statement (BK)",
        "email_body": "Notification issued 11-15-2020 at 3:53 PM.
```

The National Weather Service has issued the following: What:
Coastal Flood Statement Where: Brooklyn When: 6 AM to10 AM
on 11/15 Hazards: Above normal tidal departures may result in
minor flooding of shore roads and/or properties. Preparedness
Actions: - Avoid driving through or coming in contact with
flood waters. There could be pollutants in the water or other
hazards that you cannot see. - Coastal flood waters could
damage your vehicle. Move your car to higher ground, and wash
your car thoroughly if it makes contact with flood waters.
- New York City residents, please call 311 if you encounter
flooding that makes roads impassable, causes property damage,
or persists for more than 48 hours. Info: www.weather.gov/
okx/."

}]

The StreamName is a required parameter in the PutRecord request and determines
which stream to write the records. This name matches the logical name selected when
creating a stream.

PartitionKey is a key used to route records to different shards within a stream. The
routed records are grouped into the shard maintaining the order in which the records
were received. PartitionKey is used to create an even distribution of records across
shards so that the stream can scale. As can be seen in the following diagram, all the
records with the same PartitionKey go to the same shard:

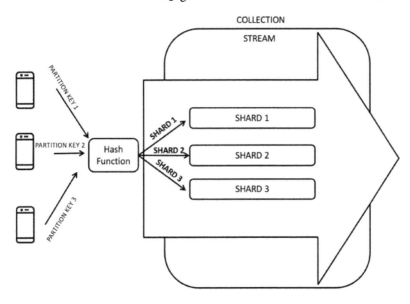

Figure 4.7 – Partition keys group records with the same partition key to the same shard

There are a number of strategies when selecting the partition key:

1. You can use a logical record data value such as **Weather** from **notificationtype** in the example emergency message. Using a data value can be a natural way to aggregate and group the data in **First In First Out** (**FIFO**) order within a shard. However, using a logical key can create "hot partition keys," where low cardinality of records for one partition key creates a situation where one shard could get a majority of the records.

2. You can also use a random partition key when records do not need to be ordered or aggregated onto the same shard. A random key creates an even distribution of records across all shards. This ensures that one shard does not get an uneven distribution (hot partition keys) of records.

> **Note**
>
> The `SequenceNumberForOrdering` parameter is an optional parameter that you can use to define your sequence for ordering. If the `SequenceNumberForOrdering` parameter is not set, `SequenceNumber` will be automatically created for the stream based on the record arrival time. The `SequenceNumberForOrdering` parameter can be used in cases where you want to use pre-existing serial keys for shard ordering.
>
> `ExplicitHashKey` is another optional parameter that can be used to create specific mapping of the record to a shard. This can be used in certain scenarios where you want greater control of the distribution of records.

The following sample `PutRecord` API HTTP POST includes the required parameters for sending our notification message into the `smartcity-emergency-system-events` stream. In the following example, `PartitionKey` is set as a random value, so records are distributed evenly across the shards. The data parameter in the **POST** request is the full contents of the JSON notification message:

```
POST / HTTP/1.1
Host: kinesis.<region>.<domain>
Content-Length: <PayloadSizeBytes>
User-Agent: <UserAgentString>
Content-Type: application/x-amz-JSON-1.1
Authorization: <AuthParams>
Connection: Keep-Alive
X-Amz-Date: <Date>
```

```
X-Amz-Target: Kinesis_20201121.PutRecord
{
  "StreamName": "smartcity-emergency-system-events",
  "Data": "": The full emergency systems JSON message…",…",
  "PartitionKey": "d17a06d5-0f83-40f6-acc5-840e7cd9aa8f"
}
```

Once the API accepts the PutRecord API POST, a return response will include the unique SequenceNumber and ShardId for the record.

The following is an example PutRecord response for the data record added to the emergency events stream. The payload includes ShardId, where the record is stored, and the stream assigned the SequenceNumber record:

```
POST / HTTP/1.1
Host: kinesis.<region>.<domain>
Content-Length: <PayloadSizeBytes>
User-Agent: <UserAgentString>
Content-Type: application/x-amz-JSON-1.1
Authorization: <AuthParams>
HTTP/1.1 200 OK
x-amzn-RequestId: <RequestId>
Content-Type: application/x-amz-JSON-1.1
Content-Length: <PayloadSizeBytes>
Date: <Date>
{
  "SequenceNumber": "41269329789653657946712963403768482178",
  "ShardId": "shardId-000000000000"
}
```

The `PutRecords` API performs the same function as `PutRecord`. However, `PutRecords` supports sending up to 500 records in a single request. Each record in the `PutRecords` API request can be up to 1 MB and as large as 5 MB for the entire `PutRecords` request:

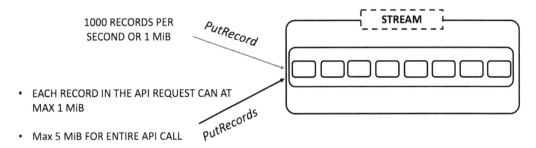

Figure 4.8 – PutRecords POST adds multiple data records to a stream. PutRecord POST adds a single data record to a stream

The `PutRecord` and `PutRecords` API requests have similar capabilities. The `PutRecord` API is designed for single records, and the `PutRecords` API is intended for a batch. When sending records as a single record or in batch, there are several considerations for order and error handling, as outlined in the following table:

PutRecord	PutRecords
Sends one record per HTTPS call	Batches multiple records and sends them in a single HTTPS request called the *Collection*
SequenceNumberForOrdering - records are coarsely ordered based on arrival time.	PutRecords doesn't guarantee the ordering of records. If you need to read records in the same order they are written to the stream, use PutRecord instead, and write to the same shard.
PutRecord throws *ProvisionedThroughputExceededException* when the request rate for the stream is too high, or the requested data is too large for the available throughput.	If 50 records are sent over single HTTPS and 10 failed, the call would still succeed with the response *FailedRecordCount* and the involved error message, producer can retry. These failed records can hamper the ordering of records as those 10 records would be sent behind the successful 40 records.

Figure 4.9 – PutRecords POST adds multiple data records to a stream. PutRecord POST adds a single data record to a stream

> **Note**
> Once you write a record to a stream, you cannot modify the record or its order. When a record is written to the stream, the record cannot be altered or deleted.

Producing data with the AWS SDK for Python (Boto3)

Boto3 is the AWS SDK for Python. The **Boto3** library allows you to quickly write software that uses services such as Amazon S3, Amazon EC2, and Amazon KDS. The following example Python code uses the Boto3 client interface to write the stream's emergency weather notification record.

Let's create a Python Boto3 producer that will write an emergency message to the stream we created previously, `smartcity-emergency-system-events`:

1. Let's start by creating a Python script called `producer.py` with the following code. In the script, there is a sample notification JSON message that we will write to the stream. This hardcoded example represents a message that could come from a file, database, or other data source:

```
import json
import uuid
import boto3
stream_name = "smartcity-emergency-system-events"
message_json = {
    "record_id": "18742",
    "date_and_time": "2020-11-14T15:53:00.000",
    "notificationtype": "Weather",
    "notification_title": "Coastal Flood Statement (BK)",
    "email_body": "Notification issued 11-15-2020 at
3:53 PM.   The National Weather Service has issued the
following: What: Coastal Flood Statement Where: Brooklyn
When: 6 AM to10 AM on 11/15 Hazards: Above normal tidal
departures may result in minor flooding of shore roads
and/or properties. ..."
}
kinesis = boto3.client('kinesis')
    data = json.dumps(message_json)
    partition_key = str(uuid.uuid4())
resp = kinesis.put_record(
        StreamName=stream_name,
```

```
        Data=data,
        PartitionKey=partition_key)
print(json.dumps(resp))
```

The computer or server running this code may require IAM permissions for stream actions, including kinesis:PutRecord, kinesis:PutRecords, and kinesis:DescribeStream. An example IAM policy is available in the book's GitHub repository for this chapter.

2. Run the producer script producer.py:

```
$ python producer.py
```

3. The producer script will write the record into the stream and print out the return response with shardID:

```
{
    "ShardId": "shardId-000000000000",
    "SequenceNumber": "4960090227335754091598993125690150
6243878407835297513618",
    "EncryptionType": "KMS"
}
```

4. You can check that the record is in the stream with the AWS CLI. The first command will get shard-id, and the second command will get ShardIterator. Lastly, we will execute get-records with the value of $SHARD_ITERATOR:

```
$ SHARD_ID=$(aws kinesis describe-stream --stream-
name smartcity-emergency-system-events | jq
'.StreamDescription.Shards[].ShardId' | tr -d '"')
$ SHARD_ITERATOR=$(aws kinesis get-shard-iterator
--shard-id $SHARD_ID --shard-iterator-type TRIM_HORIZON
--stream-name smartcity-emergency-system-events --query
'ShardIterator')

$ aws kinesis get-records --shard-iterator $SHARD_
ITERATOR
```

5. The response will return an array of records. The array will include the record that was previously added to the shard. The record data parameter will be `Base64` encoded; for example:

```
{
    "Records":[ {
        "Data":"VGhlIGZ1bGwgbWVzc2FnZSBiYXNlNjQgZW5jb2RlZC4=",
        "PartitionKey":"07142004.98660644726",
        "ApproximateArrivalTimestamp": 1.441215410867E9,
        "SequenceNumber":"4954498525690737002757088586640
6557770302265263859643187 4"
    } ],
    "MillisBehindLatest":9211972,
    "NextShardIterator":"AAAAAAAAAEDOW3ugseWPE4503kqN1yN1Ua
odY8unE0sYslMUmC61X9hlig5+t4RtZM0/
tALfiI4QGjunVgJvQsjxjh2aLyxaAaPr+LaoENQ7eVs4EdYXg
KyThTZGPcca2fVXYJWL3yafv9dsDwsYVedI66dbMZFC8rPMWc79
7zxQkv4pSKvPOZvrUIudb8UkH3VMzx58Is="
}
```

> **Note**
>
> There are pre-developed SDKs and agents designed to manage the complexity of producing records and interacting with the PutRecords API with efficiency and scale. They have several built-in features and efficiencies that help with the performance, monitoring, and recovery of a producer.
>
> The Amazon KPL performs many tasks common to creating efficient and reliable producers. When you use the KPL, you do not need to reinvent the wheel every time you create a new data ingestion application. The KPL, `https://github.com/awslabs/amazon-kinesis-client`, is open source software written in Java and C++ and is supported by Amazon for production use.

Producing data with Amazon Kinesis Agent

Amazon Kinesis Agent (`https://github.com/awslabs/amazon-kinesis-agent`) is a standalone, Java-based application that can write data into KDS and Amazon Kinesis Firehose without any producer code. The agent can monitor a filesystem directory for file patterns and send the data to a stream. The agent can handle routine maintenance, such as file rotation, restart recovery, and monitoring.

In addition to writing records to the stream, the agent also supports the preprocessing of data. The agent can convert the data from CSV format to JSON, log formats to JSON, and convert multiline records to a single line. The agent supports installation on Linux-based operating systems. You can use the AWS Cloud9 environment, described in the *Technical requirements* section, to install the Linux-based Kinesis Agent.

We will install, configure, and run Amazon Kinesis Agent on Linux in the following steps:

1. Install the agent on Linux with yum:

   ```
   $ sudo yum install -y aws-kinesis-agent
   ```

2. Let's now modify the agent configuration. Edit the configuration file in the following location: /etc/aws-kinesis/agent.json:

   ```
   {


     "cloudwatch.emitMetrics": true,
     "kinesis.endpoint": "",
     "firehose.endpoint": ""
   {
     "flows": [
       {    {
                 "filePattern": "/tmp/messages/*",
                 "kinesisStream": "smartcity-emergency-system-
   events", "
          "partitionKeyOption": "RANDOM"   }
         } ]
   }
     ]
   }
   ```

3. Start the agent manually. Using the following Linux commands, you can set the agent to start up automatically if the agent system is rebooted:

   ```
   $ sudo service aws-kinesis-agent start
   $ sudo sudo chkconfig aws-kinesis-agent on
   $ sudo service aws-kinesis-agent status
   ```

4. Monitor the agent logs. Lastly, check the logs for the status of the running agent:

```
$ tail -n 10 /var/log/aws-kinesis-agent/aws-kinesis-
agent.log
2021-02-27 20:21:38.989+0000 (Agent STARTING) com.amazon.
kinesis.streaming.agent.Agent [INFO] Agent: Startup
completed in 22 ms.
```

5. Now, if you can move data into the /tmp/messages/ directory, such as the example system message, smartcity_system_message.json, using the following Linux commands, you will be able to move the file:

```
$ sudo cp smartcity_system_message.json /tmp/messages/
```

6. Monitor the agent logs that record what was parsed and processed:

```
$ tail -n 10 /var/log/aws-kinesis-agent/aws-kinesis-
agent.log
 2021-02-27 15:24:31.147+0000
(FileTailer[kinesis:smartcity-emergency-system-
events:/tmp/messages/*]) com.amazon.kinesis.
streaming.agent.tailing.KinesisParser [INFO]
KinesisParser[kinesis:smartcity-emergency-system-events:/
tmp/messages/*]: Continuing to parse /tmp/messages/
smartcity_system_message.json.
```

Optimizing your producer

Record batching, aggregation, and compression are best practices that can increase the efficiency and capacity of reads and writes to a shard. These optimizations maximize the number of records in the payload and decrease the overall size of the request. Aggregation applies when many smaller files need to be written into the stream. Aggregation groups smaller files into a single record to maximize the number of records in a single PutRecords batch. Combining batching and aggregation maximizes the number of records that can be written into the stream at once.

Compressing and encoding records can also reduce the record payload size. As the size of the payload is reduced, the number of required shards can be reduced. In the example of SmartCity notification JSON messages, the small JSON messages could be aggregated and compressed to increase the number of records sent into a single PutRecords batch. The Amazon KPL has integrated support for aggregating multiple records into a single record for efficient puts.

Now that we have learned how to write records into the stream, let's review how records can be consumed. We will use an **AWS Lambda serverless** function to read the data records with sub-second latency.

Creating a stream consumer application

An Amazon Kinesis application is a data consumer that gets data from the stream and performs additional processing to the data records (data processing). Similar to producer applications, there are several options to help you get started creating a consumer. These options include REST APIs, SDKs, and agents that can help you create a stream consumer for your application.

Amazon Kinesis application options include the following:

- **Amazon Kinesis Data Analytics**
- **Amazon Kinesis Data Firehose**
- **AWS Lambda**
- The **Amazon Kinesis API**
- The **Amazon KCL**
- Third-party connectors/agents
- **AWS Mobile SDKs**
- Open source data process technologies, such as Apache Spark and Apache Flink

As shown in the following diagram, the **Amazon Kinesis REST API**, **AWS Lambda**, and **Amazon Kinesis Firehose** are a few of the many options for data ingestion:

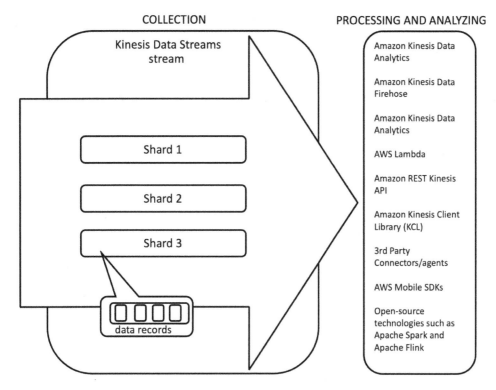

Figure 4.10 – There are several Amazon Kinesis application SDKs and Amazon services
that can process records from a stream

In the next section, we will discuss how consumer applications use the **Amazon KDS
REST API** to read and process records efficiently.

Using the GetRecords API

The consumer SDKs, agents, and other tools all simplify the steps in terms of using the
`Amazon KDS ListShards`, `GetShardIterator`, and `GetRecords` APIs. With
the `GetRecords` API, a consumer can request a batch of records of up to 10,000 records
per shard. As you can see in the following diagram, records are pulled from a shard by
a consumer application using the `GetRecords` API:

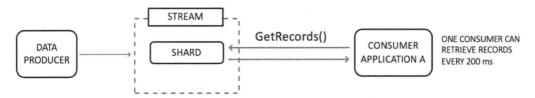

Figure 4.11 – With the GetRecords API, records are pulled by the consumer

The first step to creating a consumer is to use the `ListShards` API to get the stream's shards. For each retrieved shard, we will use the `GetShardIterator` API to obtain the shard position to start reading data records sequentially for the shard. Its position is specified using the sequence number of the data record in a shard. As shown in the diagram, the `GetShardIterator` API is first called for a given shard, followed by the retrieval of records with `GetRecords`:

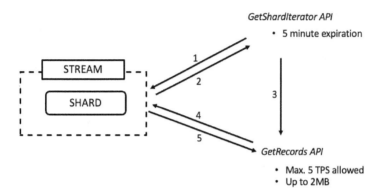

Figure 4.12 – GetShardIterator request (1) retrieves a ShardIterator (2), while the GetRecords API uses the returned ShardIterator (3) to request (4) and retrieve the records (5)

There are several different types of iterators:

1. `AT_TIMESTAMP` is used to read records from a specific point in time.

2. `TRIM_HORIZON` will get the oldest unread record in the shard. This iterator will return the oldest data records that the consumer application has not yet read.

3. `LATEST` will retrieve the most recent data in the shard.

4. `AT_SEQUENCE_NUMBER` and `AFTER_SEQUENCE_NUMBER` can be used to get records at specific order sequence positions in the shard.

    After using the `GetShardIterator` API, we will get a `ShardIterator` value and use it with the first `GetRecords` request. With subsequent `GetRecords` reads, we will use the `NextShardIterator` value returned in each `GetRecords` response. The following is an example `GetShardIterator` POST requesting 100 records with the specified `ShardIterator`:

```
POST / HTTP/1.1
Host: kinesis.<region>.<domain>
Content-Length: <PayloadSizeBytes>
User-Agent: <UserAgentString>
```

```
Content-Type: application/x-amz-JSON-1.1
Authorization: <AuthParams>
Connection: Keep-Alive
X-Amz-Date: <Date>
X-Amz-Target: Kinesis_20131202.GetRecords
{
  "ShardIterator": "AAAAAAAAAAETYyAYzd665+8e0X7JTsASDM
/Hr2rSwc0X2qz93iuA3udrjTH+ikQvpQk/1ZcMMLzRdAesqwBGPnsth
zU0/CBlM/U8/8oEqGwX3pKw0XyeDNRAAZyXBo3MqkQtCpXhr942B
RTjvWKhFz7OmCb2Ncfr8Tl2cBktooi6kJhr+djN5WYkB38Rr3akR
gCl9qaU4dY=",
  "Limit": 100
}
```

Once the GetRecords API POST is accepted successfully, a return response
includes a list of the records. The following is an example GetRecords response
for data that will be added to the emergency events stream. The response
includes the ShardId where the record is stored, and the stream assigned to
SequenceNumber for the record:

```
HTTP/1.1 200 OK
x-amzn-RequestId: <RequestId>
Content-Type: application/x-amz-JSON-1.1
Content-Length: <PayloadSizeBytes>
Date: <Date>
{
  "MillisBehindLatest": 2100,
  "NextShardIterator": "AAAAAAAAAAHsW8zCWf9164uy8Epu
e6WS3w6wmj4a4USt+CNvMd6uXQ+HL5vAJMznqqC0DLKsIj
uoiTilBpT6nW0LN2M2D56zM5H8anHm30Gbri9ua+qaGgj+
3XTyvbhpERfrezgLHbPB/rIcVpykJbaSj5
tmcXYRmFnqZBEyHwtZYFmh6hvWVFkIwLuMZLMrpWhG5r5hzkE=",
  "Records": [
    {
      "Data": "<base64 encoded data>",
      "PartitionKey": "d17a06d5-0f83-40f6-acc5-
840e7cd9aa8f",
      "ApproximateArrivalTimestamp": 1.441215410867E9,
      "SequenceNumber": "4126932978965365794671296340376848 2
```

```
178"
    }
]
}
}
```

Creating an EFO consumer with Lambda

As we reviewed in the previous examples, standard consumer applications can easily read data from the stream using various agents and SDKs. However, when the number of standard consumers grows, they can increase record processing latency, as they all share and compete for the same 2 MB GetRecords API limit. EFO is a KDS feature that enhances consumers' capabilities by adding dedicated logical throughput between the consumers and shards. This capability allows you to further scale the number of applications that can read from the data stream. The following diagram shows a dedicated pipe connection being established between a shard and a consumer using the SubscribetoShard API:

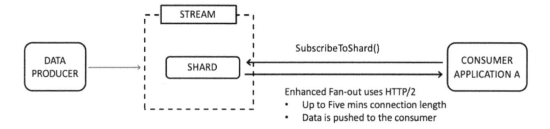

Figure 4.13 – With EFO, records are pushed to the consumer rather than pulled

The EFO consumer increases consumers' read capacity from a shared 2 MB/second to a dedicated 2 MB/second for each consumer. Utilizing an HTTP/2 WebSocket event stream, the message delivery from producer to consumer can be reduced to as little as 70 milliseconds. The following diagram shows how a dedicated EFO connection is established:

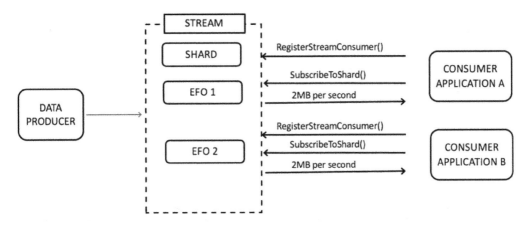

Figure 4.14 – With EFO, each consumer gets a dedicated connection

In the following steps, we will walk through code for a Lambda-based consumer that receives the stream record events as an EFO consumer:

1. We first write a Lambda-based consumer that reads the records as events. We will name the function KinesisNotificationApplication:

```
import boto3
import json
import logging
import base64


logger = logging.getLogger()
logger.setLevel(logging.INFO)


def lambda_handler(event: dict, _context):

  if event and "Records" in event:
    for record in event["Records"]:

      try:
        body = record['kinesis']
        data_in_stream_time =
body['approximateArrivalTimestamp']
        data = body["data"]
        message_JSON = base64.b64decode(data)
```

```
        message_JSON = json.dumps(message_JSON)
        partition_key = {body['partitionKey']}

        logger.info(f"Record consumed with partition key:
{partition_key} with an approximateArrivalTimestamp :
{data_in_stream_time}")
        logger.info(message_JSON)
    except KeyError as err:
        logger.error(err)
        raise err
```

2.   Once we have a Lambda function saved, we will add a trigger to the function. The trigger creates the event source mapping for a Kinesis stream to the function. The following screenshot shows an added trigger:

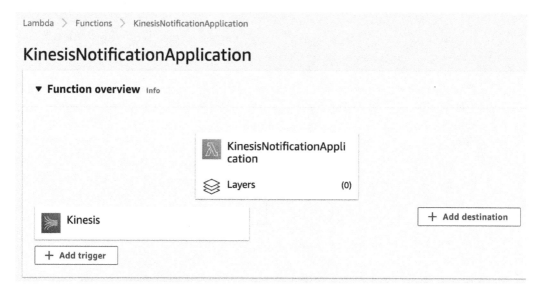

Figure 4.15 – Screenshot of a Lambda event trigger

3.   Using the AWS CLI, register the fan-out consumer (replace with `stream-arn` with your stream ARN):

```
aws kinesis register-stream-consumer \
    --stream-arn <your-stream-arn-here> \
    --consumer-name KinesisConsumerApplication
```

4. In the **Enhanced fan-out** section of the console for the specified stream, it will show as a registered consumer:

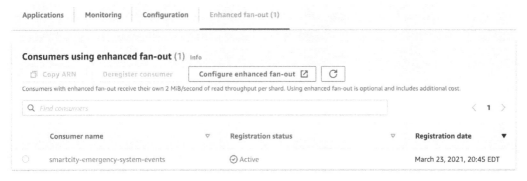

Figure 4.16 – Screenshot of the registered fan-out consumer

Performance improvements and batching with parallel Lambda invocations

When using Lambda as an EFO consumer, you can use `ParallelizationFactor` for the `EventSourceMapping` to have your Lambda function pull from a shard concurrently with multiple parallel invocations. Each parallelized invocation contains messages with the same partition key and maintains order. The invocations complete each record batch before processing the next batch with the following parallel invocation. Parallelization increases the per-shard read consumption. Through parallelization, it can process messages with up to 10 parallelized Lambda invocations per Lambda consumer. As shown in the following screenshot, you can set the concurrent batches per shard:

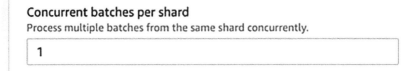

Figure 4.17 – Screenshot of the batch Lambda parallelization size

You can also gain performance improvements by setting a larger batch size that consumers process in each invocation. When setting the EventSourceMapping batch size, you can select the maximum number of records that Lambda retrieves from the stream when invoking the function. Lastly, setting maxBatchingWindow can adjust the time to wait for gathering the batch records before invoking the function. As shown in the following screenshot, these settings can be applied to the Lambda consumer application:

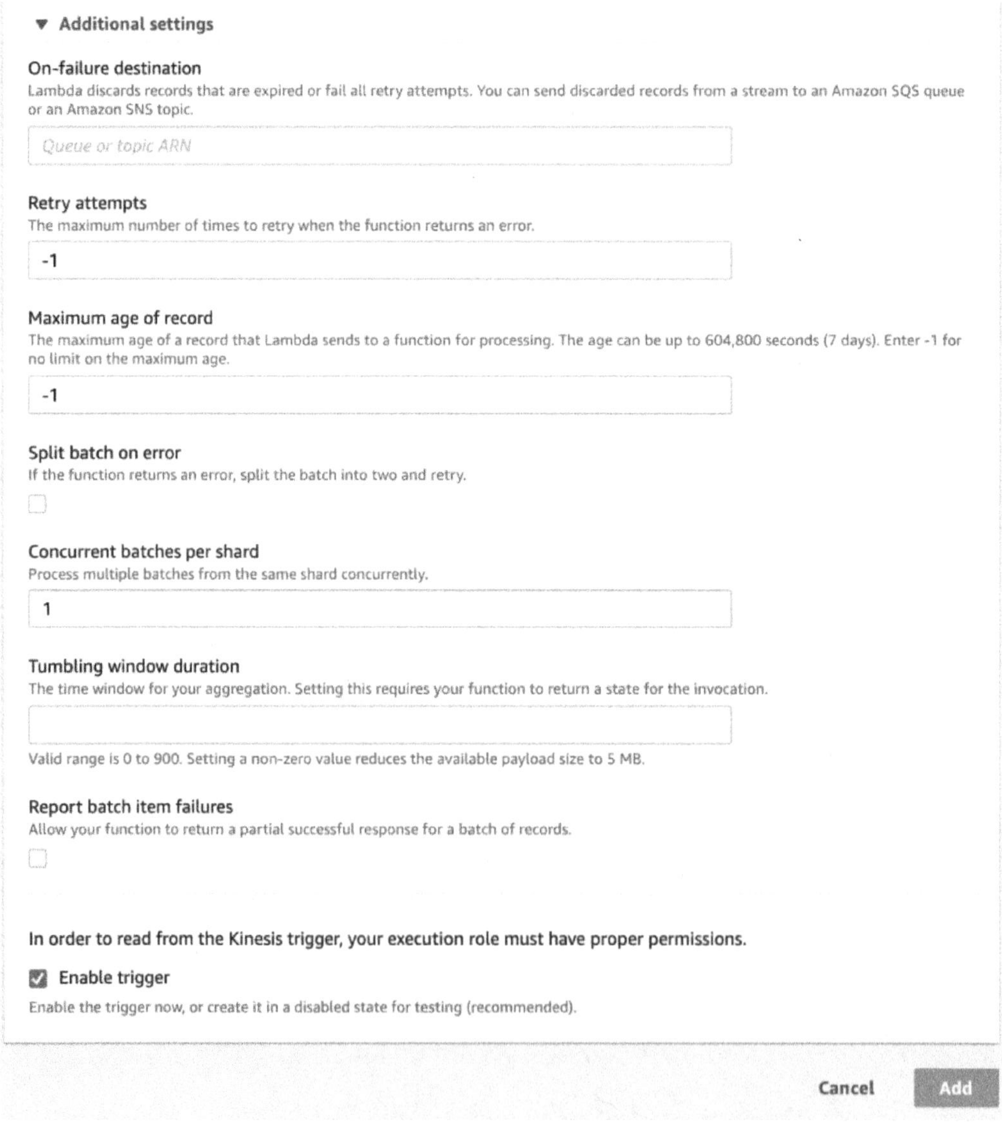

▼ **Additional settings**

On-failure destination
Lambda discards records that are expired or fail all retry attempts. You can send discarded records from a stream to an Amazon SQS queue or an Amazon SNS topic.

Queue or topic ARN

Retry attempts
The maximum number of times to retry when the function returns an error.

-1

Maximum age of record
The maximum age of a record that Lambda sends to a function for processing. The age can be up to 604,800 seconds (7 days). Enter -1 for no limit on the maximum age.

-1

Split batch on error
If the function returns an error, split the batch into two and retry.

☐

Concurrent batches per shard
Process multiple batches from the same shard concurrently.

1

Tumbling window duration
The time window for your aggregation. Setting this requires your function to return a state for the invocation.

Valid range is 0 to 900. Setting a non-zero value reduces the available payload size to 5 MB.

Report batch item failures
Allow your function to return a partial successful response for a batch of records.

☐

In order to read from the Kinesis trigger, your execution role must have proper permissions.

☑ **Enable trigger**
Enable the trigger now, or create it in a disabled state for testing (recommended).

Cancel   Add

Figure 4.18 – Screenshot of the Lambda EventSourceMapping configuration

Each of these performance settings enables you to tune the performance of the processing of the stream. As we tune the performance with settings such as these, the data becomes available with more real-time delivery.

Handling failed records in a batch of "poison pills" with parallel Lambda invocations

Although batching can improve processing performance by handling records in ordered groups, it can become more challenging to handle failures, such as when one record in a batch has an issue. These errors can lead to batch retries and duplicate record processing. For example, a single erroring record can block the processing of other records in the shard. As the records are being consumed in order, the continuous processing of the errored record prevents all the records behind it from being processed. The combination of the order guarantee and the failing record creates a scenario referred to as a *poison pill*.

Lambda `EventSourceMapping` has `ReportBatchItemFailures`, which will checkpoint the most recent successful processed record. It starts the batch from the point of the unsuccessful failed record. This continues until the maximum number of retries is reached. When `ReportBatchItemFailures` is enabled and a failure occurs, Lambda will prioritize checkpointing over other set mechanisms to minimize duplicate processing.

In the following diagram, you can see how `ReportBatchItemFailures` continuously sets checkpoints to continue processing around erroring records:

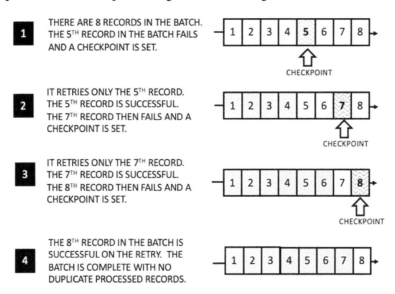

Figure 4.19 – The ReportBatchItemFailures feature tracks record level checkpoints to avoid duplicate processing when processing batches

> **Note**
>
> The `ReportBatchItemFailures` checkpointing setting is the most efficient method to avoid the blocking of processing ("poison pill") and reduce duplicate record processing.
>
> A Lambda EFO consumer also has built-in support through `EventSourceMapping` for sending old or exhausted retries to an on-failure destination such as a **Simple Queue Service** (**SQS**) queue or a **Simple Notification Service** (**SNS**) topic. The **Retry Attempts** setting sets the maximum number of times to retry if the function returns an error.

Now that we have learned how to produce and consume stream data, let's review how we can use producers, consumers, and streams to create a data pipeline for SmartCity's bike-sharing service.

Data pipelines with Amazon Kinesis Data Streams

As we have learned how to create streams, producers, and consumers, we will design a simple data pipeline for SmartCity. A data pipeline is a series of processing steps applied to data flowing from the source to the target destination. The processing steps could include automation for copying, transforming, routing, and loading source data to destinations such as business systems, data lakes, and data warehouses. A data pipeline should support the requirements for data throughput, reliability, and latency. A well-architected design will prevent many of the common problems that can occur when collecting and loading data, such as data corruption, bottlenecks, conflicts between sources, and the creation of duplicate entries.

Data pipeline design (simple)

With this first design, this demonstrates receiving data from a single source of data. The data source producer is using **Amazon Kinesis Agent** deployed in the SmartCity data center. The data is collected in a single stream with a single shard. The following design shows the flow of data from the producer to the consumer application, which pushes the message to the SmartCity rider's mobile devices:

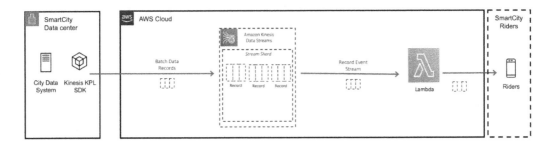

Figure 4.20 – City data system emergency message producer and AWS Lambda consumer

The pipeline has a Lambda function consumer subscribed to the stream data events. The consumer processes the message and then sends it as a push message to the SmartCity mobile app.

Data pipeline design (intermediate)

In the last design, we received data from only a single source of data. This design incorporates the SmartCity mobile app as a second source of data for the pipeline. The mobile app has a feature called **RiderAlert**, which enables riders to send emergency notifications such as excessive bike lane traffic, weather alerts, unsafe road conditions, and criminal activity. In this design, additional data producers from the rider's devices were added:

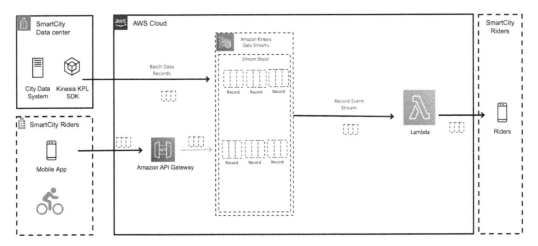

Figure 4.21 – Multiple producers are adding to the stream

As the KPL SDK is not a compatible platform with SmartCity mobile application, the app will use a simple HTTPS-based REST API to send data to the pipeline. To support this requirement, we will set up an HTTPS endpoint for the mobile application to send data to Amazon API Gateway. Amazon API Gateway allows developers to easily create an HTTP endpoint to send records to KDS. API Gateway also has support for authentication to secure access to the endpoint.

As the data rate increases, we will add a shard to the stream. The data from both sources will use the same JSON message format and a random value partition key to prevent "hot partition keys." We will use the same subscribed Lambda consumer to process the stream data events. The consumer processes the records and sends them to the mobile application as a push message to the SmartCity mobile app.

Data pipeline design (full design)

In the last design, we started receiving data from two different sources of data. In this next design, we will incorporate several AWS **Well-Architected Analytics Lens** design principles: https://docs.aws.amazon.com/wellarchitected/latest/ analytics-lens/welcome.html. The **Well-Architected Analytics Lens** is a collection of AWS recommended best practices that facilitate good design with data applications. We will also introduce additional purpose-built services with strong KDS integrations:

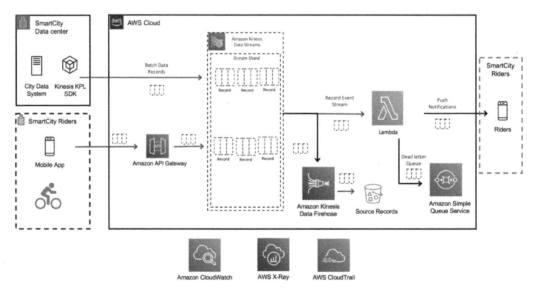

Figure 4.22 – Monitoring, security auditing, tracing, and error handling added

To prevent data volume or velocity from impacting the production pipeline, we will incorporate several design principles. We will preserve the original incoming source data, design for duplicates and failures, trace the data flow between different data systems, and monitor and optimize for reliability and scalability. We will use the Amazon CloudWatch service to monitor and log application events for observability of the pipeline. We will use AWS X-Ray to trace the application for bugs and application performance bottlenecks. Amazon SQS will be used as a **Dead Letter Queue (DLQ)** to collect records that have failed to process. Amazon **Kinesis Data Firehose (KDF)** will collect source records and store them in an Amazon S3 data lake. AWS **Identity and Access Management (IAM)** and AWS CloudTrail will govern and secure the data. In the next sections, we will walk through how these principals can benefit the pipeline.

Designing for scalable and reliable analytics pipelines

Asynchronous messaging has some unique challenges when handling errors. Data streams require mechanisms for managing the data, while also maintaining the flow and integrity of processed data. When data fails after repeated attempts, the consumer can move the erroring records into a DLQ.

Producer and consumer retries are some of the reasons why records may be delivered more than once. KDS does not automatically remove duplicate records. The destination endpoint application must anticipate and handle the processing of individual records multiple times in the most appropriate manner for the destination system. If the destination requires a strict guarantee, the record should include a primary key. In most cases, the destination can also mitigate duplicate messages by processing the same message multiple times in a way that produces the same result (idempotence). For example, the features that Lambda provides for failures, DLQs, and batching all help with the heavy lift associated with scalable pipelines.

A typical consumer failure is when a destination endpoint is not performing or unavailable. With this scenario, the consumer can back off and later retry when the destination endpoint is available. The failure of a single destination endpoint should not impact the performance of the entire system.

Preserving original sources of data

We preserve raw ingested data because having raw data allows us to repeat the processing in failure situations. We will not perform transformational processing on the original data files, so original source data is maintained. This enables us to debug issues and, if needed, reprocess the collected data. We can use Amazon Kinesis Firehose as a stream consumer to ingest and store data to an Amazon S3 bucket. KDS data retention duration can also act as storage when records need to be replayed. A new consumer could subscribe to the stream and process all the records, or from a point in time. The stream data retention duration can be set for up to 1 year.

Automating data ingestion

When designing data pipelines, we can automate data ingestion through scheduling, event-based triggers, and change detection. When we automate the ingestion, it allows data to maintain a consistent flow and reduces errors introduced through manual processes.

The Kinesis Agent can detect new files and automatically write the records to the stream as they arrive. The agent will also retry sending to the stream if a record fails. The mobile application will need to have similar logic to retry Amazon API Gateway endpoint requests if they fail.

Establishing data lineage

Data pipelines need to be able to trace data from the data source to its destination. The data pipelines should simplify the time and effort required to trace data latency and errors as it flows through each stage, including the producers, streams, consumers, and any transformations. AWS X-Ray is an example of a distributed tracing tool used to trace and analyze the data's performance throughout the data pipeline. This can include tracing the data from the producer applications into the stream and through the consumer applications. For example, you can trace whether issues with a producer are impacting downstream consumers.

In the *X-Ray tracing with Amazon KDS* section, we will review how AWS X-Ray can help to establish data lineage.

Monitoring and scaling with Amazon Kinesis Data Streams

When we design the data pipelines, we want to make each stage of the pipeline reliable and scalable. As the volume or velocity of data spikes, the system should adapt and scale, so data flow is maintained and the changes do not impact the flow of data. For example, when we use the Kinesis Data Stream Scaling Utility, it will enable the stream to adjust the shard count with a change in data volume and velocity.

In the next section, we will review the metrics and monitoring capabilities available in CloudWatch and AWS X-Ray.

CloudWatch metrics for Amazon Kinesis Data Streams

Amazon KDS and Amazon CloudWatch are tightly integrated services. There is minimal effort to collect, view, and analyze metrics for the data streams, the producers, and consumers with CloudWatch. Upon the creation of a stream, the stream level metrics are turned on by default. For example, we can monitor CloudWatch for `IncomingBytes` and `OutgoingBytes` metrics to determine the correct number of shards required in the stream. We can monitor whether producers and consumers exceed the stream's capacity with `WriteProvisionedThroughputExceeded` and `ReadProvisionedThroughputExceeded` metrics. The `MillisBehindLatest` metric can tell you how far behind the `GetRecords` response is from the stream's head. You can also monitor additional shard-level metrics by turning on **Enable Enhanced Metrics** for a stream.

Stream metrics are automatically collected and sent to CloudWatch every minute. There is no additional cost for the default metrics; however, enhanced metrics do entail an additional cost.

The stream metrics that CloudWatch can monitor include record throughput, consumer latency, and failures. You can use these metrics to trigger dynamic scaling processes to increase write or read capacity through increased shards or other consumer settings, such as the fan-out consumer Lambda `ParallelizationFactor` or batch size. The following screenshot shows the KDS integrated CloudWatch metrics:

Figure 4.23 – Example KDS integrated CloudWatch metric monitoring dashboard

CloudWatch metrics and logs are available for streams, shards, producers, agents, and consumers.

A summary of these is as follows:

- **CloudWatch metrics**: Kinesis Data Streams sends Amazon CloudWatch metrics with detailed monitoring for each stream and, optionally, the shard level.

- **Kinesis Agent**: The Kinesis Agent sends custom metric data to CloudWatch so you can monitor producer performance and stability.

- **API logging**: Kinesis Data Streams sends the API event data to AWS CloudTrail.

- **The KCL**: The KCL sends custom metrics to monitor consumer performance and stability.
- **The KPL**: The KPL sends custom metrics to monitor the producer application's performance and stability.

Several metrics are recorded in CloudWatch. These metrics can be used to monitor healthy stream and scaling needs.

Some of the metrics include the following:

- `PutRecord.Bytes`: The total number of bytes put in to the Amazon Kinesis stream over the specified time period.
- `PutRecord.Latency`: This metric monitors the performance of the `PutRecord` operation, measured over the specified time period.
- `PutRecord.Success`: This metric provides a count of successful `PutRecord` operations measured over the specified time period.
- `WriteProvisionedThroughputExceeded`: This metric provides the number of records rejected due to exceeded write capacity.
- `GetRecords.IteratorAgeMilliseconds`: This metric can be used to monitor the performance of the flow of data processing. This metric provides the age of the last read record from the `GetRecords` API calls to a stream, measured over the specified time period. When this metric's value is close to zero, this indicates that consumers have caught up with the stream's data.

X-Ray tracing with Amazon Kinesis Data Streams

As records flow through multiple devices, producers, the stream, and consumers, it is essential to have the capability to trace data from its origin to the destination. Data lineage is tracking the data origin and its flow between different data systems. When applications use AWS X-Ray, they have greater visibility for tracing errors and can monitor performance. AWS X-Ray provides the capability to track and view data as it moves from the source to the processed destination. As demonstrated in the following screenshot, AWS X-Ray provides a visual map of errors with links to insights that can help find the root causes of issues:

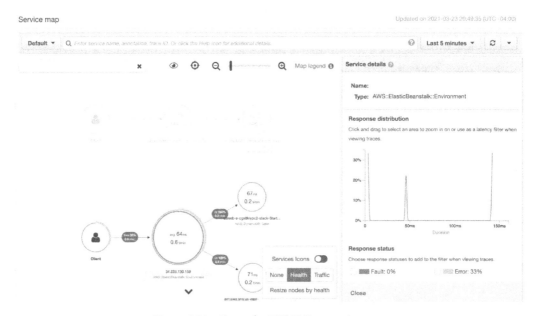

Figure 4.24 – Example AWS X-Ray service map

AWS X-Ray has several capabilities that can be used to trace both development and production applications. X-Ray works by adding tracing markers to the requests and logs. Applications can also use the application code in the AWS X-Ray SDK to include custom tracing annotations to incorporate custom context data in the tracing analytics.

Scaling up with Amazon Kinesis Data Streams

Kinesis manages much of the scaling and complexity associated with operating a data stream. This includes data storage, data security, replication across Availablility Zones, sharding operations, and monitoring. However, KDS does not provide out-of-the-box shard autoscaling based on data velocity. We want to maintain the pipeline's reliability and scalability as the flow of data changes. The Kinesis Scaling Utility (`https://github.com/awslabs/amazon-kinesis-scaling-utils`) is an open source, Java-based utility that scales Amazon Kinesis Data Streams shard counts up or down in a hands-off automated manner. As the stream shards approach capacity intervals, the utility will automatically increase or decrease the shard count. This utility helps with use cases such as handling seasonal data spikes for SmartCity weekday morning and evening peak usage patterns.

Securing Amazon Kinesis Data Streams

When building data pipelines, the data and infrastructure should be secured based on business requirements. Security begins with fine-grained controlled access for authorized users. We want to provide each user and service in the pipeline with only the required privileged access required to perform the designated task or function. The data should be protected at rest and in-flight as it flows in and out of the data pipeline. Lastly, we want to maintain and monitor an audit log of user and service access.

Amazon KDS provides several security features that can be used to implement data pipeline security policies. The following are some of the best practices and general guidelines.

Implementing least-privilege access

When granting permissions to the data pipeline, we need to decide what permissions are required for users and integrated services. For example, a producer application may only need write access to the stream and does not require read access. The consumer application may require read access to the stream data but does not require write actions. When implementing data stream security, implement the least-privilege access necessary for the principal resource granted. When we implement least-privilege access policies, it helps to reduce risks, such as malicious intent or an erroneous event.

Using IAM roles

When granting permissions with least-privilege access, we are controlling access through IAM policies. These policies determine the actions that can be performed on the data stream.

When developing consumer and producer applications with the KCL and KPL, they require permissions for services such as CloudWatch, DynamoDB, and KDS. When granting these permissions, applications should not be granted long-term credentials. Long-term credentials can lead to compromised access to the data, resulting in a significant business impact.

Rather than granting long-term credentials, grant IAM roles to the producer and consumer applications. Roles provide temporary credentials that are short-lived and automatically rotated. The role can be applied directly to the EC2 instance or Lambda function.

Implementing server-side encryption in dependent resources

Security best practice suggests always encrypting data when in-transit and at rest. When data is at rest in a stream, the data requires server-side encryption. Amazon KDS uses the **AWS Key Management Service (AWS KMS)** to provide a managed and secure system for data key management and data encryption. KMS encrypts the KDS when written into the stream using a **Customer-Managed Key (CMK)**. When a consumer application reads data from the stream, the data is decrypted from storage.

We have reviewed how least-privileged access, temporary credentials, and data encryption are essential security practices. These should be implemented to protect the data in KDS.

Summary

As you can see, KDS is a powerful service for collecting and processing data with high velocity and low latency. KDS is a managed service that handles much of the heavy lifting associated with maintaining high performance and highly reliable data streams. KDS is also highly customizable, offering several serverless and customizable tools for ingesting and processing for almost any source and destination.

In this chapter, you learned about Amazon KDS and how to design a data pipeline solution with multiple producers and consumers. You learned how to monitor, scale, and secure KDS utilizing well-architected best practices and integrated AWS tools and services.

In the next chapter, you will learn to consume and process data with other KDS services. You will learn how to ingest, transform, and process data with another purpose-built streaming technology. Amazon KDF has built-in capabilities to automatically ingest data from sources such as KDS, AWS IoT, Amazon CloudWatch Logs, and Amazon CloudWatch Events. KDF can apply **Extract, Transform, Load** (**ETL**) transformations and deliver the data to several preconfigured destinations such as AWS S3, Redshift, Amazon Elasticsearch, and other third-party destinations.

Further reading

- Amazon Kinesis Data Streams: `https://aws.amazon.com/kinesis/data-streams/`
- Amazon Kinesis Data Streams API reference: `https://docs.aws.amazon.com/kinesis/latest/APIReference/Welcome.html`
- Amazon Kinesis Data Streams developer guide: `https://docs.aws.amazon.com/streams/latest/dev/introduction.html`
- Using AWS Lambda with Amazon Kinesis: `https://docs.aws.amazon.com/lambda/latest/dg/with-kinesis.html`
- Writing to Amazon Kinesis Data Streams Using Kinesis Agent: `https://docs.aws.amazon.com/streams/latest/dev/writing-with-agents.html`
- Security Best Practices for Kinesis Data Streams: `https://docs.aws.amazon.com/streams/latest/dev/security-best-practices.html`

5
Kinesis Firehose

In this chapter, we take an in-depth look at Amazon **Kinesis Data Firehose** (**KDF**). This is a fully managed serverless service for the ingestion of large volumes of data from a number of sources and delivery to an ever-increasing number of integrated destinations. It provides an easy way to enable a number of big-data use cases by delivering data (without any coding requirements) to a data lake; a high-capacity and high-performance parallel data warehouse service; a search-and-analytics service; **HyperText Transfer Protocol** (**HTTP**) endpoints; and a number of third-party providers. It also allows a number of inline **Extract-Transform-Load** (**ETL**) transformations that enable high-velocity and high-throughput transformations, enabling near-real-time use cases. We also take a look at how KDF can be used in the data pipeline described in the chapter on **Kinesis Data Streams** (**KDS**), with the SmartCity use case.

The following topics will be covered in this chapter:

- Discovering Amazon KDF
- Understanding encryption in KDF
- Using data transformation in KDF with a Lambda function
- Understanding delivery stream destinations
- Understanding data format conversion in KDF
- Understanding monitoring in KDF
- Use-case example – Bikeshare station data pipeline with KDF

Let's get started!

Technical requirements

First, let's take a quick look at the technical requirements for running the examples in this book.

Setting up the AWS account

You will need to get an **Amazon Web Services** (**AWS**) account to run the examples included in this chapter. If you do not have an account already, you can go to `https://aws.amazon.com/getting-started/` to create an account. AWS accounts offer a **Free Tier** (`https://aws.amazon.com/free`). The AWS **Free Tier** allows you to use many AWS services for free within specified usage limits. Some of the services' examples in this chapter are outside of the AWS **Free Tier** and will incur some charges for service usage.

Using a local development environment

You will need a working Python 3.x environment. You can install Python 3.x by downloading and running the installer (`https://www.python.org/downloads/`) for your environment's operating system. Be careful not to use Python 2.7 as it is no longer maintained.

You can set up the AWS **software development kit** (**SDK**) for Python using the following link: `https://aws.amazon.com/sdk-for-python/`. The AWS SDK for Python includes several of the tools for developing in AWS with Python and includes libraries such as `boto3`.

You can also install the **AWS Command-Line Interface** (**AWS CLI**) version 2 on your computer using the following link: `https://docs.aws.amazon.com/cli/latest/userguide/install-cliv2.html`.

Using an AWS Cloud9 development environment

As an alternative to setting the aforementioned packages up in your local development environment, you can also set up and create an **AWS Cloud9** development environment with the help of this link: `https://docs.aws.amazon.com/cloud9/latest/user-guide/setting-up.html`.

AWS Cloud9 is an **integrated development environment** (**IDE**). The AWS Cloud9 IDE has rich code-editing capabilities, with support for several programming languages and runtime debuggers. It also has a built-in terminal and tools to code, build, run, test, and debug code examples.

You can use the following guide to set up your Python environment on AWS Cloud9:

`https://docs.aws.amazon.com/cloud9/latest/user-guide/sample-python.html`

Code examples

Code examples for this book are available on GitHub at `https://github.com/PacktPublishing/Streaming-Data-Solutions-with-Amazon-Kinesis`. You will need a Git client to access them (`https://git-scm.com/`).

Discovering Amazon Kinesis Firehose

The core construct in KDF is a **delivery stream**. Data is ingested into a delivery stream from a source, and data is then delivered by the delivery stream to a configured destination.

The following diagram illustrates producers sending data to Amazon KDF and the delivery destinations it supports:

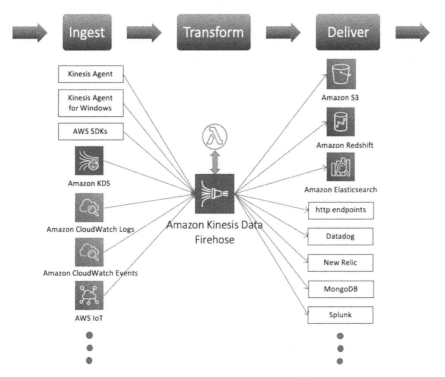

Figure 5.1 – Producers sending data to Amazon KDF and the delivery destinations it supports

Let's talk about the delivery stream itself first, and then we will talk about each of the supported destinations in detail, followed by the various mechanisms to send data to KDF.

Understanding KDF delivery streams

The purpose of using a KDF delivery stream is to deliver streaming data to one of the supported destinations. Each delivery stream supports a single destination, so if the requirement is to send the same streaming data to multiple destinations, you need to create multiple delivery streams, each pointing to a single destination you need to send the data to. A delivery stream buffers incoming records as per the configuration provided, which differs by the type of destination, performs the configured transformations and compressions, and then delivers to the configured destination. Each delivery stream is associated with a certain amount of capacity based on the ingestion method. There are two ingestion methods available. Let's have a look at these methods in detail.

Direct PUT

In this mode, the service provides the `PutRecord` and `PutRecordBatch` **application programming interfaces** (**APIs**) to send records one by one and in batches, respectively. The `PutRecordBatch` API can take up to 500 records or 4 **mebibytes** (**MiB**) per call, whichever is smaller. This is a hard limit and cannot be changed.

The default delivery stream capacity is based on the choice of the **AWS Region**. For US East (N. Virginia), US West (Oregon), and Europe (Ireland), it is 5,000 records/second, 2,000 requests/second, and 5 MiB/second. For many other regions, it is 1,000 records/second, 1,000 requests/second, and 1 MiB/second. The important thing to note here is that these are soft limits, and if the throughput for a particular use case is higher than the specified limits, a limit increase support ticket needs to be submitted and the service raises the limit for the delivery stream. The three dimensions scale proportionally. In addition, the service is able to auto-scale up to the delivery stream capacity limit. There is one other important limit that deserves a mention here. The maximum size of an individual record before Base64 encoding is 1,000 **kibibytes** (**KiB**). However, there are some strategies that can be employed to handle messages larger than the maximum size.

Strategies to handle messages larger than 1,000 KiB

The first and obvious strategy is to compress the message. KDF can handle binary payloads, and it does not need to inspect or read the actual message payload unless certain transformations are specified. A side effect of this strategy is that messages delivered to the destination are also compressed and need to be decompressed during read.

The second method is to break up the message into multiple parts and have an ID that groups the messages together so that these messages can be reassembled at the destination.

Both these strategies require some postprocessing of messages after KDF delivers the messages to the configured destination.

Rounding up the size of ingested records

From a pricing standpoint, you pay for the volume of data ingested into the delivery stream, which is the number of records/second * the size of each record. However, the size of each record is rounded up to the nearest 5 **kilobyte** (**KB**) boundary. So, if the record size is 23 KB, it will be rounded up to 25 KB, and if the record size is 497 KB, it will be rounded up to 500 KB. So, the volume of data ingested is really the number of records/second * the size of each record, rounded up to the nearest 5 KB.

So, what does this mean for you? It means that you pay more than you expect to pay if the size of your records is not close to or equal to a 5 KB boundary. If the volume of data flowing through is large, this could become quite significant. To address this on the producer side, you can concatenate records with a record separator such as \n and create larger records to be sent to KDF, or use some other method or format to pack the user records into bigger records to be sent to KDF, which are less than or equal to the nearest 5 KB boundary. Concatenating the records with a \n separator has the advantage of not requiring any postprocessing. KDF delivers the records to the destination as is. Using some other method or format to pack records may require postprocessing in the destination.

Concatenation is the method used by the Kinesis Agent for Linux, which is a tool that can be installed and used on Linux platforms to tail files and send data to Amazon KDS and Amazon KDF.

Amazon KDS as a source

There is tight integration between Amazon KDS and Amazon KDF, which allows you to specify an Amazon KDS stream as a source. The delivery stream capacity is the capacity of the source Amazon KDS stream and the service can auto-scale up to that limit. Since the capacity of an Amazon KDS stream in shards is known, it is possible for the service to create a KDF stream supporting that capacity. When this mode is chosen, the `PutRecord` and `PutRecordBatch` APIs are disabled. Data or messages in the KDS stream are sent to the configured destination. The KDF service reads from the KDS stream approximately once per second for each shard in the KDS stream.

> **KDF reading from the KDS stream**
>
> The KDF service starts reading the KDS stream from the *latest* position in the stream, which means the end of the stream. Any existing data or messages in the KDS stream present before the creation of the KDF delivery stream are not sent to the configured destination.

Currently, when reading from an Amazon KDS stream, KDF employs a standard consumer. Given that a KDS stream can support up to five standard consumers and if the KDF service determines that it is falling behind in reading from the stream, it can catch up by starting additional consumers. It is important not to overload the KDS stream with standard consumers if a KDF delivery stream is configured to use the KDS stream as a source. Typically, it is recommended not to have more than one or two standard consumers in addition to a KDF delivery stream reading from the KDS stream.

Rounding up the size of ingested records

As mentioned for the `Direct PUT` method, records ingested into a KDF delivery stream are rounded up to the nearest 5 KB boundary for pricing purposes. Correspondingly, for a KDS stream, there is a pricing component called **PUT payload unit**. This is a 25 KB payload chunk that comprises a record. If the size of a record is less than or equal to 25 KB, it contains 1 PUT payload unit. If the size of a record is greater than 25 KB, the size is rounded up to the next 25 KB boundary and divided by 25 KB to get the number of PUT payload units. For KDS, PUT payload units are charged per million.

So, how does this affect the cost of a KDS stream? It means that you pay more than you expect to pay if the size of your records is not close to or equal to a 25 KB boundary as you're paying more for PUT payload units for the volume of ingested data. To address this, you need to pack more user records into a record sent to KDS. This is implemented in the **Kinesis Producer Library** (**KPL**). If the KPL is used to send messages to the KDS stream and the `AggregationEnabled` configuration parameter is set to `true`, multiple user records are packed into a single `KinesisDataStream` record, thus increasing the size of an ingested record to a number close to a multiple of 25 KB.

Since 25 KB is a multiple of 5 KB, which is the boundary that KDF rounds up a record to, reading records sent to a KDS stream using the KPL with aggregation turned on provides good utilization of the round-up. At its end, the KDF service upon ingesting the aggregated records automatically de-aggregates the records before they're sent to the destination, so the records are delivered to the destination as they're sent to the KPL.

Understanding encryption in KDF

KDF supports both **encryption in transit** and **encryption at rest**. KDF has a REST API that supports secure HTTP (that is, HTTPS). For encryption at rest, the method employed depends on the data ingestion mechanism. As explained in the *Understanding KDF delivery streams* section, there are two ways to ingest data into KDF: Direct PUT and a KDS stream as a source. In addition, KDF has integrations with a number of other AWS services, such as Amazon CloudWatch Logs, Amazon CloudWatch Events, AWS **Internet of Things** (**IoT**), or Amazon **Simple Notification Service** (**SNS**), which allows those services to send data to KDF.

For Direct PUT using either PutRecord or PutRecordBatch APIs and for other AWS services sending data to KDF, you can enable encryption at rest (or server-side encryption) using an AWS **Key Management Service** (**KMS**) **customer master key** (**CMK**). The CMK can be either an AWS-owned CMK or a customer-managed CMK. AWS-owned CMKs are not in your account. They are a collection of CMKs owned by a service and are used to encrypt resources in your account. You don't create or manage these CMKs and cannot view, track, or audit them. You also don't pay for them. Customer-managed CMKs are in your account, and you create and manage them. You can also use, view, audit, and rotate them, and can control who has access to them and pays for them.

You can enable or disable server-side encryption through the StartDeliveryStreamEncryption and StopDeliveryStreamEncryption APIs respectively. An example of enabling it using the AWS CLI for a delivery stream with the name of KDFS3DeliverLogs is shown here:

```
aws firehose start-delivery-stream-encryption --delivery-
stream-name KDFS3DeliverLogs
```

Server-side encryption can also enabled at the time of delivery stream creation by specifying the DeliveryStreamEncryptionConfigurationInput configuration, shown in the following code block:

```
"DeliveryStreamEncryptionConfigurationInput": {
        "KeyARN": "",
        "KeyType": "CUSTOMER_MANAGED_CMK"
    }
```

The KeyARN value is the **Amazon Resource Name (ARN)** of the AWS CMK, and the KeyType value can be either CUSTOMER_MANAGED_CMK for a CMK managed and provided by you or AWS_OWNED_CMK for an AWS-owned CMK.

The AWS Console also provides the ability to enable server-side encryption at the time of delivery stream creation. The following screenshot shows server-side encryption enabled for source records in the delivery stream:

Server-side encryption for source records in the delivery stream

You can use AWS Key Management Service (KMS) to create and manage customer keys (CMKs) and to control the use of encryption across a wide range of AWS services and in your applications.

☑ Enable server-side encryption for source records in delivery stream

Encryption type

⦿ Use AWS-owned CMK
  AWS-owned CMKs are not in your AWS account. They are part of CMKs that AWS owns and manages for use in multiple AWS accounts.

○ Use customer managed CMK
  Customer managed CMKs are CMKs that you can create, own, and manage.

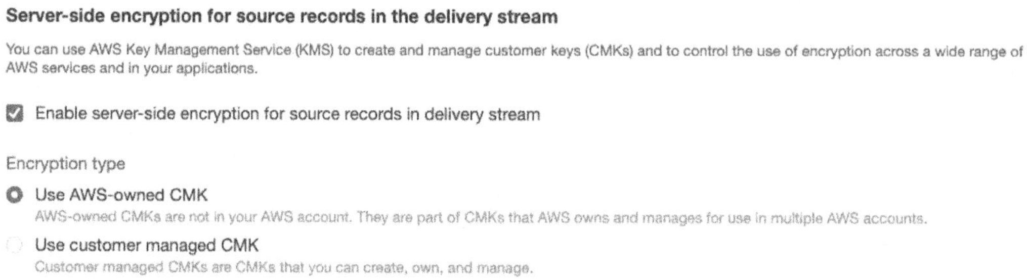

Figure 5.2 – Configuration of server-side encryption for a delivery stream during creation via the AWS Console

When a KDF delivery stream uses a KDS stream as a source, it does not employ server-side encryption but rather depends on server-side encryption being enabled for the KDS stream. When KDF reads data from the KDS stream, the KDS service first decrypts the data and then sends it to KDF. KDF buffers the data in memory and delivers it to the configured destination without storing the data at rest.

Using data transformation in KDF with a Lambda function

KDF provides the ability to transform ingested records inline through integration with the AWS Lambda service, which allows KDF to invoke a **Lambda function** (called a **Lambda transform**) to do custom processing as long as the code adheres to a data transformation and status model. By default, data transformation is disabled and needs to be enabled in the delivery stream configuration. The following diagram illustrates how data transformation works in KDF:

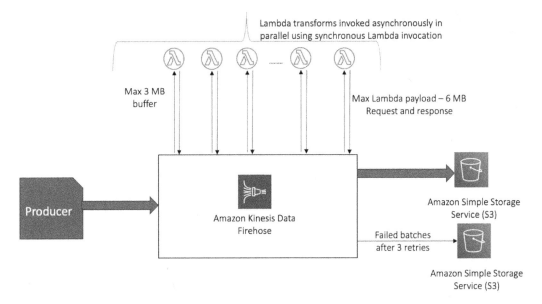

Figure 5.3 – Data transformation with Lambda invocations

Once enabled, the incoming records are buffered up to 3 **megabytes** (**MB**) by default. The buffering size can be adjusted using the ProcessingConfiguration API using the BufferSizeInMBs processor parameter (the AWS Console only supports the BufferSizeInMBs and BufferIntervalInSeconds parameters) available as textboxes and lets you choose from a drop-down list of Lambda functions available in the same account that you have access to, but you cannot set the NumberOfRetries function, which is the number of times KDF tries to retry invoking the Lambda function with the same payload of records if it either encounters an error in invoking the Lambda function or receives an error from the code in the Lambda function that was not handled in the Lambda function. The NumberOfRetries function can be set using the CLI and a **JavaScript Object Notation** (**JSON**) configuration. An example of JSON configuration is included in the code examples available with this book at https://github.com/ PacktPublishing/Streaming-Data-Solutions-with-Amazon-Kinesis. Once a buffer is full, KDF invokes the specified Lambda function with the payload of incoming records. This Lambda function invocation is synchronous, which means it is in a request/response mode, and KDF waits for the Lambda function to execute and return a response. However, KDF keeps ingesting additional records and filling additional buffers sequentially, and invokes a new instance of the Lambda function when those buffers are full. The maximum amount of time that KDF waits for a Lambda function to execute is 5 minutes, after which you get an error.

The following diagram shows the transformation model and the data transformation:

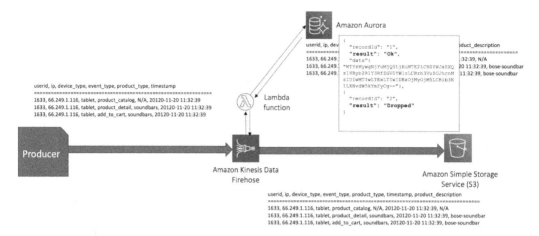

Figure 5.4 – Data transformation model and data transformation

The payload that KDF invokes the Lambda function with has some metadata in addition to the Base64-encoded data records. The metadata includes a `recordId`, which is generated by KDF for each ingested record. After the Lambda function processes the payload, KDF expects the function to return an array of records, each with the following fields:

- `recordId`—This is the same `recordId` that KDF passed to the Lambda function. Every `recordId` that was included in the payload needs to be in the returned array of records. Any `recordId` not included in the returned array is treated as a data transformation failure, having a status of `ProcessingFailed`.

- `result`—This represents the status of data transformation for the record. The possible values are these:

  a) `Ok`, which means data transformation was successful and needs to necessarily include the Base64-encoded transformed data in the data field.

  b) `Dropped`, which means the record was intentionally dropped, providing a mechanism for filtering incoming records so that only relevant records are delivered to the destination, and may or may not include data in the data field.

  c) `ProcessingFailed`, which means data transformation was unsuccessful for this record and may or may not include data in the data field. The Lambda function can log records with a `ProcessingFailed` status to CloudWatch Logs.

- `data`—The Base64-encoded data after data transformation.

If KDF encounters an error invoking the Lambda function due to a network timeout or the Lambda invocation limit being reached, or the Lambda service is not available. And, if there is an error from the Lambda function or the Lambda service, it by default retries the Lambda function thrice (unless a different number of retries is set, as mentioned earlier) with the same payload, and if there is an error for all of the retries, it skips data transformation and data delivery to the configured destination for the batch. KDF allows you to enable CloudWatch Logs error logging for the delivery stream to log these errors in CloudWatch Logs. It treats the records in the failed batch as having the transformation status of `ProcessingFailed`. KDF then delivers all the records with a status of `ProcessingFailed` for the various types of failures to the specified **Simple Storage Service (S3)** bucket with the prefix provided under the S3 error prefix. This provides you with the ability to inspect the issue with the batch and to re-process the records later.

In addition, KDF provides the ability to enable source-record S3 backup in the delivery stream configuration, which delivers the source records (before transformation) to the backup S3 bucket with the specified backup S3 bucket prefix.

The AWS Lambda console provides a number of blueprints that can be used as a starting point for creating the Lambda function for data transformation, which provides the necessary bootstrapping code to read the payload and return the output. The blueprints include `kinesis-firehose-syslog-to-json` in Node.js; `kinesis-firehose-cloudwatch-logs-processor-python` in Python 2.7 (since Python 2.7 has been deprecated, you can copy the code and use it as a starting point with Python 3.8); `kinesis-firehose-cloudwatch-logs-processor` in Node.js; and generic blueprints to process records in `kinesis-firehose-process-record` in Node.js and `kinesis-firehose-process-record-python` in Python 2.7 (as before, it is recommended to copy the code and use it with Python 3.8).

A number of features and configurations of KDF are specific to a destination. So, let's take a look at those features and configurations in the context of destinations.

Understanding delivery stream destinations

Delivery stream destinations are where KDF has the ability to land or send the ingested data. This is how KDF packages stream storage, data processing, and delivery into one neat tool that requires no code. KDF supports a number of destinations, and the KDF service has been adding additional destinations over time. Now, let's take a detailed look at the supported destinations.

Amazon S3

The first—and most popular—destination is Amazon S3. S3 is a serverless object-storage service that is highly scalable, highly durable, and highly available, and provides industry-leading performance and security features. It is designed for 99.999999999% (or 11 9s) of durability and provides storage for almost any amount of data. It provides the ideal storage at an affordable price point for use cases such as a data lake, and hence is an ideal destination for KDF. The most popular use case for using KDF is to populate a data lake that uses S3 as a destination.

Buffering

KDF buffers the incoming records based on the buffering configuration and concatenates the buffered records before delivering them to S3 as an S3 object. It is therefore advisable to append a record separator (usually a \n separator) to a record before sending the record to KDF. Doing that allows you to differentiate the records in the S3 object.

The number of records to buffer and, correspondingly, the frequency of delivery of the S3 object to S3 are determined by the **Buffer size** and **Buffer interval** values configured for the delivery stream. Note that these are referred to as **buffering hints**, and while KDF tries to adhere to it, the resulting object sizes in S3 may not be exactly the size specified. For the S3 destination, **Buffer size** can be between 1 and 128 MB, and **Buffer interval** can be between 60 and 900 seconds (or 1 minute and 15 minutes). Whichever configured value is hit first triggers the delivery of the S3 object. However, if the service determines that it is falling behind in delivering data to the destination in comparison to the rate of data ingestion, it automatically raises the buffer size to catch up and deliver data to the destination. For the purposes of a data lake, it is recommended that the S3 object sizes be greater than 100 MB.

In the AWS KDF console, the buffering hints can be configured for the S3 destination after selecting the destination type, under **Configure settings**.

The following screenshot shows the buffering hints with the default values populated:

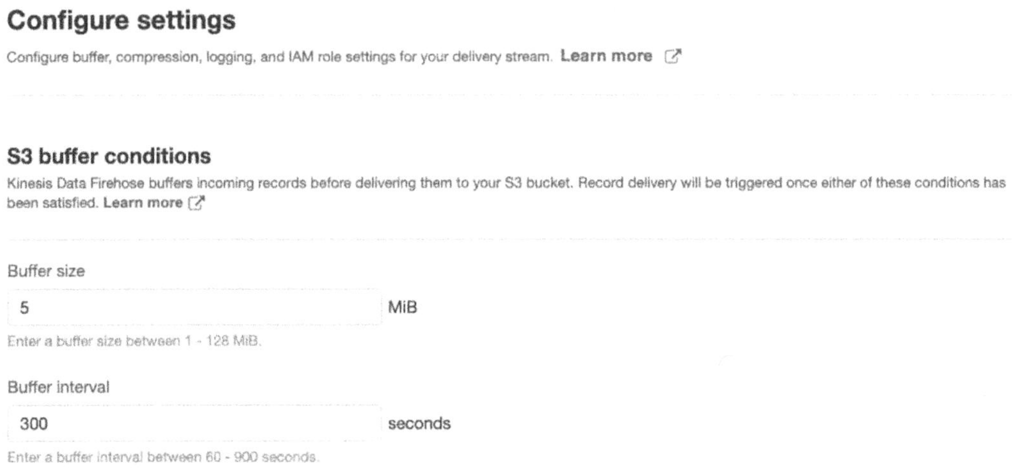

Configure settings

Configure buffer, compression, logging, and IAM role settings for your delivery stream. **Learn more** ☑

S3 buffer conditions

Kinesis Data Firehose buffers incoming records before delivering them to your S3 bucket. Record delivery will be triggered once either of these conditions has been satisfied. **Learn more** ☑

Buffer size

| 5 | MiB |

Enter a buffer size between 1 - 128 MiB.

Buffer interval

| 300 | seconds |

Enter a buffer interval between 60 - 900 seconds.

Figure 5.5 – Screenshot of the S3 destination buffering hints

The `ExtendedS3DestinationConfiguration` configuration can be used with the AWS CLI to configure the S3 destination. The `BufferingHints` configuration appears under the `ExtendedS3DestinationConfiguration` configuration and is presented as follows:

```
"BufferingHints": {
        "IntervalInSeconds": 5,
        "SizeInMBs": 300
    }
```

As the name suggests, the buffering hints act as hints. While KDF makes the best effort to adhere to the hints, KDF can raise the buffer size if the rate at which records are being ingested exceeds the rate at which records are delivered.

S3 encryption of delivered objects

KDF supports delivering objects to S3 with server-side encryption at rest, using a KMS key. The key can be either a service-managed CMK key such as aws/s3, which is the default key for the service for your account, or a customer-managed CMK that you specify. In the console, you can pick the key from a drop-down list, while in the configuration file, you have to specify the ARN of the key. You also need to provide access to this key to the **Identity and Access Management (IAM)** role that KDF assumes to deliver data to the S3 destination.

The following screenshot shows the S3 destination encryption configuration in the AWS KDF console:

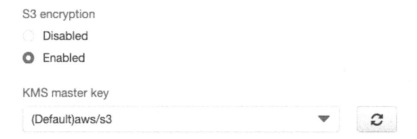

Figure 5.6 – S3 encryption setting for the S3 destination in the AWS Console

It is recommended that you use a customer-managed CMK as there are a number of advantages to using it, including the ability to control key rotation, use or upload your own key material, and control access and permissions on the key.

Compression

KDF provides the ability to compress S3 objects before delivery to S3. The supported compression formats are **Gzip**, **Snappy**, **Hadoop-Compatible Snappy**, and **ZIP**.

Understanding default and custom S3 prefixes with KDF

When storing data in S3, it is a common practice to group data in folders, especially by time, commonly known as **data partitioning**. This allows for better performance and cost optimization when querying data stored in S3 by filtering data by date and by eliminating the scanning of data in folders that are not being queried, a practice called **partition pruning**.

In the specified S3 bucket, KDF by default delivers S3 objects in a **Coordinated Universal Time (UTC)**-based folder structure in the *YYYY/MM/DD/HH* format. The UTC time used for this is the time records ingested into KDF, and the time is made available in a metadata field called `ApproximateArrivalTimestamp`. This creates a hierarchical folder structure. However, this folder structure is not compatible with Apache Hive naming conventions, which require the folder structure to be in a `/partitionkey=partitionvalue` format. The Apache Hive naming format allows the easy addition of new partitions to a table with data stored in an S3 folder through a single command such as `MSCK REPAIR TABLE`, as opposed to adding partitions one by one. It also enables partition-naming schemes such as `/date=20201-01-02/` that are helpful in reducing the number of partitions as more data is added. In order to achieve this in KDF, you need to use custom S3 prefixes.

As the name suggests, custom S3 prefixes allow you to specify S3 prefixes to alter the virtual folder structure of the objects delivered to S3. Here are two types of prefixes that can be specified:

- **S3 prefix**—This refers to the prefixes for objects delivered by KDF to S3.

- **S3 error prefix**—This refers to the prefixes of objects delivered to S3 by KDF when it encounters an error. This error could be related to a data transformation error when trying to invoke a Lambda function to perform inline ETL or a data format conversion error when trying to convert the incoming records from a JSON format to either Parquet or **Optimized Row Columnar (ORC)** format. When KDF encounters those error conditions and is unable to deliver the records after retries, it delivers the records together with some metadata to the specified S3 bucket using the folder structure specified for the S3 error prefix. It is recommended to use an error prefix that makes it easy to identify and re-process failed records, such as a date format similar to the one used for the S3 prefix except under a separate folder.

Custom prefixes utilize expressions of the form `!{namespace:value}`, where the namespace is either a timestamp or a firehose object. The Firehose namespace provides the ability to specify folder names that are not timestamp related and can have values that are either a random string or an error-output type. The error-output-type value can only be used in the `ErrorOutputPrefix` and depends on the configuration of the delivery stream, type of destination, and reason for failure. It can have the following values:

- `processing-failed`: Denotes processing failed for a Lambda transformation

- `elasticsearch-failed`: Denotes a failure in delivering records to an AWS Elasticsearch destination

- `splunk-failed`: Denotes a failure in delivering records to a Splunk destination

- `http-endpoint-failed`: Denotes a failure in delivering records to an HTTP endpoint destination
- `format-conversion-failed`: Denotes a failure in converting the format of incoming records from JSON to Parquet or ORC

The timestamp namespace can have a date pattern in the Java `DateTimeFormatter` pattern (`https://docs.oracle.com/javase/8/docs/api/java/time/format/DateTimeFormatter.html`). The two namespaces can be combined in a single expression to create a complex pattern for the prefix.

It is important to understand the origin of the timestamp used for the expression. The timestamp is not the timestamp when the incoming record was generated at the source (called the `Event` timestamp), and it is not any arbitrary timestamp value in the incoming record. It is an internal timestamp used by KDF called `ApproximateArrivalTimestamp`, which is a UTC timestamp associated with every record when it is ingested into KDF.

> **KDF S3 custom prefix expressions use ingestion time**
>
> The only timestamp available for expressions in S3 custom prefixes is the ingestion-time timestamp or `ApproximateArrivalTimestamp`. Further, since KDF buffers multiple records and delivers them together in a single object to S3, it is possible that individual records could have different ingestion timestamps. KDF uses the ingestion timestamp of the oldest record in the S3 object being written, to evaluate the prefix expression.

Assuming that you want to store log data in S3 objects in hourly folders (partitions), here is an example of an S3 prefix:

```
logs/year=!{timestamp:yyyy}/month=!{timestamp:MM}/
day=!{timestamp:dd}/hour=!{timestamp:HH}/
```

So, if you have an ingestion time of `1609808228` in Epoch time (`https://en.wikipedia.org/wiki/Unix_time`), which is Tuesday, January 5, 2021 12:57:08 A.M. in UTC, the preceding expression evaluates to a prefix, as shown here:

```
logs/year=2021/month=01/day=05/hour=00/
```

Similarly, assuming that you want to store the data with errors, by error type in hourly folders, here is an example of an S3 error-output prefix:

```
logs/!{firehose:error-output-type}/!{timestamp:yyyy/MM/dd/HH}/
```

So, if you have an ingestion time of `1609808228` in Epoch time, which is Tuesday, January 5, 2021 12:57:08 A.M. in UTC, and assuming the error was due to a Lambda transform failure, the preceding expression evaluates to an error prefix, as shown here:

```
logs/processing-failed/2021/01/05/00/
```

Even though custom S3 prefixes cannot use fields in the incoming data in expressions to create custom partitioning schemes, it does provide an easy way to query the delivered data in time-based partitions using ingestion time.

Next, let's take a look at how S3 delivery failures are handled in KDF.

S3 delivery failures

KDF stores incoming records for 24 hours in case it is unable to deliver the data to the destination. For S3, there can be multiple reasons why KDF may be unable to deliver S3 objects, including a change to the permissions preventing access to S3, deletion of the configured S3 location, unavailability of the S3 service (which is highly unlikely), or some other networking issue. In those situations, KDF continues to try to deliver the objects every 5 seconds, up to 24 hours. It also logs the error in Amazon CloudWatch Logs, if it is enabled in the configuration of the delivery stream. If it is unable to deliver the records beyond 24 hours, the data is lost. So, it is important to keep an eye on the KDF metrics available in Amazon CloudWatch for the S3 destination, particularly `DeliveryToS3.Success`, which is a ratio of the sum of successful Amazon S3 `PUT` commands over the sum of all Amazon S3 `PUT` commands and should be close to `1`. If it consistently starts falling, this indicates a problem with the destination. Similarly, the `DeliveryToS3.DataFreshness` metric indicates in seconds the age of the oldest record in KDF not delivered to S3. If this number starts going up consistently, this indicates an issue. Further, if this number starts approaching 86,400 seconds (or 24 hours), there is a potential for data loss. It is advisable to set an alarm on this metric in Amazon CloudWatch to get notified if this value crosses a threshold, to give you adequate time to investigate and fix the issue.

S3 backup

KDF provides the ability to back up the source records to a different S3 location if either data transformation or data format conversion is enabled. This allows you to preserve the source data as ingested into KDF for debugging or other business use cases. The S3 location can be a completely different bucket and prefix from the one specified for the delivery destination.

Security

KDF needs an IAM role with a permissions policy that allows it to perform actions on behalf of your AWS account. It needs permissions to access the S3 locations specified for the delivery of the data as well as the backup location, if data transformation or data format conversion is enabled and S3 backup is also enabled. If S3 server-side encryption is enabled using an AWS KMS customer-managed CMK key, access to the KMS key is also required. If CloudWatch logging of data delivery failures is enabled, it also needs access to CloudWatch Logs. In addition, if data transformation is enabled, it needs access to the Lambda function specified for data transformation and access to the AWS Glue Data Catalog, if data format conversion is enabled. Further, if the source of data is a KDS stream, then access to the KDS stream also needs to be included in the permissions policy. In order to enable cross-account access, additional permissions—as described in the *Understanding cross-account delivery deployment patterns with KDF* section of this chapter—also need to be included.

A sample policy is included in the code samples associated with this book and available on GitHub at `https://github.com/PacktPublishing/Streaming-Data-Solutions-with-Amazon-Kinesis` in the `KDFSmartCityDeliveryStreamPolicy.json` file.

Understanding cross-account delivery deployment patterns with KDF

It is common for enterprises to have a multiple-AWS-accounts set up for data management. An AWS account provides security and billing isolation from other accounts, though mechanisms exist to manage the accounts, their security, and their billing as a whole through the use of AWS Organizations, consolidated billing, and management using AWS Control Tower. An example strategy could be to have a central AWS account to host the data lake, which includes the S3 bucket to hold data and multiple client accounts either writing data to the central account or reading data from the central account. With KDF, you need to be aware of a few key aspects to set up a multi-account strategy properly.

The following screenshot illustrates such a scenario:

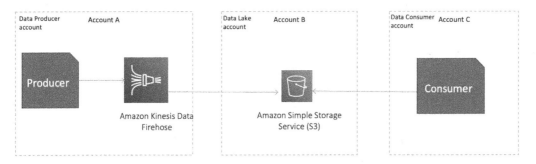

Figure 5.7 – Multi-account data-lake scenario

With this account structure, you have one or more S3 buckets in **Account B** holding the data in the data lake. **Account A** hosts the KDF delivery stream that delivers data to the S3 buckets in **Account B**, and **Account C** hosts the processes that read the data from the S3 buckets in **Account B**.

The delivery stream configuration for an S3 destination requires you to specify a bucket for delivering the S3 objects. If the bucket is in the same AWS account as the KDF delivery stream, it is available to select in the AWS KDF console. If it is in a different AWS account, you need to use the AWS CLI to create the delivery stream as the console does not allow you to specify an S3 bucket in a different account. If using the AWS CLI, the bucket ARN—whether in the same account or in a remote account—needs to be specified. In addition, the delivery stream configuration needs to specify an IAM role the KDF service can assume that allows the service to access resources in the account the KDF delivery stream is running in—in this case, **Account A**. For the purpose of writing to an S3 bucket in **Account B**, the specified IAM role needs to have access to the S3 bucket. It is important to understand the mechanism by which this access is provided and its side effects.

> **bucket-owner-full-control**
>
> It is important to understand the ownership of objects in S3. While objects written to S3 buckets in **Account B** by a user or role in **Account B** are owned by **Account B**, objects written to S3 buckets in **Account B** by a user or role in **Account A** are owned by **Account A**. **Account B** has no object permissions on those objects and has to be explicitly granted access by the owner of the objects.
>
> The object owner can grant the bucket owner full control of the object by specifying an updated **access-control list** (**ACL**) with `bucket-owner-full-control`. Once the bucket owner gets access to the objects, it can then delegate access to other identities in the same account. However, the bucket owner is still unable to delegate access to identities outside of the account. So, in order to enable clients in **Account C** to read the objects, the bucket owner can create an IAM role in **Account B** with permissions to access the objects and grant **Account C** permissions to assume the role to access the S3 objects. This is illustrated in *Figure 5.8*.

Let's take a look at the steps involved in providing KDF with cross-account access to an S3 bucket in **Account B**:

1. Create an IAM role in **Account A** that can be assumed by the KDF service. This is the IAM role specified when a delivery stream is created. However, this is just the role without any permissions policy attached.

2. Attach a bucket policy to the S3 buckets in **Account B**, which provides access to the S3 buckets, to the IAM role created in *Step 1* with a condition to check that the `bucket-owner-full-control` ACL is specified. This will ensure that only objects with that ACL set are allowed to be written to the S3 buckets. An example policy is shown as follows:

```
{
    "Version": "2012-10-17",
    "Statement": [
        {
        "Sid": "KDF-test-bucket",
        "Effect": "Allow",
        "Action": [
            "s3:AbortMultipartUpload",
            "s3:GetBucketLocation",
            "s3:ListBucket",
            "s3:ListBucketMultipartUploads",
            "s3:GetObject"
        ],
        "Resource": [
            "arn:aws:s3:::s3-datadelivery-1",
            "arn:aws:s3:::s3-datadelivery-1/*"
        ],
        "Principal": {
            "AWS": "arn:aws:iam::123456789012:role/KDF_
delivery_role"
        }
    },
        {
        "Sid": "KDF-test-object",
        "Effect": "Allow",
        "Action": [
            "s3:PutObject",
            "s3:PutObjectAcl"
        ],
        "Resource": [
            "arn:aws:s3:::s3-datadelivery-1",
```

```
                "arn:aws:s3:::s3-datadelivery-1/*"
            ],
            "Condition": {
                "StringEquals": {
                    "s3:x-amz-acl": "bucket-owner-full-
control"
                }
            },
            "Principal": {
                "AWS": "arn:aws:iam::123456789012:role/KDF_
delivery_role"
            }
        }
    ]
}
```

3. In **Account A**, delegate permissions to the role to access the S3 buckets in **Account B** in an IAM policy. KDF, when writing to the remote bucket in **Account B**, automatically adds the `bucket-owner-full-control` ACL.

In order to do that, it needs an additional permission, `s3:PutObjectAcl`, on the destination bucket. A sample policy with the additional permission is shown in the following code block:

```
{
    "Version": "2012-10-17",
    "Statement":
    [
        {
            "Effect": "Allow",
            "Action": [
                "s3:AbortMultipartUpload",
                "s3:GetBucketLocation",
                "s3:GetObject",
                "s3:ListBucket",
                "s3:ListBucketMultipartUploads",
                "s3:PutObject",
                "s3:PutObjectAcl"
            ],
```

```
            "Resource": [
                "arn:aws:s3:::s3-datadelivery-1",
                "arn:aws:s3:::s3-datadelivery-1/*"
        ]
    }
]
}
```

4. Create an IAM policy and IAM role in **Account B** that provides permissions to read the S3 objects, and grant access to **Account C** to assume the role. This role is not for KDF to be able to deliver the objects but for consumers in **Account C** to be able to assume to read the objects in the S3 bucket delivered by KDF.

The following screenshot shows the setup as described:

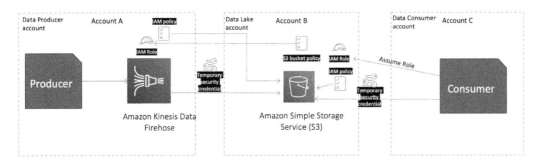

Figure 5.8 – S3 cross-account delivery setup

An alternate mechanism to achieve the same outcome could be to run the KDF delivery stream in **Account B** and create an IAM role in **Account B** with permissions to access the KDF delivery stream, and grant **Account A** permissions to assume the role. Then, producers in **Account A** sending data to the KDF delivery stream in **Account B** would first need to assume the role before sending data to the KDF delivery stream. In this case, since **Account B** owns the delivered objects in S3, it can then use a bucket policy to provide permissions to **Account C**, which can then delegate permissions to identities (for consumers) in **Account C**.

Amazon Redshift

Amazon Redshift (**Redshift**) is a fully managed, **petabyte** (**PB**)-scale, **massively parallel processing** (**MPP**) data warehouse service from AWS. It was launched in February 2013 and is an extremely popular service. It is a relational database that is based on PostgreSQL but has some important differences from PostgreSQL as it is specifically designed for **online analytical processing** (**OLAP**) workloads and is extensively used for data analysis and business intelligence applications, as opposed to transactional workloads.

It employs a distributed and shared-nothing architecture with a **leader** node that fields client connections and **Structured Query Language** (**SQL**) statements, creates a distributed query execution plan, and sends them to a number of **compute** nodes, each with independent memory, **central processing unit** (**CPU**), and storage to process the query on its own subset of data, ideally collocated with the node in its own storage. This parallelizes the query execution and data scanning and processing of large volumes of data across a number of nodes, vastly improving the performance of queries over **symmetric multiprocessing** (**SMP**) systems.

On the ingest side, when data needs to be inserted into tables in Redshift, Redshift provides a COPY command. The COPY command is able to do parallel loading of files or data directly into the compute nodes, making the ingestion process extremely fast. KDF uses the COPY command to load data into Redshift, but in order to do that, it first needs to stage the files in a temporary S3 location. It then issues the COPY command to load the data in those S3 objects into a table in Redshift. Each delivery stream is able to load data into a single Redshift table. So, if you have a requirement to load multiple tables, multiple KDF delivery streams need to be created, one for each Redshift table to be loaded. There are some other patterns that can be employed when you need to load multiple tables, as discussed in the *Security* section of this chapter.

Connecting to Redshift

In order to deliver data to a Redshift cluster, KDF needs to know the connection information for the Redshift cluster. In the AWS KDF console, there is a drop-down list that populates all the available Redshift clusters in the same account in the same AWS Region, and you can pick one cluster in the list and provide the **User name** and **Password** of a user that has insert privileges into the table and database that you specify.

The following screenshot shows the AWS Console with the Redshift cluster information filled out:

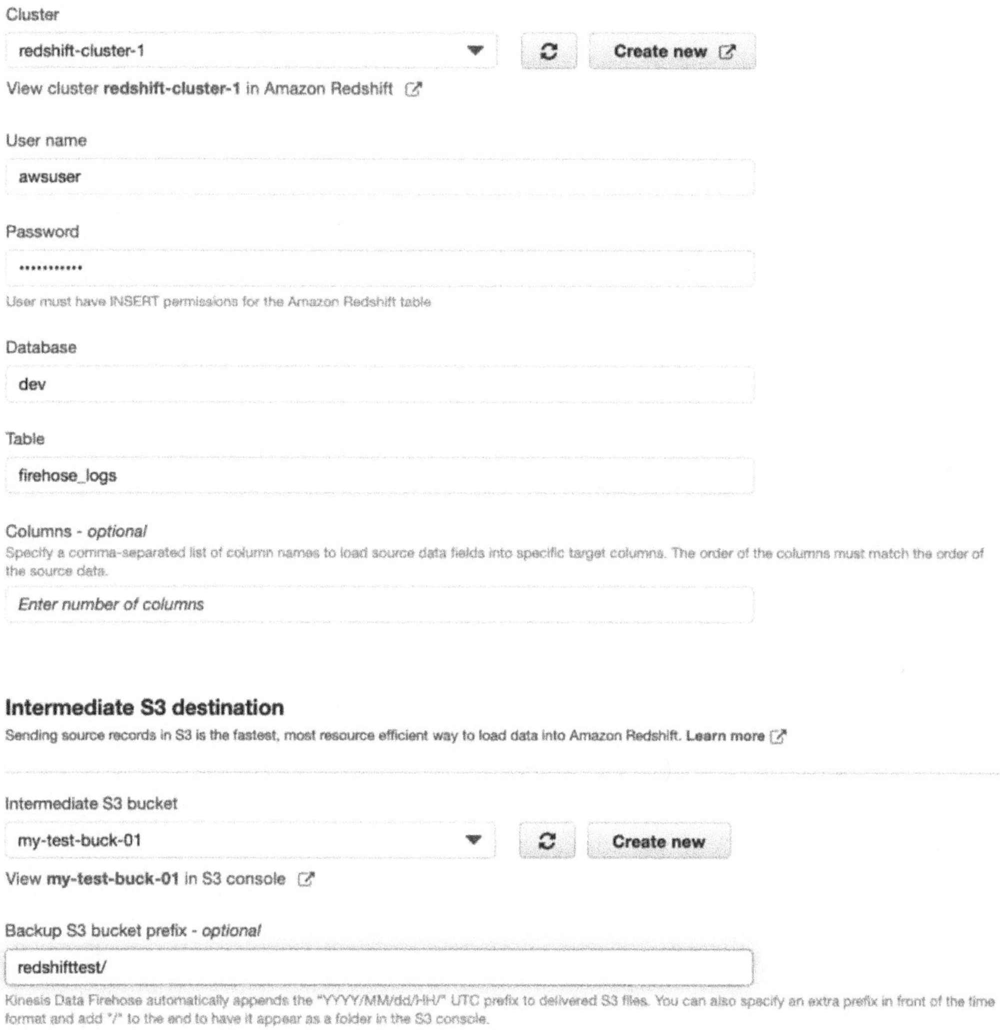

Cluster

redshift-cluster-1

View cluster **redshift-cluster-1** in Amazon Redshift

User name

awsuser

Password

••••••••••

User must have INSERT permissions for the Amazon Redshift table

Database

dev

Table

firehose_logs

Columns - *optional*

Specify a comma-separated list of column names to load source data fields into specific target columns. The order of the columns must match the order of the source data.

Enter number of columns

Intermediate S3 destination

Sending source records in S3 is the fastest, most resource efficient way to load data into Amazon Redshift. **Learn more**

Intermediate S3 bucket

my-test-buck-01

View **my-test-buck-01** in S3 console

Backup S3 bucket prefix - *optional*

redshifttest/

Kinesis Data Firehose automatically appends the "YYYY/MM/dd/HH/" UTC prefix to delivered S3 files. You can also specify an extra prefix in front of the time format and add "/" to the end to have it appear as a folder in the S3 console.

Figure 5.9 – Screenshot of KDF connection information for Redshift

In the RedshiftDestinationConfiguration configuration, you can specify the Redshift cluster information in the ClusterJDBCURL configuration parameter under RedshiftDestinationConfiguration. The **Java Database Connectivity (JDBC)** URL is in the following format:

```
jdbc:redshift://Redshift Cluster endpoint:configured port for
the Redshift cluster/database name
```

You can get the Redshift cluster JDBC URL from the AWS Redshift console from the **CLUSTERS** menu in the **Properties** tab, when you view **Connection Details** and then click **View all connection details**.

Buffering

As mentioned earlier, KDF delivers data to Redshift in two steps, first to an intermediate S3 bucket and prefix to stage the files and then to Redshift, utilizing the `COPY` command. A lot of the configuration options available for S3, explained in this chapter for the S3 destination, apply to the intermediate S3 location as well.

However, the S3 configuration for the Redshift destination uses the `S3DestinationConfiguration` property configuration as opposed to the `Extended S3DestinationConfiguration` property configuration for the S3 destination. The `S3DestinationConfiguration` property configuration supports a smaller subset of options and does not include the `DataFormatConversionConfiguration` property configuration for data format conversion, the `ProcessingConfiguration` property for specifying a Lambda transform, and the `S3BackupConfiguration` property for backing up the source data records to a different S3 location before any transformation. The `ProcessingConfiguration` and `S3BackupConfiguration` property configurations are instead directly available as part of the `RedshiftDestinationConfiguration` property configuration, which is the configuration for the Redshift destination. However, the `DataFormatConversionConfiguration` property configuration—and, hence, the ability to convert incoming records from JSON format to Apache Parquet or Apache ORC—is only available for the S3 destination and not for any other destination.

The `S3DestinationConfiguration` property configuration does provide the ability to specify the buffering hints related to the volume of data to buffer before delivering an object to the intermediate S3 location. This is available as **Buffer size** and **Buffer interval** values. The **Buffer size** value can be between 1 and 128 MB and the **Buffer interval** value can be between 60 and 900 seconds (or 1 minute and 15 minutes). KDF concatenates the buffered incoming records before delivering the records to an S3 object, so you need to make sure that the `COPY` command works on the concatenated records.

The Redshift `COPY` command provides a number of options to load various data formats, and the `RedshiftDestinationConfiguration` property configuration allows you to specify the `COPY` command options (`https://docs.aws.amazon.com/firehose/latest/APIReference/API_CopyCommand.html`).

KDF runs one `COPY` command at a time, since it is always loading the same table. If after one `COPY` command finishes there are more S3 objects containing data in the intermediate S3 bucket that remains to be loaded, it issues further `COPY` commands. It creates a Redshift `manifest` file for each load and puts it in the S3 location, under a `manifests` folder underneath the specified prefix (if specified), and uses it in the `COPY` command. Under the `manifests` folder, KDF always appends the `YYYY/MM/dd/HH` prefix using the UTC time for the delivered files.

In the `RedshiftDestinationConfiguration` property configuration, assuming the S3 bucket is `example-redshift-bucket-1` and the prefix is `logs/`, the `COPY` command is specified under `RedshiftDestinationConfiguration`, as follows:

```
"CopyCommand": {
        "DataTableName": "Sample",
        "DataTableColumns": "Col1,Col2",
        "CopyOptions": "JSON 's3:// example-redshift-
bucket-1/jsonpathsfile.txt region us-east-1'
"
        },
```

The table in the Redshift cluster (where the delivery stream needs to insert data) is specified in `DataTableName`, the columns to load are specified in `DataTableColumns`, and the `COPY` command options are specified in `CopyOptions`. The `DataTableColumns` and `CopyOptions` parameters are optional. The `JSONPaths` file is a JSON file providing information on how to interpret nested JSON fields and map the JSON keys to column names in the Redshift database tables.

Delivery failure

Since KDF delivers data to Redshift in two steps—first to a specified S3 bucket and prefix and then to Redshift—delivery failures can occur in either step. For delivery failures to the intermediate S3 location, the same retry behavior exists as for the S3 destination, and since KDF stores the ingested data for 24 hours, if KDF is unable to deliver the data to S3 for more than 24 hours, data loss can occur. For the second step, for the Redshift destination you can set a retry duration between `0` and `7200` seconds in the delivery stream configuration.

The default is `3600` seconds, or `1` hour. If KDF is unable to deliver the data to Redshift due to permissions issues, network problems, cluster unavailability, or any other reason, it retries the `COPY` command up to the configured retry duration. If all the retries fail, it skips the batch of records and delivers a `manifest` file with information on all the skipped objects to an `errors` folder. This enables you to easily load the skipped data using the `manifest` file later, after fixing whatever error was causing the load to fail. If CloudWatch logging is enabled for the Redshift destination, the error is also logged to CloudWatch Log. The retry configuration is illustrated in the following code snippet:

```
"RetryOptions": {
        "DurationInSeconds": 6000
    }
```

In the `RedshiftDestinationConfiguration` configuration, the retry duration is specified under `RedshiftDestinationConfiguration` under `RetryOptions`.

Security

When you create a Redshift cluster, you have to provide **virtual private cloud** (**VPC**) information and the subnet group (you can create a subnet group in the AWS Redshift console or using the AWS CLI), which is a group of subnets in the VPC where Redshift can create a cluster. Redshift chooses one of the subnets in the subnet group to create the cluster nodes. The subnets specified can either be **private subnets** or **public subnets**. If they are private subnets, the cluster endpoint is not accessible from the internet. If the subnets are public subnets and you configure the cluster to be publicly available, the cluster endpoint is accessible from the internet. In that case, you can also optionally specify an **Elastic Internet Protocol** (**Elastic IP**) address to connect to the cluster from the internet. In order to protect the cluster from a networking standpoint, you need to associate a security group (which is like a firewall) to the cluster and only grant inbound access to the IP addresses or security groups that you deem necessary. The inbound access rules should allow access to the database port configured for the cluster so that SQL client tools such as MySQL Workbench can connect to the cluster. There can be up to five security groups associated with a cluster. It is recommended that to provide inbound access to the cluster, you create an additional security group and associate it with the cluster in addition to the initial security group associated with the cluster, which provides minimal access.

> **Elastic IP address**
>
> An Elastic IP address is a public IPv4 address reachable from the internet that can be allocated to an AWS account and associated with an **Elastic Compute Cloud** (**EC2**) instance or an **Elastic Network Interface** (**ENI**).

For KDF to be able to deliver data to your Redshift cluster, it has to be accessible from the internet since KDF is unable to access a private cluster. Consequently, you need to configure your Redshift cluster to be publicly accessible and optionally associate an Elastic IP address with it. In addition, create another security group that provides access to the IP addresses KDF uses for the region your KDF delivery stream is running in and associate it with your Redshift cluster. The list of IP addresses to allow for each region is specified at this link: `https://docs.aws.amazon.com/firehose/latest/dev/controlling-access.html#using-iam-rs`.

If it is against your security policy to have publicly accessible Redshift clusters, you can instead use the S3 destination and deliver the data to S3 and then use `COPY` commands in an EC2 instance (**virtual machine (VM)** in AWS) in the same VPC as the Redshift cluster (with access to the S3 bucket) to run the `COPY` command, or use a Lambda function with VPC access to run the `COPY` command. This architecture can also be used if you want to load multiple different Redshift tables, which KDF doesn't support with a single delivery stream. Note that the architecture mentioned here needs to be augmented with a management framework with retries, failure management, and making sure S3 objects are only loaded once. A good example is available at `https://github.com/awslabs/aws-Lambda-redshift-loader`.

In addition to securing the network, you need to provide a Redshift database username and password for KDF to use to connect to the specified database in the Redshift cluster and insert the data in the specified table. The user also needs to have an `INSERT` privilege on the specified table.

KDF also needs access to the S3 bucket to write and read the intermediate files, to CloudWatch Logs if error logging is enabled, to the Lambda function if the Lambda transform is enabled, and to the KMS key specified if encryption is enabled for S3. As with the S3 destination, this access is provided via an IAM role that needs to be specified when creating a delivery stream. The AWS Console provides an option to create the IAM role during creation of the delivery stream. The IAM policy looks similar to the one for the S3 destination.

Compression

The Redshift destination configuration provides the option to compress the objects delivered to the intermediate S3 location. However, the Snappy and ZIP compression formats supported by the **S3Configuration** are not supported. This option is not available in the AWS Console.

Amazon Elasticsearch Service

Amazon Elasticsearch Service (**AES**) is a fully managed service that offers Elasticsearch as a service and makes creating, managing, securing, and scaling Elasticsearch clusters easy and cost-effective. AES was launched in October 2015. Elasticsearch is a RESTful (where **REST** stands for **REpresentational State Transfer**), distributed, scalable, and fast search-and-analytics engine based on Apache Lucene. AES supports the Elasticsearch APIs, provides integration with other AWS services as well as Logstash, offers managed Kibana, and supports alerting and SQL querying. It is possible to set up an AES cluster in minutes using the AWS AES console, or the AWS CLI, or AES APIs.

Elasticsearch is a distributed document store and it stores JSON documents. The documents are indexed to make them searchable. Elasticsearch uses an inverted index wherein every word in a document is indexed to all documents that have them. The key/value pairs in the JSON documents are fields within the documents, and they have datatypes and are searchable. Each document has an `_id` field that can be used to uniquely identify it, and the field is indexed for fast lookups.

Traditionally, each document was also assigned a mapping type in a `_type` field. The mapping type was meant to identify the type of document based on content or classification—for example, a JSON document with customer information could have a mapping type of `customers`. Each document could only be assigned to a single type and a single index. If we compare to relational databases, the index is a database, the mapping type is loosely a table (although this analogy is problematic due to which mapping types are deprecated in Elasticsearch 7.0, but is useful for a person new to Elasticsearch to understand the correlation between the different Elasticsearch entity types), the JSON document is a row in the table, and the fields are columns.

The integration between KDF and AES provides a very easy mechanism to provide search and analytics on large volumes of data without writing code, whether the data is coming from external sources or the log data is coming from other AWS services integrated with KDF.

In AES, the first step to provision an Elasticsearch cluster is to create a domain, which is the same thing as a cluster and includes the associated instances (nodes), storage, and configuration settings. The following information is needed for the AES destination:

- **Domain**—In the AWS Console, you can pick from a drop-down list that populates all the AES domains in the same AWS account and the same region. In the `ElasticsearchDestinationConfiguration` configuration used with the AWS CLI, you need to provide either the ARN of the AES domain or the domain endpoint. For cross-account delivery of data to an AES domain in a different AWS account, see the section on cross-account delivery to an AES destination.

- **Index**—The name of the index to be used when indexing data. KDF creates a new index if an index with the specified name does not exist. In the `ElasticsearchDestinationConfiguration` configuration, this appears as `IndexName`.

- **Type**—The mapping type name of the documents indexed. If the AES domain is for Elasticsearch 6.x, there can only be one type per index, so if a new type name is provided here for an existing index, KDF can return a runtime error. For Elasticsearch 7.x, since mapping types are deprecated, you should not specify a value for **Type**. In the `ElasticsearchDestinationConfiguration` configuration, this appears as `TypeName`.

- **Index rotation**—The frequency with which the indexes should be rotated. This is provided so as to expire data, making it easier to manage storage in AES. The valid values are `NoRotation`, `OneHour`, `OneDay`, `OneWeek`, and `OneMonth`. KDF appends a portion of the UTC KDF ingestion timestamp (`approximateArrivalTimestamp`) to the index name and rotates it.

> **AES document IDs**
>
> KDF does not support providing AES document IDs, which are generated by KDF on the fly. This means that updates to existing documents in the index are not possible, and everything is an insert.

Once a domain is created, you can retrieve the domain ARN and use it configure the AES destination in KDF.

Understanding the KDF deployment pattern of delivering to AES in a VPC

AES can be configured to run both as a publicly accessible cluster in a service-managed VPC and as a non-public cluster in your own VPC. KDF has the ability to deliver data to an AES cluster in both modes. In order to deliver to a publicly accessible AES cluster, the KDF delivery stream needs to know either the AES domain ARN or the public cluster endpoint. It also needs IAM permissions to be able to access the cluster, which is described in the next section. For an AES cluster inside a VPC, there is an additional configuration that needs to be supplied for the delivery stream, which includes the VPC information. Specifically, you need to provide the VPC subnets you want KDF to access. KDF drops an ENI in each of the specified subnets. You can specify a single subnet or multiple subnets across multiple **Availability Zones (AZs)**, to have resilience for AZ failures. These ENIs get a private IP address from the **Classless Inter-Domain Routing (CIDR)** block of the associated subnets.

Since the AES domain in the VPC also drops ENIs in one or more subnets specified for the AES domain, KDF is able to communicate with the AES cluster. It is important that the required subnet routing tables are appropriately set up to allow network traffic to flow from the subnets specified for KDF to the subnets specified for AES. In general, by default, each routing table has a default route that allows traffic to the entire VPC CIDR block. In addition, the VPC configuration for the delivery stream needs to specify one or more security groups to be applied to the ENIs to restrict traffic. They should allow outbound HTTPS traffic to the security group for the AES domain.

The following diagram shows the architecture for KDF delivering data to an AES domain in a VPC:

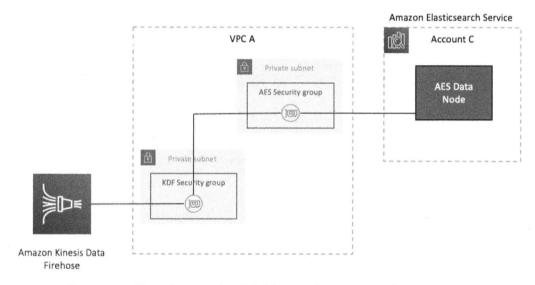

Figure 5.10 – The architecture for KDF delivering data to an AES domain in a VPC

The ElasticsearchDestinationConfiguration configuration can be used with the AWS CLI to configure the AES destination, as illustrated in the following code snippet:

```
"VpcConfiguration": {
        "SubnetIds": [
            ""
        ],
        "RoleARN": "",
        "SecurityGroupIds": [
            ""
        ]
    }
```

The VpcConfiguration configuration appears under the ElasticsearchDestinationConfiguration configuration and allows the specification of subnets, security groups, and an IAM role.

Buffering

For the AES destination, KDF buffers incoming records according to the buffering hints provided in the delivery stream configuration. The **Buffer size** parameter can have values between 1 and 100 MB and the **Buffer interval** parameter can have values between 60 and 900 seconds (or 1 minute and 15 minutes). Whichever value is hit first triggers sending the batch of records to AES. It is required that the incoming records are in JSON format, flattened to single-line JSON objects, and UTF-8 encoded. After buffering, KDF generates an Elasticsearch bulk index request to send and index the records in AES. Bulk indexing (_bulk API) greatly reduces indexing overhead and increases the speed of indexing. Also, the rest.action.multi.allow_explicit_index option on the AES cluster needs to be set to true to allow AES to accept bulk indexing requests with an explicit index specified. This is set to true, by default, for an AES domain.

In the AWS KDF console, the buffering hints can be configured for the AES destination after selecting the destination type under **Configure settings**.

The following screenshot shows the buffering hints with the default values populated:

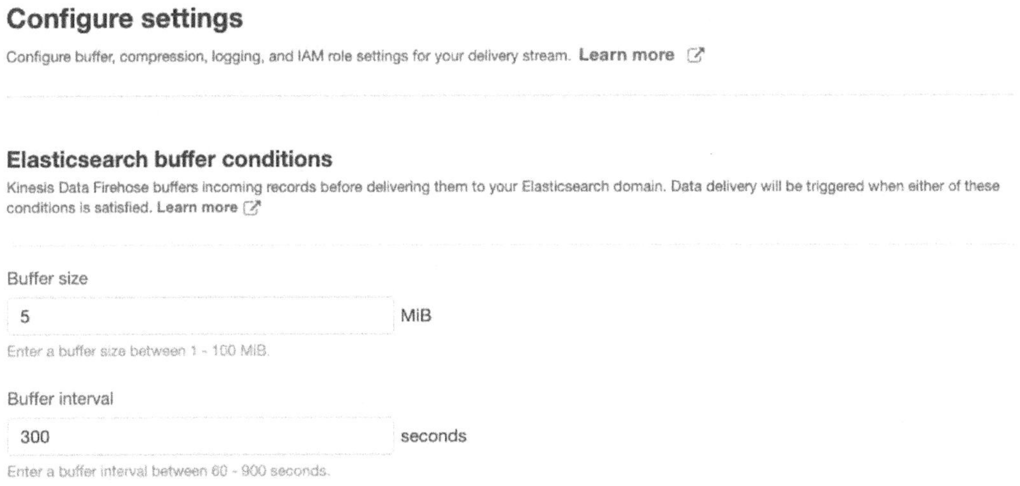

Configure settings

Configure buffer, compression, logging, and IAM role settings for your delivery stream. **Learn more** ☑

Elasticsearch buffer conditions

Kinesis Data Firehose buffers incoming records before delivering them to your Elasticsearch domain. Data delivery will be triggered when either of these conditions is satisfied. **Learn more** ☑

Buffer size

| 5 | MiB |

Enter a buffer size between 1 - 100 MiB.

Buffer interval

| 300 | seconds |

Enter a buffer interval between 60 - 900 seconds.

Figure 5.11 – Screenshot of the AES destination buffering hints

In the `ElasticsearchDestinationConfiguration`
configuration, the `BufferingHints` configuration appears under
`ElasticsearchDestinationConfiguration` and is presented as follows:

```
"BufferingHints": {
        "IntervalInSeconds": 5,
        "SizeInMBs": 300
    }
```

As the name suggests, the buffering hints act as hints, and KDF tries to adhere to the hints
as much as possible but can increase the size of the buffer if the rate of data delivery is
falling behind the rate of data received.

Data transformation and data format conversion

Data transformation using a Lambda transform is supported with the AES destination.
However, data format conversion is not supported. The configuration for data
transformation is similar to what was described earlier in this chapter.

Delivery failure

Data delivery to the AES destination can fail for a number of reasons, such as network
issues, unavailability of the AES domain, or permissions issues. In addition, there could be
issues with having multiple types for a single index, or having fields with the same name
specified for multiple mapping types having different field data types. On encountering
an error, KDF retries the bulk indexing request for a configurable duration between 0 and
7,200 seconds (or 0 to 2 hours). If all the retries fail, it skips the bulk indexing request
and moves forward. However, it delivers the skipped documents, together with some
metadata, including the error code and error message, to an `elasticsearch_failed`
folder (prefix) in the S3 bucket configured under **S3 backups**. This enables you to inspect
the documents and the error codes and messages, fix the problem, and retry sending the
documents.

S3 backup

For the AES destination, KDF offers two modes of backing up incoming data, as follows:

- **Failed Documents Only**—In case of delivery failures and after exhausting all
  retries, KDF delivers the failed records to the specified S3 bucket prepended
  with the `elasticsearch_failed/` prefix (essentially delivering to an
  `elasticsearch_failed` folder).

- **All Documents**—KDF delivers all incoming records to the specified S3 bucket. In case there are delivery failures, the failed records are also delivered to the S3 bucket prepended with the `elasticsearch_failed/` prefix. The ability to deliver all incoming records to the S3 bucket is important as, unlike with the Redshift destination, the incoming records are not staged in S3 before delivering to AES, and this allows you to maintain a copy of the incoming records for later analysis and reconciliation with the data loaded into AES.

If data transformation is enabled using a Lambda transform, any records for which processing failed are also delivered to the S3 bucket specified for the backup S3 configuration.

The following screenshot shows the S3 backup configuration for the AES destination using the AWS Console:

S3 backup

To prevent against data loss, Kinesis Data Firehose can back up records to your S3 bucket while delivering it to your Elasticsearch cluster. **Learn more**

Backup mode

O Failed records only

All records

Backup S3 bucket

Choose a bucket   Create new

Backup S3 bucket prefix - *optional*

Enter a prefix

Kinesis Data Firehose automatically appends the "YYYY/MM/dd/HH/" UTC prefix to delivered S3 files. You can also specify an extra prefix in front of the time format and add "/" to the end to have it appear as a folder in the S3 console.

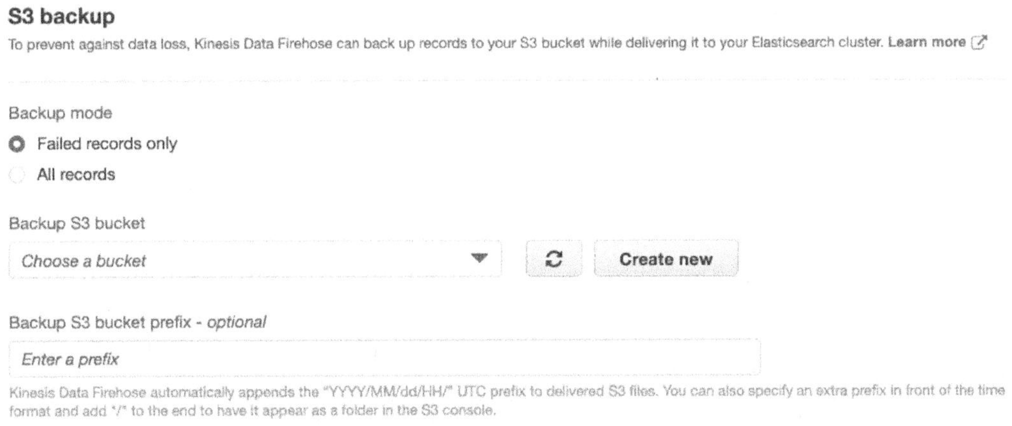

Figure 5.12 – Screenshot showing the S3 backup configuration for the
AES destination using the AWS Console

S3 backup provides an important safety feature to store a copy of all incoming records as they were at the time of ingestion. The backed-up records can also be used as an input to development or test environments.

Security

For the AES destination, KDF needs access to the AES domain. In addition, it needs access to the S3 bucket to write and read all or failed records depending on how the delivery stream is configured, to CloudWatch Logs if error logging is enabled, to the Lambda function if the Lambda transform is enabled, and to the KMS key specified if encryption is enabled for S3. This access is provided via an IAM role that needs to be specified when creating a delivery stream. The AWS Console provides an option to create the IAM role during creation of the delivery stream. The IAM policy looks like the one for the S3 destination, with the addition of the policy for access to the AES domain. For an AWS account with account ID 123456789012 and an AES domain of loganalytics in the us-east-1 AWS Region, the policy looks like this for a publicly accessible domain:

```
{
    "Version": "2012-10-17",
    "Statement": [{
        "Effect": "Allow",
        "Action": [
            "es:DescribeElasticsearchDomain",
            "es:DescribeElasticsearchDomains",
            "es:DescribeElasticsearchDomainConfig",
            "es:ESHttpPost",
            "es:ESHttpPut"
        ],
        "Resource": [
            "arn:aws:es:us-east-1:123456789012:domain/
loganalytics",
            "arn:aws:es:us-east-1:123456789012:domain/
loganalytics/*"
        ]
    }, {
        "Effect": "Allow",
        "Action": [
            "es:ESHttpGet"
        ],
        "Resource": [
            "arn:aws:es:us-east-1:123456789012:domain/
loganalytics/_all/_settings",
            "arn:aws:es:us-east-1:123456789012:domain/
```

```
loganalytics/_cluster/stats",
            "arn:aws:es:us-east-1:123456789012:domain/
loganalytics/index-name*/_mapping/type-name",
            "arn:aws:es:us-east-1:123456789012:domain/
loganalytics/_nodes",
            "arn:aws:es:us-east-1:123456789012:domain/
loganalytics/_nodes/stats",
            "arn:aws:es:us-east-1:123456789012:domain/
loganalytics/_nodes/*/stats",
            "arn:aws:es:us-east-1:123456789012:domain/
loganalytics/_stats",
            "arn:aws:es:us-east-1:123456789012:domain/
loganalytics/index-name*/_stats"
        ]
    }]
}
```

If the AES domain is in a VPC, the following permissions need to be added to the policy. They provide access to the VPC and the ability to create and manage ENIs in the VPC:

```
{
    "Effect": "Allow",
    "Action": [
            "ec2:DescribeVpcs",
"ec2:DescribeVpcAttribute",
"ec2:DescribeSubnets",
"ec2:DescribeSecurityGroups",
"ec2:DescribeNetworkInterfaces",
"ec2:CreateNetworkInterface",
"ec2:CreateNetworkInterfacePermission",
"ec2:DeleteNetworkInterface"
    ],
    "Resource": [
            "*"
    ]
}
```

KDF is also able to deliver data to an AES domain that is in a different AWS account from the KDF delivery stream. However, the AES domain needs to be publicly accessible. In order for KDF to be able to do cross-account delivery of data to an AES destination, the IAM role that is supplied in the delivery stream configuration (and that KDF assumes) needs to have access to the AES domain in the remote account. Just as with the cross-account access described for S3 earlier, there are a few steps that need to be followed.

The following diagram shows cross-account delivery of records from KDF to AES:

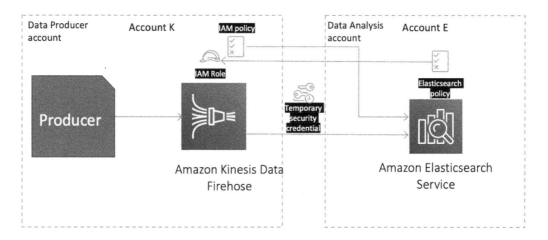

Figure 5.13 – Cross-account delivery of records from KDF to AES

Assuming the account that has the KDF delivery stream is **Account K** and the account that hosts the `loganalytics` AES domain is **Account E**, proceed as follows:

1. Create an IAM role in **Account K** to be used by the KDF delivery stream and associate an IAM policy, as described previously. Make sure the account ID specified (`123456789012` in the example) is the account ID for **Account E** and the domain name is the domain for the AES domain in **Account E**.

2. AES supports resource-based IAM policies, which are IAM policies that can be associated with resources as opposed to identities such as users, groups, and roles. The resource-based policies allow you to specify the actions that can be performed on that resource by the identities that you specify in the policy. In **Account E**, specify a resource-based policy for the AES domain. In the AWS Console for AES, click on **Actions** then **Modify Access policy**, and put the access policy in the textbox provided. The access policy should look like this:

```
{
    "Version": "2012-10-17",
```

```
    "Statement": [
      {
        "Effect": "Allow",
        "Principal": {
          "AWS": "arn:aws:iam::Account-K:role/firehose_
delivery_role"
        },
        "Action": "es:ESHttpGet",
        "Resource": [
          "arn:aws:es:us-east-1:Account-E:domain/
loganalytics/_all/_settings",
          "arn:aws:es:us-east-1:Account-E:domain/
loganalytics/_cluster/stats",
          "arn:aws:es:us-east-1:Account-E:domain/
loganalytics/roletest*/_mapping/roletest",
          "arn:aws:es:us-east-1:Account-E:domain/
loganalytics/_nodes",
          "arn:aws:es:us-east-1:Account-E:domain/
loganalytics/_nodes/stats",
          "arn:aws:es:us-east-1:Account-E:domain/
loganalytics/_nodes/*/stats",
          "arn:aws:es:us-east-1:Account-E:domain/
loganalytics/_stats",
          "arn:aws:es:us-east-1:Account-E:domain/
loganalytics/roletest*/_stats"
        ]
      },
      {
        "Effect": "Allow",
        "Principal": {
          "AWS": "arn:aws:iam::Account-K:role/firehose_
delivery_role"
        },
        "Action": [
          "es:DescribeElasticsearchDomain",
          "es:DescribeElasticsearchDomains",
          "es:DescribeElasticsearchDomainConfig",
          "es:ESHttpPost",
```

```
        "es:ESHttpPut"
    ],
      "Resource": [
        "arn:aws:es:us-east-1:Account-E:domain/
  loganalytics",
        "arn:aws:es:us-east-1:Account-E:domain/
  loganalytics/*"
      ]
    }
  ]
}
```

3. Use the AWS CLI or KDF APIs to create the delivery stream and specify the AES cluster endpoint instead of the AES domain ARN. It is not possible to do this using the AWS Console, which only allows you to choose from a pre-populated drop-down list of domains in the same account and the same region.

Cross-account delivery of records to an AES domain is very beneficial if you have a multi-AWS account set up to centralize search and data analysis using AES in one account, and data ingestion and delivery with KDF in multiple other accounts.

Splunk destination

Splunk is a software platform commonly used by many large and small enterprises to collect, search, analyze, and visualize large volumes of data from myriad data sources such as websites, machines, logs, devices, sensors, and business applications. KDF offers Splunk as a destination to make it easier for enterprises that have standardized their search-and-analytics platform on Splunk to be able to send data from all of those sources, as well as many AWS services integrated with KDF, to Splunk for easy analysis.

Splunk is available as a destination in KDF under **Third-party service provider**, which has a number of other third-party providers listed.

The following screenshot shows a screenshot of the Splunk destination available under **Third-party service provider**:

Destination

○ **Amazon S3**
Object storage built to store and retrieve any amount of data from anywhere.

○ **Amazon Redshift**
An enterprise-level, petabyte scale, fully managed data warehousing service.

○ **Amazon Elasticsearch**
An open-source search and analytics engine for use cases such as log analytics, real-time application monitoring, and click stream analytics.

○ **HTTP Endpoint**
A way to deliver data to your custom destination.

◉ **Third-party service provider**
Choose from a list of third-party service providers.

Third-party service provider

Splunk ▼

Figure 5.14 – Screenshot of the Splunk destination available under Third-party service provider in the AWS Console

In order to use Splunk as a destination, you need to have Splunk already set up with an active and available Splunk index. KDF supports both **Splunk Enterprise** and **Splunk Cloud**. There are a few prerequisites on the Splunk side before the integration works. The Splunk add-on for Amazon Kinesis Firehose needs to be installed, the **HTTP Event Collector** (**HEC**) needs to be set up and enabled, and an HEC token with indexer acknowledgments enabled needs to be created. The HEC provides a mechanism to send events and data to Splunk over HTTP or HTTPS (secure HTTP) protocols and makes it easy to send events to Splunk by removing the need to set up Splunk forwarders.

The HEC token is a means to authenticate clients connecting to Splunk and delivering data. Each token is a 128-bit, 32-character **globally unique identifier** (**GUID**), which is presented by clients to HEC, which when authenticated allows clients to send data to Splunk in text
or JSON format. The token configuration has the source, source type, and index, which the Splunk indexers then use to index the incoming data.

Buffering

KDF concatenates the incoming records and buffers them.

> **Buffering hints**
> The **Buffer size** and **Buffer interval** values for the Splunk destination are set to 5 MB and 60 seconds respectively and are not configurable.

If you need any record separators in the data, you have to add them to the record sent to KDF and make sure Splunk understands how to parse the data.

Data transformation and data format conversion

Data transformation using a Lambda transform is supported with the Splunk destination. However, data format conversion is not supported. The configuration for data transformation is similar to what was described earlier in this chapter.

Understanding KDF deployment patterns for Splunk

In order for KDF to deliver data to Splunk, it needs access to the Splunk environment. KDF can deliver to any publicly accessible endpoint. For Splunk installations running in a VPC, Splunk recommends having an **Elastic Load Balancer** (**ELB**) fronting the indexers that is exposed to the internet to proxy traffic to the indexers. KDF only supports the **Classic Load Balancer** (**CLB**) with duration-based sticky sessions enabled and cookie expiration disabled. In that case, the ELB **Domain Name System** (**DNS**) name is the Splunk cluster endpoint. If you don't have an ELB and are directly exposing one or more HEC endpoints to KDF from within your VPC, you need to make sure there is a public IP address attached and that they're in a public subnet so that they can be accessed from the internet. In addition, the security group attached should have inbound rules to provide access to the KDF IP addresses. The CIDR block to provide access to the IP addresses is available at this link: `https://docs.aws.amazon.com/firehose/latest/dev/controlling-access.html#using-iam-splunk-vpc`.

Delivery failure

As explained earlier, the HEC set up on the Splunk side needs to have an HTTP event collector token with indexer acknowledgments enabled. This allows Splunk to send back acknowledgments to KDF on successful delivery of data. KDF depends on these acknowledgments to deal with delivery failure. When KDF sends data to Splunk, it starts an acknowledgment timer. If KDF receives a delivery error or the acknowledgment does not arrive within the acknowledgment timeout period, KDF retries the request and starts a retry duration counter.

The retry and HEC acknowledgment timeout durations can be configured in the Splunk destination configuration and can be between 0 and 7,200 seconds (or 0 and 2 hours) for the retry duration and between 180 and 600 seconds (or 3 minutes and 10 minutes) for the HEC acknowledgement timeout duration. KDF keeps retrying, resetting the acknowledgment timeout period before each retry, and waiting for the acknowledgment until the retry duration expires. Even if the retry duration expires while KDF is still waiting for an acknowledgment, it still waits until the acknowledgment timeout period expires and then checks to see if there is any time left in the retry duration.

If it is unable to deliver after the retry duration expires, it sends the data to the configured backup S3 bucket in a `splunk-failed` folder. The S3 backup configuration can be configured to either just back up the failed events or all events. Just as with the AES destination, since the incoming records are not staged by KDF in a S3 bucket, backing up all the incoming data to a S3 bucket is useful to inspect the data or reload the data, if needed.

Splunk destination configuration

In order to setup the Splunk destination in KDF, you need the following:

- **Splunk cluster endpoint**—This is the endpoint to connect to. This endpoint needs to be publicly accessible. For further information on configuring and retrieving the endpoint, see `https://docs.splunk.com/Documentation/AddOns/ released/Firehose/ConfigureFirehose`.

- **Splunk endpoint type**—The available values are RAW, which is the most common format and can parse most formats, or `Event`, which requires a specific JSON format. When using `Event`, you need to use a Lambda transform to properly format the incoming events in the proper JSON format.

- **Authentication token**—This is the HEC token that KDF needs to authenticate with the HEC.

- **HEC acknowledgement timeout**—The timeout period for the HEC acknowledgment.

- **Retry duration**—The time period in seconds that KDF retries sending data in case there is a delivery failure or there is no acknowledgment from the Splunk HEC.

The following screenshot shows the Splunk destination configuration in the AWS Console:

Splunk cluster endpoint

> https://xyz.splunk.com:8088

Format: https://xyz.splunk.com:8080

Splunk endpoint type

◉ Raw endpoint
   Capable of parsing most common log formats. View supported log formats ↗.

◯ Event endpoint
   Requires specific JSON formatting ↗. Use the Kinesis Data Firehose data transformation feature to properly format source data.

Authentication token

> Enter your authentication token

☐ Show token

HEC acknowledgement timeout
Specify how long Kinesis Data Firehose waits for index acknowledgement from Splunk. If Splunk doesn't send the acknowledgment before the timeout, Kinesis Data Firehose considers it a data delivery failure and backs up the data to your S3 bucket.

| 180 | seconds |

Enter a timeout duration from 180 - 600 seconds.

Retry duration
Specify how long Kinesis Data Firehose retries sending data to Splunk. Kinesis Data Firehose first waits for an acknowledgment from Splunk. If the acknowledgment doesn't arrive and your retry duration is greater than 0, Kinesis Data Firehose starts the retry duration counter and keeps retrying until the retry duration runs out. After that Kinesis Data Firehose considers it a data delivery failure and backs up the data to your S3 bucket.

| 300 | seconds |

Enter a retry duration from 0 - 7200 seconds.

Figure 5.15 – Screenshot of the Splunk destination configuration in the AWS Console

You need to have the Splunk cluster information handy before you set up the KDF delivery stream for the Splunk destination.

Security

For the Splunk destination, KDF needs access to the HEC, as explained earlier. In addition, it needs access to the S3 bucket to write and read all or failed records (depending on how the delivery stream is configured), to CloudWatch Logs if error logging is enabled, to the Lambda function if the Lambda transform is enabled, and to the KMS key specified if encryption is enabled for S3. This access is provided via an IAM role that needs to be specified when creating the delivery stream. The IAM policy looks similar to the one for the S3 destination.

HTTP endpoint destination

The HTTP endpoint destination enables KDF to send data to any HTTP endpoint over HTTPS over the internet. The destination endpoint can be in a different AWS account or in a different AWS Region, or it can be in your own enterprise data center or anywhere else as long as it is accessible. This is an extremely powerful feature that opens up possibilities for data ingestion and processing. You don't have to wait for additional destinations for software platforms that you use, and KDF doesn't need support to come online. You can now expose an HTTP endpoint and get KDF to send data to the endpoint, and you can receive the data and send it to any software platform you want. AWS provides a service called **Amazon API Gateway**, which is a serverless, fully managed service that allows you to build and deploy secure and scalable APIs.

Since the data sent to the APIs you deploy can be either proxied (for some supported AWS services) or processed by a Lambda function and then sent to other AWS services, this opens up integration with a number of other AWS services with KDF, such as **Amazon DynamoDB**, which is a serverless, highly scalable NoSQL database, and **Amazon Relational Database Service** (**Amazon RDS**), which is a fully managed relational database service that offers multiple different database engines. In addition, since you can send data to endpoints in other AWS Regions, you can have a managed, configuration-based way to replicate data to multiple AWS Regions across the globe.

The HTTP endpoint destination also forms the basis for a number of third-party vendors to be able to integrate with KDF and make it easy to consume data, to then offer their own processing, analyzing, and visualization capabilities. A number of vendors already have integrations with KDF, including **Datadog**, **New Relic**, and **MongoDB**, and can be considered to be special cases of the HTTP endpoint destination. In the AWS Console, these integrations are available under **Third-party service provider**, together with Splunk.

Buffering

Similar to other destinations, KDF buffers the incoming data before delivering it to the destination. For the HTTP endpoint destination and the third-party destinations mentioned, the **Buffer size** hint can be between 1 and 64 MiB and the **Buffer interval** value can be between 60 and 900 seconds (or 1 minute and 15 minutes). KDF concatenates the incoming records before delivering, and you need to make sure the data format being delivered is acceptable to the HTTP endpoint or to the third-party endpoints. If needed, you can use a Lambda transform to transform incoming records to the format needed.

Data transformation and data format conversion

Data transformation using a Lambda transform is supported with the HTTP endpoint destination. However, data format conversion is not supported. The configuration for data transformation is similar to what was described earlier in this chapter.

Delivery failure

The delivery failure behavior for the HTTP endpoint is similar to the Splunk destination. When KDF sends data to an HTTP endpoint, it expects an acknowledgment and starts an acknowledgment timer. If it encounters an error or the acknowledgment doesn't come within the acknowledgment timeout period, it retries the request and starts a retry duration counter. It keeps retrying until it succeeds or the retry duration (this can be between 0 and 7,200 seconds) expires. If all retries fail, it sends the data to the specified S3 backup bucket, to a `http-endpoint-failed` folder. When configuring the backup S3 bucket, you can choose if you want to send all data to the S3 backup location or only the failed data. The S3 backup configuration is similar to other destinations.

Security

The KDF integration with an HTTP endpoint includes the option of providing an access key or an API key that KDF sends to the endpoint and that can be utilized by the endpoint for authentication. For example, the **Datadog** destination enables you to specify an API key. In addition, it needs access to the S3 bucket to write and read all or failed records, depending on how the delivery stream is configured, to CloudWatch Logs if error logging is enabled, to the Lambda function if the Lambda transform is enabled, and to the KMS key specified if encryption is enabled for S3. This access is provided via an IAM role that needs to be specified when creating the delivery stream. The IAM policy looks similar to the one for the S3 destination.

The following screenshot shows the HTTP endpoint configuration in the AWS Console:

HTTP endpoint configuration

HTTP endpoint name - *optional*

```
HTTP endpoint
```

HTTP endpoint URL

```
https://api.httpendpoint.com
```

Format: https://xyz.httpendpoint.com

Access key - *optional*
Contact the endpoint owner to obtain the access key required to enable data delivery to their service from Kinesis Data Firehose. **Learn more** ☐

```
Enter access key
```

☐ Show access key

Content encoding
Kinesis Data Firehose uses content encoding to compress the body of a request before sending it to the destination.

◉ Disabled

○ GZIP

Parameters - *optional*
Kinesis Data Firehose includes these key-value pairs in each HTTP call. **Learn more** ☐

No parameters to display.

Add parameter

You can add up to 50 parameters.

Retry duration
The time period during which Kinesis Data Firehose retries sending data to the selected HTTP endpoint. **Learn more** ☐

```
300
```
seconds

Enter a retry duration from 0 - 7200 seconds.

S3 backup

Specify the S3 bucket backup plan for the data the Kinesis Data Firehose delivers to the selected destination. You can back up all data or only the data that Kinesis Data Firehose could not deliver to the selected destination. **Learn more** ☐

S3 backup mode

◉ Failed data only

○ All data

S3 bucket

```
Choose a bucket                          ▼
```
↻   **Create new**

Backup S3 bucket error prefix - *optional*
All failed data is backed up in the specified S3 bucket error prefix.

```
Enter a prefix
```

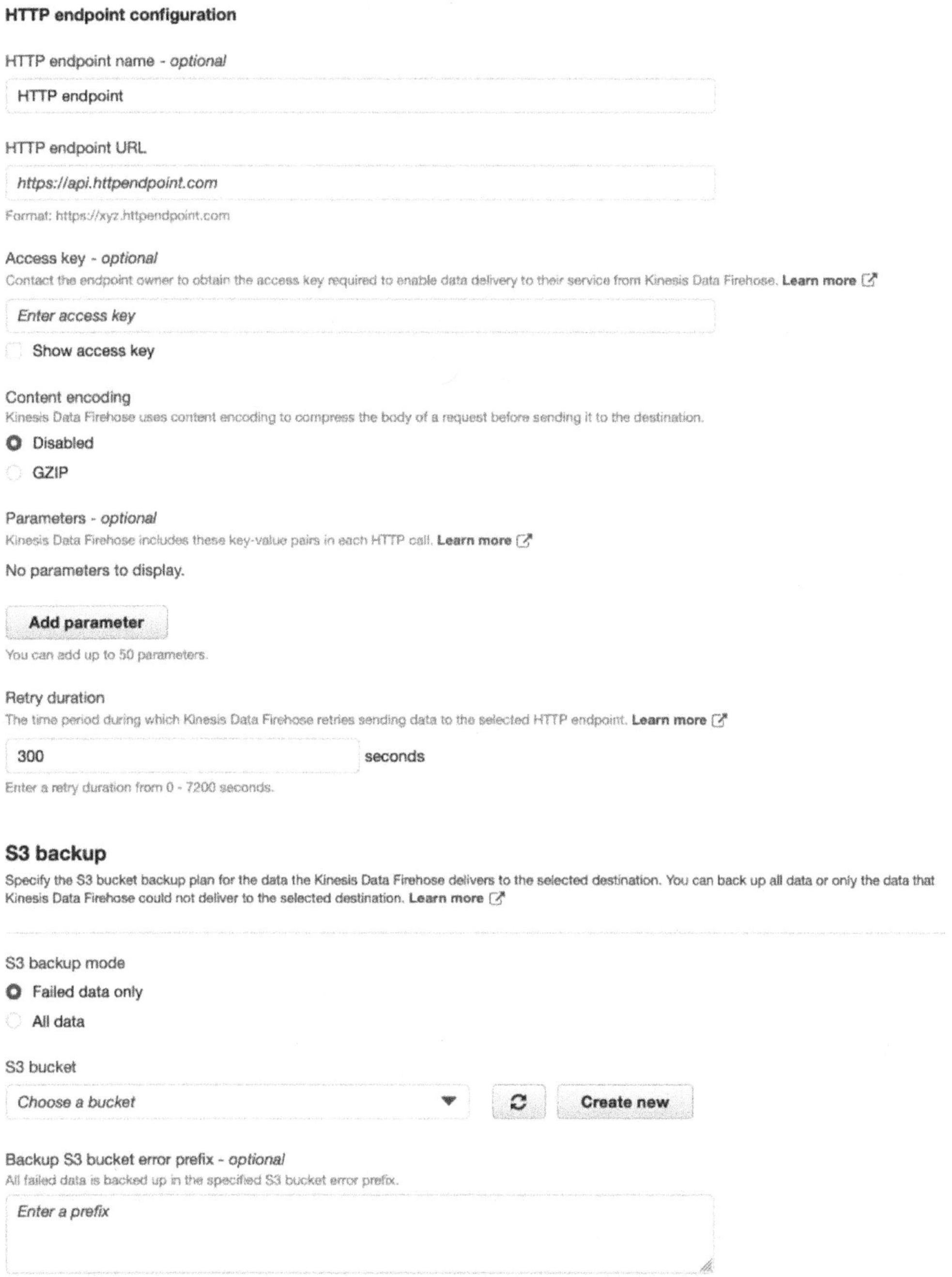

Figure 5.16 – Screenshot of the HTTP endpoint configuration in the AWS Console

It is important to note that KDF can only send data to a publicly accessible endpoint and not in an AWS VPC. For example, using a public API Gateway endpoint as a proxy or with Lambda integration can provide a serverless option to expose your own services or send data to other AWS services using KDF HTTP endpoints. The third-party provider destinations based on the HTTP endpoint have similar configurations.

That wraps up the destinations supported by KDF. Now, let's take a brief look at how data format conversion works in KDF.

Understanding data format conversion in KDF

KDF allows the conversion of incoming data from JSON to either **Apache Parquet** (**Parquet**) or **Apache ORC** (**ORC**) format. Parquet and ORC are popular **columnar formats** as opposed to JSON or **Comma Separated Values** (**CSV**), which are row formats. Columnar formats provide several advantages for storage and faster querying compared to row formats, especially in big-data use cases. In row formats, data for all columns in a row is stored together, which means that when querying a subset of columns, the data for all columns needs to be read and the unneeded columns filtered out. In columnar formats, data is stored by columns. This provides the ability to only retrieve data for the columns specified. This results in less data scanned for returning query results, and more sequential reads, resulting in better performance. In addition, since data in a column tends to be similar, columnar formats allow for better compression as well. This results in space saving in storage and also more data read in each **input/output** (**I/O**), resulting in better performance and cost savings in storage. The decision on whether to use Parquet or ORC is use-case specific, and specific to the tools being used to read and query the data. Certain tools perform better with Parquet, and others with ORC. A thorough discussion on the merits of each is beyond the scope of this book.

Data format conversion is not enabled by default in the configuration of the delivery stream and is only available for the S3 destination. If you enable it, S3 compression configuration for the delivery stream is disabled. By default, the Parquet objects being delivered to S3 are compressed using **Snappy compression** (`https://github.com/google/snappy`), which is an open source compression/decompression library from Google that targets faster compression and decompression and offers reasonable compression performance that can result in compressed files being 20% to 100% bigger than other compression libraries such as `zlib`. In addition, the `SizeInMBs` configuration in the buffering hints, specifying the amount of data to be buffered in KDF before delivering an object to S3, cannot be set to a value less than 64 MB. This is done to ensure that the size of Parquet objects delivered to S3 (after compression) is not too small, as that leads to higher cost and lower performance when AWS services such as Amazon Athena are used to query the records.

KDF only supports JSON as the format for incoming records for data format conversion. If the incoming records have any other format, then a Lambda transform can be used to first convert the data to JSON before the data format conversion. Lambda transforms are applied to the incoming records before data format conversion, which means that any filtering, transformation, or decorating of records needed can be combined with data format conversion.

There are three steps in data format conversion, listed as follows:

1. **Deserialization**—This is the conversion of bytes to an object in memory. In the context of KDF data format conversion, which uses Apache Hive compatible deserializers, this reads the JSON of the incoming data.

2. **Schema to interpret the data**—A schema is needed to provide information to KDF on how to interpret the incoming JSON record.

3. **Serialization to Parquet or ORC**—Conversion of the data to the specified columnar data format.

> SerDe
>
> **SerDe** stands for **Serializer-Deserializer**. A serializer converts objects in memory or, in the case of Apache Hive, a **row** into bytes to be stored in a file or sent over a network. A deserializer does the reverse—it converts bytes into objects in memory or, in the case of Apache Hive, a row.

Deserialization

KDF supports the following two types of deserializers:

- OpenX JSON SerDe
- Apache Hive JSON SerDe

OpenX JSON SerDe

This is the recommended SerDe deserializer to be used with data format conversion in KDF, with some caveats. It only handles date fields that are in Epoch seconds, Epoch milliseconds, Epoch floating-point seconds, the `yyyy-MM-dd'T'HH:mm:ss[.S]'Z'` format, where the fractional seconds can have up to nine digits, or the `yyyy-[M]M-[d]d HH:mm:ss[.S]` format, where the fractional seconds can have up to nine digits. If the timestamps are in any other format, then Apache Hive JSON SerDe should be used.

This SerDe also provides options to convert dots (`" . "`) in JSON keys to underscores, which can be important since Apache Hive does not allow dots in column names, and also to convert JSON keys to lowercase before deserialization, which can be important if you have a naming standard to only have lowercase column names. One other import option is to be able to map column names to JSON keys. This is a very useful feature to circumvent Apache Hive limitations. For example, if the incoming data has JSON keys that are Apache Hive-reserved keywords, they cannot be column names. So, if the schema definition for the table specifies a different column name, there has to be a mechanism to map the incoming JSON key to the column name.

These options are only available when the KDF delivery stream is created using the AWS CLI and not in the AWS Console.

For more information, see `https://github.com/rcongiu/Hive-JSON-Serde`.

> **Hyphens in the JSON key of a complex data type**
>
> If the incoming JSON record has a JSON key in a struct that has a hyphen, Apache Hive throws an error. Since KDF uses AWS Glue for schema information and AWS Glue is an Apache Hive-compatible metastore, KDF throws an error as well when it encounters a hyphen in the key of a nested struct during data format conversion. However, you can get past this error by modifying the schema in AWS Glue and either removing the hyphens or converting them to underscores, and then utilizing the column name to the JSON Keys mapping feature of the OpenX JSON SerDe.

Apache Hive JSON SerDe

This SerDe is a part of Apache Hive and supports timestamps in formats other than the ones listed for the OpenX JSON SerDe. It provides an option to specify the timestamp format in the pattern syntax of Joda-Time's `DateTimeFormat` format strings (`https://www.joda.org/joda-time/apidocs/org/joda/time/format/DateTimeFormat.html`). If no format is specified, then by default KDF uses `java.sql.Timestamp::valueOf`, which converts the `String` object (incoming string representing the timestamp) to a `java.sql.Timestamp` value.

For more information, see `https://cwiki.apache.org/confluence/display/Hive/LanguageManual+DDL#LanguageManualDDL-JSON`.

Schema

KDF needs to be provided the location of a schema in the AWS Glue Data Catalog. The schema can either be created manually using the AWS Glue console or using the CLI or SDK, or by first creating a delivery stream that delivers a small number of sample records to an S3 location in JSON format and then using AWS Glue crawlers to crawl the data, infer the schema, and create a table with the inferred schema in the AWS Glue Data Catalog in a specified database. You can then create a new delivery stream or update an existing delivery stream with data format conversion enabled, with the AWS Glue crawler-created schema. If the S3 location specified for the crawler (which is the same location where the sample records were delivered) is used as the destination for the delivery stream, you can easily use the AWS Glue Data Catalog table to query the data (delete the objects with the sample records first). The crawler can also be run on a schedule, and it can identify and add additional partitions to the AWS Glue Data Catalog table as more data and partitions are added over time.

Serializer

There are two supported serializers, Apache ORC and Apache Parquet.

Data format conversion errors

As mentioned earlier in the chapter under S3 prefixes, the KDF delivery stream configuration provides an option to specify an S3 error prefix where KDF delivers records that failed transformation or data format conversion. If KDF encounters a data format conversion error, such as being unable to read and parse a record or being unable to successfully deserialize a record, or encounters schema errors or Hive errors due to unsupported structures in the schema, it writes the records together with some metadata in S3 objects in the `S3 prefix` (folder) specified in the S3 error prefix configuration. If the S3 bucket or the prefix location is unavailable due to permission issues or networking issues, KDF continues to retry indefinitely and stops making any progress in delivering subsequent records. Since KDF stores incoming records for a period of 24 hours, if it blocks for more than 24 hours, there could be data loss. In order to prevent data loss and to get notified of the issue and take corrective measures well in time, it is imperative to monitor the KDF CloudWatch `SucceedConversion.Records`, `SucceedConversion.Bytes`, `FailedConversion.Records`, and `FailedConversion.Bytes` metrics and create an alarm on `FailedConversion.Records`.

Next, let's take a deeper look at monitoring KDF.

Understanding monitoring in KDF

KDF is tightly integrated with Amazon CloudWatch. We have seen how KDF sends error messages to CloudWatch Logs when enabled. In addition, KDF sends metrics to CloudWatch as well. These help with monitoring different aspects of KDF, depending on the feature enabled and destination configured. You can also set alarms on these metrics to either get notified when the alarms trigger or take some automated action using Lambda functions. Some metrics are common for all destinations and some are specific to each destination. I called out some metrics that are relevant to some destinations earlier. In addition, here are some metrics that KDF supports, to keep an eye on:

- `IncomingBytes`—The number of bytes ingested successfully into the delivery stream over the specified time period. Compare this with what you expect the producer to be sending to KDF for reconciliation.

- `IncomingRecords`—The number of records ingested successfully into the delivery stream over the specified time period. Compare this with what you expect the producer to be sending to KDF for reconciliation.

- `IncomingPutRequests`—The number of successful `PutRecord` and `PutRecordBatch` requests over the specified period of time.

- `KinesisMillisBehindLatest`—This is relevant when the ingestion is from a KDS stream as a source and indicates the number of milliseconds that the last read record is behind the newest record in the Kinesis data stream. This metric is important to monitor and put an alarm on, to see if KDF is falling behind in reading from the KDS stream. If it falls behind more than the retention period of the KDS stream (the default is 24 hours), there can be missing data in the KDF destination.

- `RecordsPerSecondLimit`—This indicates the current limit set for KDF for records per second, beyond which there could be throttling, and is relevant for ingestion via `Direct PUT` and is good to compare with the `IncomingRecords` metric to figure out when to request a limit increase for the KDF delivery stream.

- `BytesPerSecondLimit`—This indicates the current limit set for KDF for bytes per second, beyond which there could be throttling, and is relevant for ingestion via `Direct PUT` and is good to compare with the `IncomingBytes` metric to figure out when to request a limit increase for the KDF delivery stream.

- `PutRequestsPerSecondLimit`—This indicates the current limit set for KDF for `PUT` requests (`PutRecord` and `PutRecordBatch`) per second, beyond which there could be throttling, and is relevant for ingestion via `Direct PUT` and is good to compare with the `IncomingPutRequests` metric to figure out when to request a limit increase for the KDF delivery stream.

- `ThrottledRecords`—The number of records that were throttled because data ingestion exceeded one of the delivery stream limits. A steadily increasing number of throttled records indicates that you need to request a limit increase. It is recommended to create an alarm for this metric.

- `DeliveryTo<Destination>.Success`—This is available for all destinations and indicates the ratio of successful deliveries over unsuccessful deliveries. It needs to be monitored to identify failures.

- `DeliveryTo<Destination>.DataFreshness`—The age of the oldest record in KDF. Any record older than this age has been delivered to the destination. This indicates the latency in delivery to the destination. It is recommended to create an alarm for this metric and notify when it goes over the specified buffering limit in the destination configuration.

KDF is also integrated with **AWS CloudTrail**, which when enabled logs all the API calls made against the KDF APIs and can deliver those events to an S3 bucket. It logs all control-plane API calls and includes what request was made, who made it, and from where, it can be used to audit access and actions made against the KDF APIs.

Use-case example – Bikeshare station data pipeline with KDF

The use case is to take streaming data coming from bike stations spread across multiple New York locations, decorate it with address information stored in an Amazon DynamoDB table, buffer and aggregate the data, and land it in an S3 bucket that forms a data lake for historical analysis and insights utilizing big-data query tools such as Apache Hive and Amazon Athena, which is a serverless Apache Presto service.

The architecture for delivering data to S3 in Parquet format using KDF for analysis with big-data tools is depicted in the following diagram:

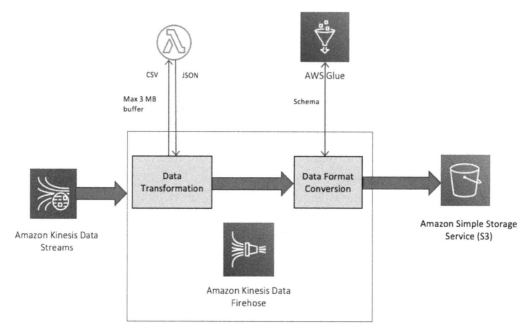

Figure 5.17 – Architecture for delivering data to S3 in Parquet format

This architecture is a part of the architecture described in *Chapter 4, Kinesis Data Streams*, under the *Data Pipelines with Amazon Kinesis Data Streams* section, and is a blow-up of the Amazon KDF part of the architecture.

The code and configuration files referenced here are available in the code examples available on GitHub at `https://github.com/PacktPublishing/Streaming-Data-Solutions-with-Amazon-Kinesis`. You will need a Git client to access them (`https://git-scm.com/`). It is important for you to replace the AWS account ID and the region with your own before you use those.

The KDF delivery stream is configured to ingest data using a KDS stream as a source. It uses a Lambda transform to add address information to the incoming records, and then uses KDF data format conversion to convert the incoming records to Parquet using a schema defined in the AWS Glue Data Catalog. It buffers records for 15 minutes or 128 MB (whichever comes earlier), and then delivers the S3 objects to the specified S3 bucket using a custom prefix in a Hive-style partitioning format.

Steps to recreate the example

Let's look at the steps to recreate the example, as follows:

1. The first step is to create an Amazon DynamoDB table to hold the SmartCity bike-station addresses. The following AWS CLI command accomplishes that:

```
aws dynamodb create-table \
    --table-name BikeStationAddress \
    --attribute-definitions \
        AttributeName=StationId,AttributeType=N \
    --key-schema \
        AttributeName=StationId,KeyType=HASH \
  --provisioned-throughput \
        ReadCapacityUnits=10,WriteCapacityUnits=10
```

2. The address data is in a file called station_addresses.csv in CSV format and looks like this:

```
100,7033 Summerhouse Ave. Staten Island NY 10306
110,68 Oak Ave. Staten Island NY 10312
```

3. This data needs to be loaded into the Amazon DynamoDB table. To do that, you can run the following command:

```
python3 loadDynamoDBStationAddresses.py
```

4. The next step is to create an Amazon KDS stream that will receive the streaming bike-station data, as follows:

```
aws kinesis create-stream --stream-name
KDSSmartCityBikesStream --shard-count 1
```

5. Next, we need to create a number of resources that will be used with the KDF delivery stream. First, we create a `role` and `policy` for the Lambda transform that will look up the address information and decorate the data coming from the KDS stream, as follows:

```
aws iam create-role --role-name KDFSmartCityLambdaRole
--assume-role-policy-document file://
TrustPolicyForLambda.json
```

```
aws iam create-policy --policy-name
KDFSmartCityLambdaPolicy --policy-document file://
KDFSmartCityLambdaPolicy.json
```

```
aws iam attach-role-policy --role-name
KDFSmartCityLambdaRole --policy-arn arn:aws:iam::<your-
aws-account-id>:policy/KDFSmartCityLambdaPolicy
```

6. Next, zip up and create the Lambda function, like this:

```
zip -r Lambda_function.zip KDFLookupAddressTransform.py
```

```
aws Lambda create-function --zip-file "fileb://
Lambda_function.zip" --cli-input-json file://
CreateLambdaKDFLookupAddressTransform.json
```

7. Now, it is time to create the S3 bucket that will hold the data deposited by KDF. The bucket name needs to be unique across all AWS accounts across the board. You can add a prefix to the bucket name to make it unique. Make sure you update the bucket name in other JSON configuration files as well. The code is illustrated in the following snippet:

```
aws s3 mb s3://<prefix>-kdf-smartcitybikes-data --region
<your-aws-region>
```

8. You also need to create the AWS Glue database and table that KDF can use to convert the incoming JSON data to Parquet, as follows:

```
aws glue create-database --database-input
"{\"Name\":\"smartcitybikes\"}"
```

```
aws glue create-table --database-name smartcitybikes
--table-input file://SmartCityGlueTable.json
```

9. At this point, we need to create the IAM `role` and `policy` for KDF to call the Lambda transform, access the Glue schema, and land the data in S3. This can be achieved by running the following code:

```
aws iam create-role --role-name KDFSmartCityDeliveryRole
--path /service-role/ --assume-role-policy-document
file://TrustPolicyForFirehose.json
```

```
aws iam create-policy --policy-name
KDFSmartCityDeliveryStreamPolicy --policy-document
file://KDFSmartCityDeliveryStreamPolicy.json
```

```
aws iam attach-role-policy --role-name
KDFSmartCityDeliveryRole --policy-arn arn:aws:iam::<your-
aws-account-id>:policy/KDFSmartCityDeliveryStreamPolicy
```

10. Finally, we're ready to create the KDF delivery stream, as follows:

```
aws firehose create-delivery-stream --cli-input-json
file://KDFCreateDeliveryStreamSmartCityBikes.json
```

Now, all that is left to do is send data to the KDS stream and observe the data in Parquet format, with the station address information landing in S3. Then, we can perform queries using Amazon Athena. To do this, we will use a Java producer included in the GitHub repository, which you can find at `https://github.com/PacktPublishing/Streaming-Data-Solutions-with-Amazon-Kinesis`. Clone the repository and go to the `chapter6/producer-app/ride-producer` directory, then build the application using Gradle. The build process can take a few minutes. Here is the code for this:

```
cd chapter6/producer-app/ride-producer
./gradlew build
```

The `producer` application uses the value of a `KINESIS_STREAM` environment variable to determine which Kinesis stream to send records to. Make sure to set the `KINESIS_STREAM` environment variable to `KDSSmartCityBikesStream`, as illustrated in the following code snippet:

```
export KINESIS_STREAM=KDSSmartCityBikesStream
```

Now, we're ready to start the producer application, as follows:

```
./gradlew run
```

The producer application will send data in the following format:

```
{
  "stationId":420,
  "action":"DOCKED",
  "tripDuration":145,
  "price":19.14,
  "eventUTCTime":"2020-12-25T13:19:31.000589",
  "bikeDetail":
  {
    "bikeNum":"a33492a7-d59f-4484-bb37-7431252d8099",
    "bikeType":"ADVANCED"
  }
}
```

There are few things to note about the `producer` application's event to KDS. If the action is `"RENTED"`, this indicates that someone has just taken a bike for a ride, and conversely, `"DOCKED"` indicates the bicycle being returned to the station. When the action is `"RENTED"`, the `tripDuration` and `price` fields will be empty.

After the Lambda transform runs, it will add the address information and transform it to the following:

```
{
  "stationId":420,
  --
  --
  "bikeDetail":
  {
    "bikeNum":"a33492a7-d59f-4484-bb37-7431252d8099",
    "bikeType":"ADVANCED"
  }
  "stationAddress": "101 Ridgewood Road New York NY 10020"
}
```

It might take a while for the data to show up in the S3 bucket you created since the buffering hints for the KDF delivery stream are set to 15 minutes or 128 MB. You can go to the S3 bucket and see the data that has landed.

Once landed, some sample analysis you can do on the data could include the following:

- The average price of all bike rentals, as illustrated in the following code snippet:

```
SELECT avg(price) FROM
"smartcitybikes"."bikestationsdata";
```

- The average duration bikes are docked per hour, to identify the peak hours and the non-peak hours so that prices can be assigned appropriately, as illustrated in the following code snippet:

```
SELECT hour, avg(tripduration) FROM
"smartcitybikes"."bikestationsdata" where action =
'DOCKED' group by hour order by hour;
```

- You can also identify the duration bikes are docked per hour per location, to identify inactive locations. Then, you can target promotions or relocate the stations.

Summary

In this chapter, we reviewed the features of Amazon KDF and how it can be used in data pipelines in common multi-account enterprise architectures. We saw how to do encryption, networking, authentication, and authorization with multiple Amazon and third-party services and software. We saw how Amazon KDF can be an integral part of any data analytics pipeline or data-lake architecture with its ability to easily ingest data from other AWS services including AWS IoT, Amazon CloudWatch Logs, Amazon CloudWatch Events, and KDS, do inline transformations using Lambda functions, and deliver to Amazon S3, Amazon Redshift, Amazon Elasticsearch, HTTP endpoints, and other third-party destinations. We also looked at the SmartCity bikes example and saw how to deliver records to Amazon S3 in a columnar Parquet format. It should now be clear how you can configure Amazon KDF for your use cases.

In the next chapter, we will look at other services under the Kinesis umbrella of services.

Further reading

You can use the following links for further reference:

- Amazon KDF Developer Guide:

  https://docs.aws.amazon.com/kinesisvideostreams/latest/dg/
  what-is-kinesis-video.html

- Amazon KDF API reference:

  https://docs.aws.amazon.com/kinesisvideostreams/latest/dg/
  API_Reference.html

- Analyze logs with Datadog using Amazon KDF HTTP endpoint delivery:

  https://aws.amazon.com/blogs/big-data/analyze-logs-with-
  datadog-using-amazon-kinesis-data-firehose-http-endpoint-
  delivery/

- Ingest streaming data into Amazon Elasticsearch Service within the privacy of your
  VPC with Amazon KDF:

  https://aws.amazon.com/blogs/big-data/ingest-streaming-
  data-into-amazon-elasticsearch-service-within-the-privacy-
  of-your-vpc-with-amazon-kinesis-data-firehose/

- Amazon KDF custom prefixes for Amazon S3 objects:

  https://aws.amazon.com/blogs/big-data/amazon-kinesis-data-
  firehose-custom-prefixes-for-amazon-s3-objects/

6
Kinesis Data Analytics

Amazon **Kinesis Data Analytics** (**KDA**) is a service we use to analyze streaming data, gain actionable insights, and create customer insights in near real time. KDA provides two types of analytics engines, SQL and Apache Flink. KDA is a fully managed serverless service that reduces the complexity of building, managing, and operating analytical streaming applications. In other words, we don't have to stand up, patch, or maintain any servers. Amazon Web Services also handles the scaling of underlying compute resources based on our KDA application needs.

Data has become the blood of every company, regardless of the industry. Lately, hot data usually has much more value than data at rest; *cold data*. Keeping competitive nowadays means being able to process large amounts of hot data in seconds. For example, if an online retailer has a promotion for some of its items, it's more valuable to know what's in shoppers' carts while they are actively shopping than 10 or 15 days after purchasing. While we are shopping, those online retailers can suggest items based on what is already in our shopping cart and increase their sales. Cold data isn't useless, however, as we can derive value from it when we, the shoppers, return next time.

Streaming applications commonly carry the latest data, and in this chapter, you will learn how to use KDA to derive insights from streaming data. Using KDA, we will analyze, summarize, filter, aggregate, and enhance streaming data using reference data. While building the KDA stream processing application in this chapter, we will define input sources, reference data, in-application tables (streams), windows for aggregation and transformation code, and then send KDA output to be consumed by visualization tools.

In this chapter, we're going to cover the following main topics:

- Discovering Amazon Kinesis Data Analytics
- Working on SmartCity bike share analytics use cases
- Creating operational insights using SQL Engine
- Creating operational insights using Apache Flink
- Building bike ride analytic applications
- Monitoring KDA applications

Technical requirements

There are a few things that you will need to set up and configure before we start exploring KDA. If you have already set these up in previous chapters, please skip ahead to the next section.

AWS account setup

You will need to get an AWS account to run the examples included in this chapter. If you do not have an account already, you can go to https://aws.amazon.com/ getting-started/ to create an account. AWS accounts offer a **Free Tier** (https://aws.amazon.com/free). The AWS **Free Tier** allows you to use many AWS services for free within specified usage limits. Some of the service examples in this chapter are outside the AWS **Free Tier** and incur some service usage charges.

AWS CDK

You will need an AWS **Cloud Deployment Kit** (**CDK**) to create cloud application resources required for the setup of the exercises we will perform in this chapter. You can install a CDK by executing the following on your command prompt:

```
npm install -g aws-cdk
```

For a detailed walkthrough, refer to the following link: https://docs.aws.amazon. com/cdk/latest/guide/getting_started.html.

Java and Java IDE

You will need the **Java Development Kit** (**JDK**) version 11 (`https://www.oracle.com/java/technologies/javase-jdk11-downloads.html`). We recommend using a development environment (IntelliJ Idea is what we used) to develop and compile the Apache Flink application.

You will need Apache Maven (`https://maven.apache.org/plugins/maven-compiler-plugin/`) to compile the Apache Flink application, and it must be in your working path. KDA for Apache Flink only supports Java applications that are built with Apache Maven.

Code examples

Code examples in this book are available on GitHub at `https://github.com/PacktPublishing/Streaming-Data-Solutions-with-Amazon-Kinesis`. You will need a Git client to access them (`https://git-scm.com/`).

Discovering Amazon KDA

Why do we need analytics, and what can we do with KDA? KDA allows us to understand and analyze the data flowing through our data streams. Before we dive into KDA, we recommend you take a look at how Zynga is utilizing KDA. Please watch this video (it starts around 20 minutes in): `https://www.youtube.com/watch?v=PvxlF3A-Res`. You will learn how Zynga uses KDA to extract various metrics to run their business efficiently and offer an excellent customer experience that we want to replicate for our SmartCity's bicycle fleet.

> *"Zynga is a leading developer of the world's most popular social games that are played by millions of people around the world each day."*
>
> *– Zynga.*

Given that KDA is a managed service, AWS provides a monthly uptime percentage of at least 99.9%. For us, this means we have the platform we can start working with right away. More importantly, if we determine that we no longer require KDA, we simply remove the application, and charges stop. AWS uses what they call a **Kinesis Processing Unit** (**KPU**) to measure our application's resource utilization. KPU is equivalent to 1 vCPU and 4 GB of memory. You can find further details here: `https://aws.amazon.com/kinesis/data-analytics/pricing/`.

Based on the memory and compute needs of our application, KDA will scale up or down. KDA imposes a soft limit of a maximum of 8 KPUs for SQL applications, which we can increase by contacting AWS or submitting a limit increase through the AWS Console. We can see how many KPUs our application is consuming using CloudWatch. We will go into details later in this chapter as we build our KDA application.

Once you complete this chapter, you will create your KDA applications and derive insights and value from your real-time data.

Working on SmartCity bike share analytics use cases

In this chapter, we will be using KDA to analyze SmartCity's bicycle fleet's telemetry to improve customer experience. Using a producer application, we will simulate 40 bicycle stations, and each bicycle rental or return to the station will generate an event. The producer application will then put events into our Kinesis data stream. Our KDA application will process data by aggregating multiple events over time so that we can get the following analytics:

- We will use KDA to determine whether a station that is running low on available bikes can move bicycles from other stations where there is an abundance of them.

- Management wants to know how much revenue we are generating from bicycle rentals every 30 minutes. It's not sustainable that we produce those reports manually, so we will use KDA to determine revenue generated every 30 minutes.

> **Producer application**
>
> You will not create a producer application as we have already created a producer application that you will use. We will focus on creating a KDA analytics application.

Chapter 3, Introduction to SmartCity Bike-Sharing Service, mentioned that there are two primary engines in KDA: SQL-based and Apache Flink-based. We will design an analytics solution for SmartCity using both of these engines. We will simulate real-time data produced by the users interacting with a fleet of bicycles, and then we will create actionable insights using KDA. The architecture of the solution that we will build is shown in *Figure 6.1*:

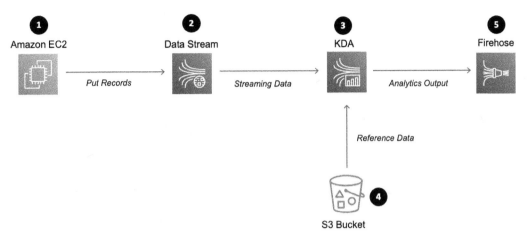

Figure 6.1 – SwipeBike streaming analytics architecture

Let's step through the SwipeBike streaming analytics pipeline:

1. The producer application will simulate bicycle rentals and returns to the bike stations.

2. We will run a producer application on an EC2 instance. The producer application will send rental events' data to a Kinesis data stream.

3. The data stream will send the data to a KDA application for processing.

4. The KDA application will perform analytics using streaming and reference data that we are storing in the S3 bucket.

5. The output of the KDA application will be sent to Firehose to be used by downstream consumers.

An example of an event created by the producer application sent to KDS is shown as follows:

```
{
    "stationId":420,
    "action":"DOCKED",
    "tripDuration":145,
    "price":19.14,
    "eventUTCTime":"2020-12-25T13:19:31.000589",
    "bikeDetail":
    {
        "bikeNum":"a33492a7-d59f-4484-bb37-7431252d8099",
```

```
        "bikeType":"ADVANCED"
    }
}
```

There are a few things to note regarding the producer's event in the Kinesis data stream. If the action is `"RENTED"`, this indicates that someone has just taken a bike for a ride, and conversely, `"DOCKED"` indicates that the bicycle has been returned to the station. When the action is `"RENTED"`, the `tripDuration` and `price` fields will be empty.

Creating operational insights using SQL Engine

Streaming SQL builds on the concepts of **Structured Query Language** (**SQL**) commonly used in various relational databases. Building on top of SQL means that SQL streaming generally has a lower learning curve for those familiar with databases. While there is no standard streaming SQL syntax, KDA uses the ANSI 2008 SQL standard with extensions that allow us to create real-time stream processing solutions. The key difference compared with the SQL database is that streaming SQL operates on a continuous data flow (stream). The following are the crucial advantages of streaming SQL:

- It's easy to learn for those who have worked with a SQL database.
- Its behavior is well understood as it uses the concepts of tables, joins, and aggregate functions.
- There is a rich ecosystem of SQL tools and code generators.

If you are thinking, "this is great, I'm going to replace my database," that's not the case. Databases are intended to process and store immense amounts of data. KDA SQL streaming can process vast volumes of data, but it does it in small chunks of data. Use cases for KDA revolve around obtaining insights or analytics on the latest data, be it data in the last few minutes or few hours.

> **SQL and streaming SQL**
> If you are familiar with databases and database SQL, you can think of streaming SQL as analogous to using database triggers to process the data. Streaming SQL adds **WINDOW** concepts to operate on a collection of events (rows), whereas database triggers work on a single row (event).

Core concepts and capabilities

We are first going to cover some of the core concepts of KDA SQL. To start with the KDA SQL application, we first define the input or source, either Kinesis Data Streams or Kinesis Data Firehose. The following diagram shows the general architecture and flow for KDA SQL's engine architecture:

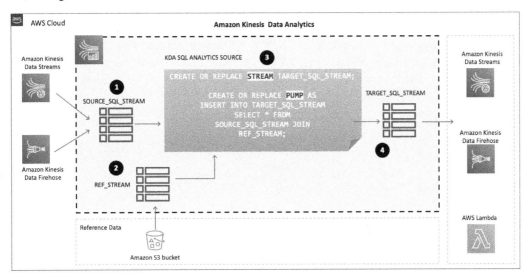

Figure 6.2 – KDA for SQL architecture

There are two possible sources for the KDA SQL engine: a Kinesis data stream or a Firehose delivery stream. Once either of these two are plugged into KDA for SQL, we process the data received as follows:

1. We map the KDA application source to an in-application stream (**SOURCE_SQL_STREAM**), which behaves like a table.

2. We can also add any reference data that we need. Adding reference data is optional.

3. In-application STREAM and PUMP is the code that we write to do the actual processing of the data. In-application STREAM is like a database table, and it holds data. PUMP is analogous to a database's SELECT * FROM ... INSERT INTO statement. PUMP operates on in-application STREAM (tables) and joins it with reference data or other in-application stream data to perform our desired business logic.

4. The outcome of PUMP is then inserted into another in-application stream, TARGET_SQL_STREAM.

We can then use TARGET_SQL_STREAM for additional analysis or send it downstream to continue processing.

Defining inputs

The KDA application takes a single input, a Kinesis data stream, or a Kinesis Firehose delivery stream. You can think of your KDA application as one of the Kinesis data stream consumers. That, in turn, means that KDA doesn't alter the data in the Kinesis data stream, and we can have another consumer reading the data from that same Kinesis data stream. When multiple KDA applications are reading from the same Kinesis data stream, please know that Kinesis data stream quotas and throughput are still applicable. For example, let's assume that we have five KDA applications reading from a single-shard Kinesis stream. Since a Kinesis shard can support up to five read transactions, assuming we even have read distribution across five KDA applications, this means that each application gets a single read per second:

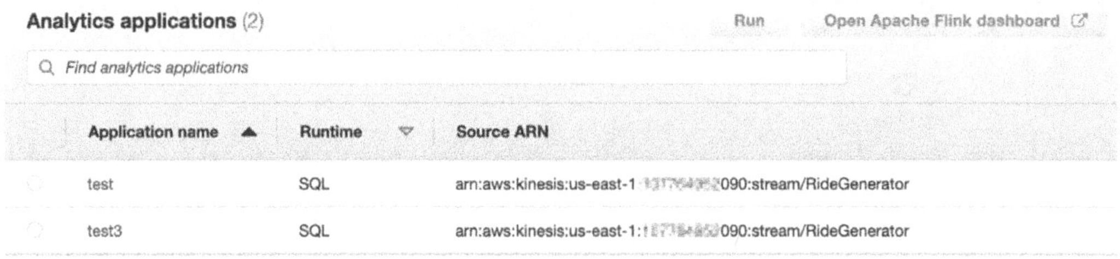

Analytics applications (2)		Run Open Apache Flink dashboard

Application name ▲	Runtime ▽	Source ARN
test	SQL	arn:aws:kinesis:us-east-1 · ·090:stream/RideGenerator
test3	SQL	arn:aws:kinesis:us-east-1:· ·090:stream/RideGenerator

Figure 6.3 – Example of the single stream used by two KDA applications

Another input to our KDA application can be *Reference Data*. If you are familiar with SQL and databases, you can think of reference data as lookup tables. An example of reference would be a table containing postal codes and their association with cities and states. Let's assume that the Kinesis data stream only has `customer-id` and `postal-code`. We can use reference data to join it with `postal-code` and output city and state for that `customer-id`.

> **Note**
>
> We must store KDA reference data in the Amazon S3 bucket as CVS or JSON files. The maximum file size is 1 GB.

Defining a SQL schema

Just like in the case of standard SQL, the KDA SQL application relies on a static schema. Input mapping is very much analogous to the database table schema definition. **Input mapping** informs our KDA application of the structure and data types of the streaming data. KDA can perform auto-discovery of the streaming data schema by reading sample data from the stream and then attempting to detect the data's format. If KDA can determine the structure, it will suggest a schema along with columns and data types. We can change the schema in case KDA has not detected the correct data type or column. Since schema discovery is only sampling data, there is a possibility that the schema will not match all the records in our stream. When KDA detects records that don't match the schema, it will send those records to an in-application error stream.

In the same way as relational databases have the maximum number of columns per table, there are limits associated with KDA SQL. The maximum size of the row (event) is 512 KB, which also includes KDA metadata. Typically, KDA metadata is under 1 KB.

Suppose you have use cases where your input data stream has new fields added after you defined the KDA schema or newly formatted messages added by the producer. In that case, KDA will not auto-discover the schema change, and KDA will not read new fields/messages. If our producers are adding new fields or message formats, that likely means there is a code change. We will need to coordinate the changes of producers and changes to the KDA SQL application. You can then infer the schema using the `DiscoverInputSchema` API.

> **Note**
>
> In order for KDA to process our streaming data, it must use either CSV or JSON format. In our examples in this chapter, we are using JSON formatted data.

Besides using Kinesis Schema Discovery or the `DiscoverInputSchema` API, we can also use the KDA API to specify the streaming data's schema. While creating a KDA application using API, we can use the `CreateApplication` API and then set the following three properties:

- `InputSchema`, which is a collection of `RecordColumns`
- `RecordEncoding`
- `RecordFormatType` as CSV or JSON

Here is an abbreviated example of how we could define the schema for our bike-rental JSON message. When we define mappings for JSON documents, we use `JSONPath`, which is a standardized way to query JSON document elements. In the following example, we use `$.stationId` JSONPath markup to map data to our schema:

```
"InputSchema": {
   "RecordColumns": [
      {
            "SqlType": "INTEGER"
            "Name": "stationId",
            "Mapping": "$.stationId"
      }
   ],
   "RecordFormat" :{
         "RecordFormatType": "JSON"
   },
   "RecordEncoding": "UTF-8"
}
```

Earlier in this chapter, we had example of an event created by the producer application. Here is a snippet:

```
"bikeDetail":
  {
     "bikeNum":"a33492a7-d59f-4484-bb37-7431252d8099",
     "bikeType":"ADVANCED"
  }
```

To get to `bikeNum`, which is nested under `bikeDetail`, we would use the JSONPath markup `$.bikeDetail.bikeNum`.

KDA SQL key constructs

Once we create a KDA SQL streaming application, and define the input and schema, KDA will create two in-application streams. In-application streams are not like Kinesis data streams or Firehose delivery streams; you can think of in-application streams as tables that exist and hold data for our KDA SQL application. When we stop, our KDA in-application stream is no longer available, but the input Kinesis data stream or Firehose delivery stream is unaffected. In-application stream `source_sql_stream_001` contains data received from the input Kinesis data stream. If our input data stream has multiple shards, in-application stream `source_sql_stream_001` will include data from all shards.

KDA SQL will try to scale our in-application streams so that it matches the amount of data being sent to it by input streams, such as the data stream of Firehose. There will be instances where we will want to set the in-application streams explicitly. We can do that by using the `InputParallelism` parameter. Assuming that the input source is a Kinesis data stream with 20 shards and we set `InputParallelism` to 4, KDA for SQL will have 4 in-application streams, each receiving data from 5 shards.

The second stream that KDA creates is `error_stream`, which will hold any records that KDA reads from the input data stream but couldn't convert using a schema that we have defined. Errors usually occur when we have different record types in our input stream. If we encounter this situation, one of the workarounds is to define our schema as a single `VARCHAR` field, read the whole record into it, and then perform parsing of that record in our code. Another alternative is to use AWS Lambda for pre-processing and standardizing the records in the same format.

We can also create our in-application streams for intermediary processing, and we will do that when we build our KDA SQL application for SmartCity. We use `CREATE OR REPLACE STREAM` syntax to create an in-application stream, and then we define the column names, data types, and precision:

```
CREATE OR REPLACE STREAM completed_bike_rides (
        stationId            INTEGER,
        tripDuration         BIGINT,
        price                REAL
    );
```

Once the in-application stream is defined, we can insert data into that stream using the `PUMP` operation. `PUMP` selects data from one or more in-application streams and then inserts it into the in-application stream:

```
CREATE OR REPLACE PUMP completed_rides_pump AS
    INSERT INTO completed_bike_rides
        SELECT STREAM
            "stationId",
            "tripDuration",
            "price"
        FROM source_sql_stream_001
        WHERE "action" LIKE 'DOCKED'
            AND ("tripDuration" > 0 AND "price" > 0) ;
```

Query for `completed_rides_pump` executes continuously over the in-application stream, `source_sql_stream_001`. The query filters events, indicating that the bicycle is `DOCKED`, trip duration, and price are greater than zero. The pump will insert results into the `completed_rides_pump` in-application stream.

Reference data

Besides using streaming data, we can also define reference data that our KDA application can then utilize. Reference data allows us to enrich or further filter the data by joining data from the data stream with reference data. To use reference data in the KDA application, we must store it in S3 in JSON or CSV format. The maximum size of the S3 file that contains reference data cannot be larger than 1 GB.

Modifying input using AWS Lambda

Often in data processing pipelines, we need to transform the raw data received. When we use KDA, this is pretty easy to achieve by creating an inline AWS Lambda function that will either convert or transform it. When we use AWS Lambda for pre-processing, we need to make sure that we conform to the record response model, shown as follows:

```
{
    "records": [
        {
            "recordId": "3636363625767804737012376 08934523",
            "result": "Ok",
            "data": "ewoic3RhdGlvbklkIjoOMjAsCiJhY3Rpb24iO=="
        }
    ]
}
```

If the Lambda put back into the data stream doesn't match the record response model, we will get an error. You can find detailed requirements pertaining to the Kinesis record response model here: `https://docs.aws.amazon.com/kinesisanalytics/latest/dev/lambda-preprocessing.html`.

> **AWS Lambda**
>
> If you are not familiar with AWS Lambda, think of it as code that you write to perform a specific function, while AWS provides all the underlying infrastructure. Our only job is to write code.

Let's now take a look at a brief example of how Lambda can be useful in transformation. The following diagram shows a simple transformation:

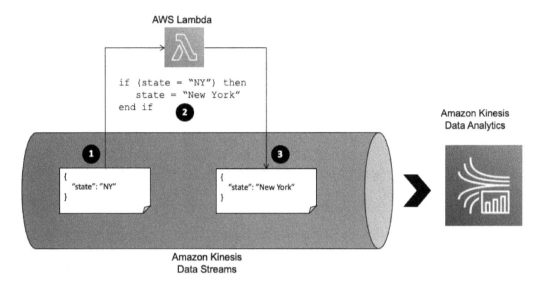

Figure 6.4 – Inline transformation using AWS Lambda

In the preceding example, we put a record into Kinesis and we send a state value as code, "NY" (**1**). In order to make the output readable to our users, we use Lambda to map that state code to the actual state name, "New York" (**2**). Once mapping is complete, we put the record back into the data stream (**3**).

Streaming SQL code

When it comes to SQL code that we write to perform streaming data processing, a few key concepts are essential. The maximum size of the SQL code for our application is 100 KB. By default, KDA will create SOURCE_SQL_STREAM_XXX, which represents the data flowing through the stream. If you are familiar with SQL and databases, think of SOURCE_SQL_STREAM as a database table populated by ongoing data inserts. We then simply write our SQL to process data from the source stream table.

> **KDA SQL reference**
>
> For further information regarding KDA SQL, you can visit the following link:
>
> https://docs.aws.amazon.com/kinesisanalytics/
> latest/sqlref/analytics-sql-reference.html.

Windows

For SmartCity use cases, we need to look at the events that happened over a certain period. The following are the events and time periods we are going to use in this example:

- Average ride duration over the last 15 minutes

- Average amount earned by rentals over the previous 10 minutes

- Count of bicycles that have been rented or returned to the station in the last 5 minutes

How do we do that, given that this is streaming data and events *come* and *go*? We will be using windows. Windows in streaming applications act like a memory cache that accumulates events over a specified period. A windows streaming application will gather individual events in this memory cache, and then we can apply various analytical functions over that collection of the events.

If our data has event time, then we can use that timestamp when performing time-based windowing operations. In the absence of the event timestamp, we have the following two options:

- Use KDA's ROWTIME timestamp

- Use the Kinesis APPROXIMATE_ARRIVAL_TIME

KDA's ROWTIME value will be the time when KDA inserted the row into our in-application stream. The Kinesis APPROXIMATE_ARRIVAL_TIME data stream is the approximate time when a record is inserted into the data stream.

Exploring the types of windows – staggering, sliding, and tumbling

Our producer application will randomly generate and insert data into the Kinesis data stream for all 40 bicycle stations. We will have records from all stations intermingled and out of order. In order for us to perform analysis or aggregation over the specific time horizon, we use windows. KDA SQL supports three types of windows, which we are going to discuss next:

- **Sliding windows**: Sliding windows keep moving with new records detected in the data stream. Sliding windows are the right choice for calculating moving averages. A fixed time INTERVAL defines the duration of the window. Depending on the velocity of records and the interval defined, sliding windows can overlap, and records can be considered for aggregation across multiple windows; there is a 1-to-n relationship between the record and window.

For example, if the interval is 5 minutes and a new record arrived at 14:20, records considered in a sliding window would be from 14:15 to 14:20. Assuming that another record arrives at 14:21, the second sliding window would be from 14:16 to 14:21, and records from 14:16 to 14:20 would be considered in both windows' aggregations as seen in the following figure:

```
SELECT STREAM STATION_ID,
    CAST( MIN(PRICE) OVER WIN AS DECIMAL(4,2)) AS min_price,
    CAST( MAX(PRICE) OVER WIN AS DECIMAL(4,2)) AS max_price,
    CAST( AVG(PRICE) OVER WIN AS DECIMAL(4,2)) AS avg_price,
    CAST( SUM(PRICE) OVER WIN AS DECIMAL(4,2)) AS earnings
FROM COMPLETED_BIKE_RIDES
WINDOW WIN AS (
    PARTITION BY STATION_ID
    RANGE INTERVAL '5' MINUTE PRECEDING);
```

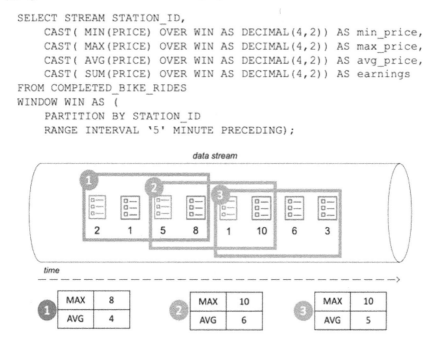

Figure 6.5 – Sliding window

- **Tumbling windows**: When we want to process streaming records over a set period in a contiguous manner, we use tumbling windows. The tumbling window will start aggregating records, and when the specified interval is over, a new tumbling window begins at that time. The tumbling window ensures that no record will be considered across two windows. There is a 1-to-1 relationship between the record and the window:

```
CREATE OR REPLACE PUMP RENTAL_COUNT_PUMP AS
  ..
FROM "SOURCE_SQL_STREAM_001"
GROUP BY "stationId",
  STEP("SOURCE_SQL_STREAM_001".ROWTIME BY INTERVAL '5' MINUTE);
```

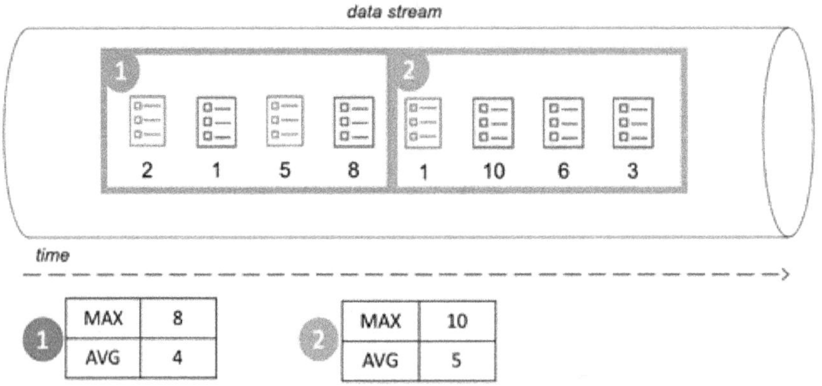

Figure 6.6 – Tumbling window

- **Staggering windows**: These are useful for aggregating records that come at varying times. The staggering window starts once KDA detects a record that matches the key defined in PARTITION BY (not to be confused with a Kinesis data stream partition). A fixed time interval establishes the duration of the window. If we wanted to count rentals at the bicycle station for 1 minute from the time the first bicycle is rented out, the tumbling window wouldn't work because the events might fall into separate windows. We could combine multiple tumbling windows to group the related events or use a staggering window. The staggering window is initiated as our KDA application receives the first event (with a RIDE_TIME of 14:06:05) for station 120 (with a ROWTIME of 14:06:30). The staggering window will expire after 1 minute, at ROWTIME 14:07:30. KDA will output results captured during the staggering window (based on ROWTIME and RIDE_TIME):

```
STATIONID,
FLOOR (RENTAL_TS TO MINUTE),
COUNT (STATIONID)
FROM ..
WINDOWED BY STAGGER (
    PARTITION BY FLOOR(RENTAL_TS TO MINUTE),
    STATIONID RANGE INTERVAL '1' MINUTE
)
```

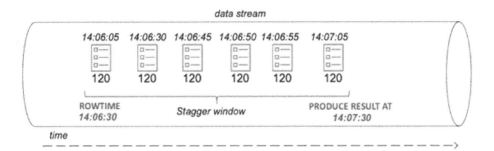

Figure 6.7 – Staggering window

Looking at the preceding diagram, our staggering window would pump the results as shown in the following table:

ROWTIME	RIDE_TIME	STATIONID	COUNT
14:06:30	14:06:00	120	5
14:07:29	14:07:00	120	1

Figure 6.8 – Results of the staggering window

In this section, we have learned about SQL Engine core concepts, such as ingesting data into in-application streams. In order to analyze data, we used three different types of windows, along with aggregation functions to achieve the desired output results. We then used data pumps to send the output from our analytics for further processing or reporting. In the following section, we are going to learn how do the same with KDA Flink engine.

Creating operational insights using Apache Flink

Amazon Kinesis Data Analytics for Apache Flink allows us to go beyond SQL and use Java or Scala as programming languages and a data stream API to build our analytics applications. In this section, we are going to focus on KDA for Flink.

> **Note**
>
> If you are not familiar with Apache Flink, we recommend you first go through the Flink overview: `https://ci.apache.org/projects/flink/flink-docs-release-1.11/learn-flink/`.

Apache Flink deserves a book in itself, and we are going to cover how to run Flink applications on KDA specifically.

When we create applications with KDA for Flink, we follow the same pattern as we did with KDA SQL, with a number of differences outlined in the following table:

	KDA SQL	KDA for Flink
Input	Specified at the creation of an application. It has to be a single Kinesis data stream or delivery stream (Firehose).	We don't specify the input at the time of application creation. The input can be a Kafka or Kinesis data stream or delivery stream (Firehose). We can build our connectors for data sources.
Processing	ANSI SQL only.	Multiple Flink operators are available. The table API is similar to KDA SQL.
Output	It has to be a Kinesis data stream, delivery stream (Firehose), or AWS Lambda.	Multiple Flink sink connectors are available, with popular ones including AWS S3, Elasticsearch, and JDBC. We can build our own sinks.
Monitoring	CloudWatch.	CloudWatch as well as the Flink dashboard.

Figure 6.9 – KDA SQL and KDA Flink comparison

KDA Flink applications come with more options and flexibility, which can be a determining factor in selecting which engine to use. For example, it is common for companies to have multiple AWS accounts where data pipelines span across those accounts. When it comes to AWS cross-account sharing and data stream consumption, that functionality currently isn't supported by Kinesis Data Analytics SQL-based applications. Assuming we have two AWS accounts, `Account01` and `Account2`, there are three options when it comes to achieving cross-account capabilities:

- The first workaround is to set up a Java application that reads from the Kinesis data stream in `Account01` and then writes to the Kinesis data stream in `Account02`. The SQL KDA application would then operate in `Account02` and process data from the Kinesis data stream in that account. Examples of using two streams can be found at the AWS site: `https://docs.aws.amazon.com/kinesisanalytics/latest/java/get-started-exercise.html#get-started-exercise-5`.

- Another way to move data from the `Account01` data stream to the `Account02` data stream is to use AWS Lambda. This solution is similar to the first one, with the critical difference being that you are using Lambda instead of writing a Java KDA application. The solution can be found at this link: `https://github.com/awslabs/kinesis-aggregation/blob/master/java/KinesisLambdaForwarder/README.md`.

- The third option, instead of using SQL KDA, is to switch to a Flink-based application: `https://docs.aws.amazon.com/kinesisanalytics/latest/java/examples-cross.html`.

> **KDA Flink processing non-AWS sources**
>
> A KDA for Flink application can make calls to Kafka or other sources supported by Flink connectors that aren't deployed on AWS; it could be on-premises or with a different cloud provider. These resources have to be accessible to KDA; we need to configure firewalls and security properly.

Kinesis data streams don't provide *exactly-once* semantics as an out-of-the-box feature. There are a few workarounds, such as using DynamoDB, S3, or ElasticCache in our consumer application to check for duplicates and avoid them. We can use KDA for Flink to achieve exactly-once semantics as Flink supports it out of the box. KDA turns on Flink's exactly-once checkpoint configuration, ensuring that checkpoints are persisted to durable storage such as S3. Exactly-once processing incurs overhead, whether we run Flink on EKS or KDA. Before you start using the exactly-once delivery feature, make sure you understand the impacts on your application. You can find details on Flink's exactly-once semantics here: `https://flink.apache.org/features/2018/03/01/end-to-end-exactly-once-apache-flink.html`.

Options for running Flink applications in AWS Cloud

Besides being able to run Flink applications on KDA, we have a few other options with AWS Cloud. It all comes down to the level of flexibility that we want to have. *Figure 6.10* shows the responsibilities of running a Flink application using different approaches:

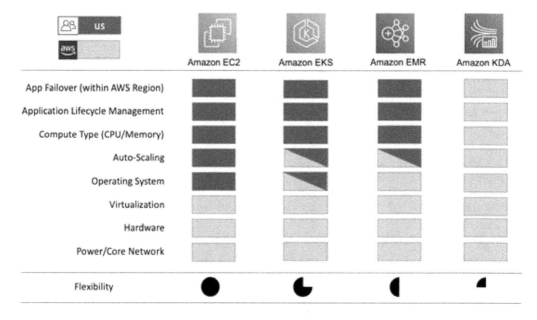

Figure 6.10 – Options for running Flink on AWS Cloud

Running our own EC2 instances with our own runtime for the Flink application provides the most significant level of flexibility, but it also requires the most effort on our side. For EC2 instances, we have classified scaling as something that we have to do ourselves. We are referring to autoscaling as it relates to our Flink application, and not autoscaling the EC2 feature. We can implement autoscaling with EC2 instances, but we have to output Flink metrics, and create a threshold and scaling policies ourselves. On the other hand, both Amazon EKS and Amazon EMR have autoscaling built in for underlying resources, and we can set up thresholds through the CLI or console.

> **EMR with EKS**
>
> EMR recently announced the ability to run big data jobs on EKS. We can now use EMR without having to worry about managing the underlying Kubernetes cluster(s).

KDA for Flink, on the other hand, is fully managed by AWS and, from our perspective, fully serverless (we don't have to worry about servers or storage). Since AWS is doing the heavy lifting to manage the Flink cluster, we can't use Flink's REST API to manage our jobs directly.

Flink applications on KDA

Earlier in the chapter, we explored KDA for the SQL Engine architecture. Let's now look at KDA Flink engine architecture shown in the following diagram:

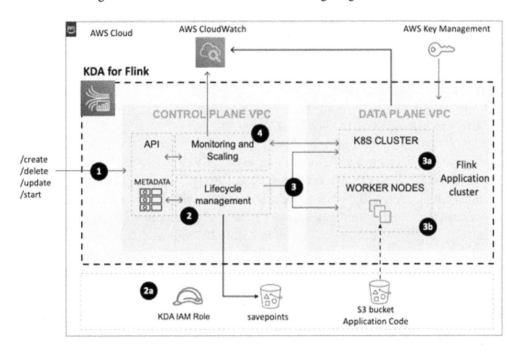

Figure 6.11 – KDA Flink engine architecture

What should stand out is that KDA Flink engine architecture is different to that of KDA SQL. There are quite a few differences, the most notable being that KDA Flink actually runs as a Kubernetes cluster. Let's now step through the data flow and examine the core components:

1. We interact with KDA for Flink using the API layer.

    AWS Console and AWS CLI use the same API; you can see this in AWSCloudTrail. The API layer receives our request, for example, CreateApplication, along with parameters, and persists that as metadata in the DynamoDB table. The architecture of the control plane is shared by both KDA engines, Flink and SQL.

2. Life cycle management takes over and orchestrates the next steps. Once KDA has metadata, it will create the IAM role (2b) that our KDA application can assume. We can also pre-create this role and just provide it as part of the metadata.

3. When we call the `StartApplication` API, the life cycle manager will instantiate our Flink application's infrastructure by creating an EKS cluster and worker nodes.

Our Flink application gets its own EKS cluster, and this configuration provides network separation of the KDA application at a Kubernetes networking level. We can choose between two templates (development and production). The template defines settings, such as whether snapshots are auto-enabled, parallelism per KPU, and logging levels. KDA will load our Flink application from S3; our application JAR file's maximum size is 512 MB.

> **Flink and Maven dependency**
>
> At the time of writing this book, KDA was supporting Flink 1.11.1. To deploy our Flink JAR, we have to build it using Maven 3.1.

Based on template settings, KDA will size up the EKS cluster for our Flink application. KDA uses the **Kinesis Processing Unit** (**KPU**), 1vCPU, 4 GB of memory, and 50 GB of storage. The basic application will start with 1 KPU. KDA will use a separate core for other components of KDA needed to run our application. KDA will load all related Flink libraries for us. Each KDA KPU receives 3 GiB of JVM heap, and the remaining memory is allocated to KDA management components. KDA encrypts data at rest as well as in transit using KMS. KMS keys are generated for each application.

KDA manages the full life cycle of our Flink application on our behalf. It will take automatic savepoints (the KDA term is **snapshot**) as we perform updates of our Flink application. KDA maintains up to 1,000 savepoints in case we need to restore from one of them. KDA applications often require us to keep the track of the state, an example being when we use windows. KDA will have to aggregate data somewhere and retain the state of that window. When we activate checkpointing, KDA will keep track of the state. Flink itself comes with three state stores: `MemoryStateBackend`, which maintains the state in the Java heap; `FsStateBackend`, which maintains the state in the filesystem; and `RocksDBStateBackend`, which stores the state in the RocksDB database.

KDA state backend is RocksDB and S3, and KDA manages it fully. You can learn more about `RocksDBStateBackend` here: `https://ci.apache.org/projects/flink/flink-docs-stable/ops/state/state_backends.html#the-rocksdbstatebackend`. To learn about RocksDB, please navigate to this link: `https://rocksdb.org/`. If you want to use a different state backend, use EKS to run your Flink application.

Savepoints in Flink are used when we want to pause processing, for example, updating our application, and they contain the state of our entire application. In that sense, you can think of them as being *heavy backup*. Savepoints are intended to provide lots of durability, and KDA stores them in S3. When we configure KDA to take automatic snapshots (`SnapshotsEnabled=true`), KDA will create a snapshot each time our application is updated, scaled, or stopped.

Scope of the savepoint (snapshot)

The scope of the savepoint is a KDA application. We can't take a savepoint created by application *A* and start it with application *B*. KDA doesn't automatically delete snapshots. We need to create our own housekeeping routine to delete old snapshots. One of the options is to create an EventBridge scheduled rule that runs on a daily basis. Set the AWS Lambda as the target. Lambda code should then invoke KDA's `ListApplicationSnapshots` API and, in the case of snapshots more than 7 days old (using the `SnapshotCreationTimestap` value), invoke the `DeleteApplicationSnapshot` API.

Checkpointing is how Flink manages recovery when something goes wrong (that is, a Java thread dies) so that we can go back to that checkpoint and continue processing. We use checkpoints to recover quickly from the failure, and in KDA, they are persisted in RocksDB. In Flink on KDA, we can only control three settings:

a. `CheckpointingEnabled`: `True` or `False`.

b. `CheckpointInterval`: The default is `60000`.

c. `MinPauseBetweenCheckpoints`: The default is `5000`.

4. Monitoring and scaling components will observe our applications for any signs of trouble or if an application requires more compute and memory resources. KDA will then scale the underlying resources by moving our application to different clusters or different instance types. Autoscaling is configurable, and we can delegate autoscaling. Automatic scaling overwrites some parallelism; for example, if operator-level parallelism is set in our application, KDA will override it. Autoscaling is the right choice when our Flink operators perform about the same amount of work and require similar resources. KDA will monitor CloudWatch for things such as CPU utilization of our KDA cluster, and it will aggressively scale up at about 5-minute intervals as required. Scale down works in a more conservative way, and KDA will look for multiple CPU utilization intervals before it scales down our KDA Flink cluster. When operators require a different level of resources, we can turn off autoscaling and set parallelism at the operator level.

We set parallelism at two levels as follows:

- The number of KPUs, which can range between 1 and 8.

- Overall parallelism, with a maximum of 256. In a nutshell, each KPU can have up to 32 with a maximum of 8 KPUs, which gives us 256.

> **KDU scaling**
>
> If we want to have 64 parallel tasks per application, we will set the KPUs to two (64/32). We can increase the limit of 8 KPUs by contacting AWS or by opening the limit increase case.

Unlike with KDA for SQL, with Flink, we can use connectors to read and write data from inputs and sources. When our KDA Flink application uses Kinesis Data Streams as the source, we can use **Enhanced Fan-Out (EFO)**. We covered EFO in *Chapter 5, Kinesis Data Streams*, in detail. The advantage of using EFO with our Flink application is that we are getting dedicated bandwidth. EFO is useful if we have multiple consumers besides our Flink application, or multiple Flink applications consuming from the same stream. To enable EFO, we need to set RECORD_PUBLISHER_TYPE and EFO_CONSUMER_NAME in our Flink application configuration. The following is a code snippet concerning how to configure an EFO consumer, and you can get a working example of an EFO consumer here: https://docs.aws.amazon.com/kinesisanalytics/latest/java/examples-efo.html:

```
consumerConfig.putIfAbsent(RECORD_PUBLISHER_TYPE, "EFO");
consumerConfig.putIfAbsent(EFO_CONSUMER_NAME, "efo-flink");
```

To write the output of the KDA SQL application, we use destinations. With KDA for Flink, we do it by using Sink. Kinesis Firehose and S3 are the most widespread sink connectors.

A KDA SQL application has a limit of three destinations, but in the case of KDA for Flink, we have multiple options. You can find the list of available Flink connectors here:

https://ci.apache.org/projects/flink/flink-docs-release-1.12/dev/connectors/.

To decouple our Flink application code from the configuration settings, we use runtime properties. For example, we can configure checkpointing using runtime properties, so when we are in development, we can turn checkpointing off, and then turn it on when in production. The following code snippet is an example of checkpointing being turned on:

```
"FlinkApplicationConfiguration": {
    "CheckpointConfiguration": {
        "CheckpointingEnabled": "true"
    }
}
```

You can find the full list of configurable items in the AWS documentation located at https://docs.aws.amazon.com/kinesisanalytics/latest/java/how-properties.html.

Building bike ride analytic applications

Let's put the described SwipeBike and KDA into action. As a first step, we will simulate bike trips; bikes being rented and returned. We have provided code that will do this for you. We will then build analytics applications using KDA SQL and KDA Flink. These applications will functionally be the same and will analyze the data for bike trips.

Setting up a producer application

If you haven't installed prerequisites, please go to the *Technical requirements* section of this chapter and install the prerequisites. Using AWS **Cloud Deployment Toolkit (CDK)**, we will create the infrastructure required, including deploying the producer application that we will use in this chapter. If you haven't done so already, go ahead and pull down the required CDK code from the GitHub repository:

```
git clone https://github.com/tmakota/kinesis-book.git
```

> **Cost**
>
> If you chose to do the exercises in this chapter, please note that you will incur AWS charges for the resources created in your AWS account.

In order to set up the producer application, perform the following steps:

1. Open up the command prompt or terminal and navigate to the directory where you cloned the code from Github. Navigate to `chapter6`, then to the `producer-cdk` directory, and then create and start the Python virtual environment:

    ```
    python3 -m venv .venv
    source .venv/bin/activate
    ```

2. Once you have the virtual environment running, install all the dependencies required by the CDK project:

    ```
    pip install -r requirements.txt
    ```

    Make sure that the CDK project synthesizes correctly before you attempt to run it:

    ```
    cdk synth
    ```

    Deploy the CDK application to create the infrastructure. Change the parameters accordingly. S3 bucket names are globally unique. If you don't change the names of S3 buckets (`kdasrcbucketname` and `kdaoutputbucketname`), the deployment will probably fail. You can leave the names of the Kinesis and Firehose streams as they are:

    ```
    cdk deploy --parameters kdasrcbucketname=kda-upload-tmak \
      --parameters kdaoutputbucketname=kda-output-tmak \
      --parameters sourceStreamName=ProducerStream \
      --parmeters deliveryStreamName=AnalyticsOutput
    ```

> **Note**
>
> By deploying the CDK application, it will create resources such as a VPC, IGW, subnets, a t3.small EC2 instance, IAM roles, a Kinesis data stream, and a Firehose delivery stream, which will incur charges from AWS for which you will be responsible.

3. Navigate to **AWS Console**, go to the **EC2** section, and then click on the **Instances** tab/link. If everything is deployed properly, we should see an EC2 instance with the name `producer-cdk/Instance`. Click the checkbox next to the instance and then click the **Connect** button. Click on the **Session Manager** tab and then click the **Connect** button again. Once you are connected, let's change the directory to `ssm-user` by using the following command:

    ```
    cd /home/ssm-user
    ```

4. The next step is to pull the Java producer-app code from Git to simulate bicycle rentals. You can clone the entire Git repository, but in this example, we will pull just the producer application directory using `sparsecheckout`:

    ```
    git init
    git remote add origin -f https://github.com/tmakota/
    kinesis-book.git
    git config core.sparsecheckout true
    echo "chapter6/producer-app/*" >> .git/info/sparse-
    checkout
    git pull --depth=2 origin master
    ```

5. Navigate to **Producer application code** under `ride-producer` and then build the application using Gradle. The build process may take a minute or two:

    ```
    cd chapter6/producer-app/ride-producer
    ./gradlew build
    ```

    A producer application uses the value of the system variable `KINESIS_STREAM` to determine the Kinesis stream in which to send the records. CDK installation will set the value of `KINESIS_STREAM` to the stream that we created previously. Before running the producer application, make sure that `KINESIS_STREAM` has your Kinesis data stream's value:

    ```
    echo $KINESIS_STREAM
    ```

    If the output doesn't have your stream name, execute the following command:

    ```
    source /etc/profile
    ```

6. Run the echo command again, and once it does have the value of your Kinesis data stream, run the producer application itself to start sending data to your stream:

```
./gradlew run
```

7. Stop the producer application for now (*Ctrl+C*). We will use it once we start building KDA applications in the *Building a KDA SQL application* section in this chapter.

In this section, we have established the prerequisites for building KDA SQL and Flink applications. Setting up a producer application will simulate bike rides and place the records in a Kinesis data stream, which we will then use as input for our analytics applications.

Building a KDA SQL application

Let's create our KDA SQL application by performing the following steps:

1. Log in to your AWS account and navigate to the **Amazon Kinesis** console. The dashboard will show your existing Kinesis streams and applications.

2. Under the **Data Analytics** section, click on the **Create Application** button. Give your application a name; we will be using kda-sql-app to refer to this application throughout this chapter.

3. Set **Runtime environment** to be SQL. Although not required, you should get into the habit of using **tags**. Tags help with many things, including cost allocations, access controls through IAM policies, or other specific usages that your company may have in place.

4. Once you are ready, go ahead and click **Create Application**. You should get a message that says **Successfully created Application kda-sql-app**.

If you prefer to use the **Command-Line Interface (CLI)**, use the following code:

```
aws kinesisanalytics create-application \
--application-name kda-sql-app \
--application-description "First KDA Application" \
--tags Key=Name,Value=KDASQLApplication
```

We used a shorthand version of the `create-application` API to create the KDA application. Please note that you can specify all the application details with the CLI command, such as source, input, and destinations, in a single command. At this point, you should be able to see your newly created KDA SQL application in AWS Kinesis Console, as shown in *Figure 6.5*:

Application name ▲	Runtime ▽	Status ▽	Created time
kda-sql-app	SQL	⏱ Ready	December 15, 2020, 13:43 EST

Figure 6.12 – Example of a KDA SQL application in AWS Console

There are a few other ways to create KDA applications, such as using AWS Console or using CloudFormation or AWS CDK. We recommend that you use the latter two, and in this chapter, in the *Deploying a Flink app* section, we are going to show you how to use AWS CDK to deploy a Flink application.

Defining inputs for a SQL application

To define inputs for our application, perform the following steps:

1. Navigate to the **AWS Kinesis** console and select kda-sql-app from the list of available applications. We are now going to connect our KDA application to the ProducerStream Kinesis data stream. We will use the stream that was created by CDK and that we insert data into using the producer application.

   > **I don't see the ProducerStream**
   >
   > If you don't see the RideGenerator stream in your Kinesis dashboard, please go back earlier in this chapter and make sure you have completed the *Setting up a producer application* section. It will walk you through a producer application setup, which we require in order to proceed with the exercises.

2. Click on the **Connect streaming data** button, and then from the list of data streams, select ProducerStream. In our use case, we aren't going to perform any record pre-processing, and we will leave it as disabled.

In order for `kda-sql-app` to access data from the `ProducerStream` data stream, it needs to have permission. Permissions in AWS are handled using **Identity Access Management (IAM)** services. KDA will, by default, offer to create the IAM role on our behalf so that our KDA application can access the data from the `ProducerStream` data stream. The IAM role name format is *kinesis-analytics-{name-of-kda-application}-{region}*.

3. Now is the time to start your producer application. Navigate to **EC2 Console**, log in to the `producer-cdk/Instance` instance, and run the producer application:

```
./gradlew run
```

Once the producer application is running, we can proceed with **Discover Schema**. KDA offers an automated way to infer the data types of the data flowing through the `ProducerStream` source data stream. We are going to use AWS Kinesis Console to discover the schema automatically. If you click the **Discover Schema** button, KDA will connect to the `ProducerStream` data stream using the IAM we specified in the previous step and read the records. After reading the data records, KDA will try to infer the column names, their data types, and sizes:

| Edit schema | Retry schema discovery | | | | | |

| Raw | Lambda output | Formatted | | | | |

| Q Filter by column name | | | | | | |

stationId INTEGER	action VARCHAR(8)	tripDuration INTEGER	price REAL	bikeNum VARCHAR(64)	bikeType VARCHAR(8)	eventUTCTime VARCHAR(32)
110	DOCKED	3532	58.870000000000005	707b7401-2a6c-40d6-a471-2548b947b192	BASIC	2021-01-01T23:06:11
110	RENTED	0	0.0	1fa99269-4894-412f-9594-989b792a428d	BASIC	2021-01-01T23:05:53
110	DOCKED	886	14.77	28a5c134-9619-40b4-aef3-2460d1d31a92	ADVANCED	2021-01-01T23:06:02
110	RENTED	0	0.0	281dc0af-fd8a-4b9e-83ad-d46da490e7bb	ADVANCED	2021-01-01T23:05:44

Figure 6.13 – KDA schema discovery tool

Sometimes, KDA will not detect the data types. In our case, KDA has discovered `eventUTCTime` as `VARCHAR(32)`. Click on the **Edit schema** button, which will allow us to change the names of the columns and their types, as well as size or precision. Change **Column Type** from `eventUTCTime` to `TIMESTAMP`, and `price` to `DOUBLE`. Click **Save schema** and update the stream samples:

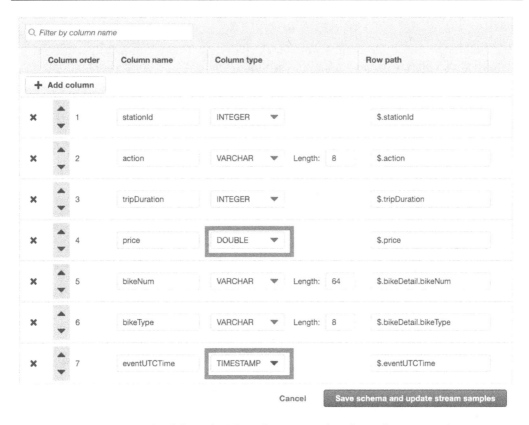

Figure 6.14 – Modifying the KDA schema using the schema discovery tool

In this example, we aren't using reference data, but we could have files in the S3 bucket. When using reference data, we specify the filename and give the reference table a name. Just like with Schema Discovery, KDA can infer the data schema of our reference data.

> **Reference data isn't refreshed automatically**
>
> Sometimes, reference data needs to be updated, and in order to do so, we would update the S3 file containing reference data. KDA will not automatically recognize that data has changed, and AWS Console doesn't have a way to refresh reference data. To update the reference data, we need to use the `update-application` CLI or the `UpdateApplication` API call.

Creating SQL code for real-time analytics

We will build SQL code to determine whether the bicycle station is running low on available bikes so that we can move bicycles around:

> **SQL code**
>
> You can find SQL code in the GitHub repository here: `https://github.com/PacktPublishing/Streaming-Data-Solutions-with-Amazon-Kinesis/tree/main/chapter6/sql-app`.

1. From the `kda-sql-app` console, click on the **Go to SQL editor** button.

2. In SQL Editor, enter SQL listed in the section below, and then click the **Save and Run SQL** button. We are using a tumbling window of 1 minute to summarize bikes that have left and arrived at each station. The `CASE` statement inspects the `action` field, and we translate the output into the `bikeCount` field:

```
CREATE OR REPLACE STREAM RENTAL_COUNT (
    STATIONID           INTEGER,
    BIKECOUNT           INTEGER,
    ASOFTIME            TIMESTAMP
);

CREATE OR REPLACE PUMP RENTAL_COUNT_PUMP AS
    INSERT INTO RENTAL_COUNT
    SELECT STREAM
        "stationId",
        SUM(CASE "action"
            WHEN 'RENTED' THEN -1
            WHEN 'DOCKED' THEN 1
            ELSE 0
        END)  "bikeCount",
        ROWTIME AS asOfTime
FROM "SOURCE_SQL_STREAM_001"
GROUP BY "stationId",
  STEP("SOURCE_SQL_STREAM_001".ROWTIME BY INTERVAL '1'
MINUTE);
```

In SQL code, we set the interval to be 1 minute so as to see the results for the
RENTAL_COUNT in-application stream quickly. In a typical application, the interval
would probably be longer than 1 minute. Please note that AWS recommends that
windowed intervals do not exceed 1 hour due to the nature of underlying storage for
in-application streams (result tables). Since we need to track our stations continuously,
how do we work around this limit? We will send the output of our KDA application to
Firehose and persist the results in S3 for more durable storage. In a real-world application,
we could keep running totals in the database and send KDA windowed operation results
to update that database:

Pause results   ﹀ New results are added every 2-10 seconds. **The results below are sampled.** ⓘ

☐ Scroll to bottom when new results arrive.

Q *Filter by column name*

ROWTIME	STATIONID	BIKECOUNT	ASOFTIME
2021-01-01 23:32:00.0	410	4	2021-01-01 23:32:00.0
2021-01-01 23:33:00.0	290	0	2021-01-01 23:33:00.0
2021-01-01 23:33:00.0	460	2	2021-01-01 23:33:00.0
2021-01-01 23:33:00.0	300	-1	2021-01-01 23:33:00.0
2021-01-01 23:33:00.0	240	-2	2021-01-01 23:33:00.0
2021-01-01 23:33:00.0	340	-1	2021-01-01 23:33:00.0

Figure 6.15 – KDA analytics in action, producing aggregation

To send data from our RENTAL_COUNT in-application stream to S3, click on the
Connect to a destination button. When prompted for the Firehose delivery stream,
select the BikeAnalyticsOutput delivery stream created by the CDK application,
which is configured to send data to the S3 bucket. For in-application streams, select
RENTAL_COUNT and then select CSV as the output format. Click **Save** and then
Continue.

Building a KDA Flink application

In the previous section, we created a SQL application using the AWS console. In this
section, we will set up the Flink KDA application in a repeatable manner using AWS
CDK. Before we start, make sure that you have completed the *Setting up a producer
application* section.

> **Note**
>
> If you haven't already pulled the source code from GitHub, please go ahead and do that now.
>
> CDK: `https://github.com/PacktPublishing/Streaming-Data-Solutions-with-Amazon-Kinesis/tree/main/chapter6/flink-cdk`.
>
> Flink code: `https://github.com/PacktPublishing/Streaming-Data-Solutions-with-Amazon-Kinesis/tree/main/chapter6/flink-app`.

We will primarily use code from the CDK section. Flink code contains the actual Java application code that uses the Flink framework to count a number of bikes that have been rented or returned, just like we did in the SQL application.

We included the JAR file in the distribution, and this is available in the `flink-app/jar` directory. If you want to build your JAR file, this is how you would do it. Open up your Java IDE and import the project from the `flink-app` directory. If you don't use the Java IDE, navigate to the `flink-app` directory using the command prompt or terminal. Execute the Maven package using the following command:

```
mvn package
```

Once `mvn package` completes, it will create a JAR file with our application. We are going to use that JAR file in the next section.

Copying a JAR file to an S3 bucket

Navigate to the directory where the JAR file is and copy it into the S3 bucket you created while setting up the producer application. This is a bucket that we defined as a `kdasrcbucket` parameter. You can also find the name of the S3 bucket from the CloudFormation console by navigating to the `flink-cdk` stack and then, under the **Outputs** tab, the S3 bucket name will be listed under the `KDASourceBucketName` key. In the following example, that bucket name is `kda-upload-tmak`; your bucket name will be different:

```
--parameters kdasrcbucketname=kda-upload-tmak
```

To upload a JAR file to an S3 bucket, you can use AWS Console and copy or use the AWS CLI:

```
aws s3 cp kda-flink-app-1.0-SNAPSHOOT.jar s3://{bucket-name}
```

Deploying a Flink app

We are now ready to deploy our Flink application using CDK. We will use nested stacks, which will show you how to set up your AWS Cloud infrastructure orchestration and deployment in a modular manner to achieve reuse and repeatability. We will use two CDK stacks; under the `flink-cdk` directory, you should see two additional directories: `main_cdk` and `kda_app`. Those two directories hold our stacks. Under `main_cdk`, there is the main stack, the `main_cdk_stack.py` Python file, which will create IAM roles and permissions, as well as log groups and streams. We created Flink application properties in the main stack so that we can show how to pass arguments to the KDA App stack. This, in turn, would make the KDA App stack reusable for any other KDA Flink application:

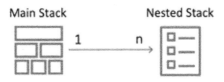

Figure 6.16 – CDK nested stacks for the flexible organization of deployments

> **Tip**
> Treat stacks as you would treat microservices or object-oriented code. Make them the smallest unit of deployment to maximize reuse.

To deploy our Flink application, let's first deploy the stack:

1. Replace `kda-upload-tmak` with the name of the S3 bucket where you uploaded the JAR file:

    ```
    cdk deploy –parameters bucketNameParm=kda-upload-tmak
    ```

2. Once the deployment is finished, let's navigate the AWS Console and examine the newly created Flink application:

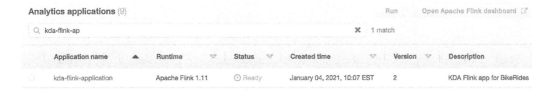

Figure 6.17 – Flink KDA application

3. Click on the application to bring up the details. Under **IAM Role**, you should see `flink-cdk-kdaIAMRoleXXXXXX`. This is the IAM role that KDA will assume as it makes a call to other AWS resources, such as reading from a Kinesis stream or sinking to a Firehose stream. Click on **Role**, and this will bring up **IAM Summary**, and then expand the `kdaIAMRoleDefaultPolicyXXXX` policy. You'll notice that policy only grants permissions required by our Flink application.

4. Under **Properties**, you will see two groups: `CustomerConfigProperties` and `OutputConfigProperties`. Our Flink application code uses **Key-value pairs** defined under these two groups to read from and sink to specific resources. We have externalized these values to minimize changes to our Flink code. In case we need to read from a different stream to the one defined as the `INPUT_STREAM` key, we would simply change the value of that key and would not need to recompile and redeploy our Flink application.

5. Start the KDA Flink application by clicking the **Run** button and start the producer application. Navigate to the Flink dashboard to see details regarding running jobs.

The following screenshot is an example of what you should be able to see in your own Flink dashboard:

Figure 6.18 – Flink dashboard

The Flink dashboard is a useful tool for monitoring the health of our KDA applications. The Flink dashboard is accessible through the KDA console or by invoking an API to obtain the URL. The dashboard allows us to see task managers as well as see the state (running, completed, canceled, and failed) of our jobs.

Securing KDA applications

Since KDA is a managed service, one of the advantages is that the shared responsibility model for KDA means that AWS assumes a greater responsibility for security. When it comes to encryption, KDA takes care of encryption at rest and in transit. Our application's code is encrypted at rest. KDA, by default, encrypts the storage of running applications, both ephemeral and durable storage, including our application code. We can't use our encryption keys; KDA uses its keys to encrypt the data. Internal in-transit data is also encrypted, including communication with other Kinesis services. KDA will not manage in-transit encryption between KDA and our Kafka cluster or other non-Kinesis sources.

As is the case with all other AWS services, KDA uses the IAM service to manage permissions. When we created our KDA application, we had to create an IAM role for KDA to assume. That IAM role has IAM policies that specify resources and permissions for those resources. The IAM role name is in the following format: `kinesis-analytics-{name-of-kda-application}-{region}`. We need to make sure that the IAM role we assign to KDA only has permissions to perform the actions required by the KDA application. For example, our KDA application will need to read data from the Kinesis `ProducerStream` data stream and output/sink data to the Firehose delivery stream, `BikeAnalyticsOutput`. IAM policy for the KDA IAM role will then specify these two as resources so that our KDA application doesn't mistakenly read/write from/to incorrect streams.

We can tighten security further by making our KDA for Flink application be VPC bound. Let's assume that the KDA application needs access to the database residing in our VPC. Commonly, databases are set up so that they are in the private subnet of our VPC so that they aren't exposed to the internet. KDA applications are unable to access our database unless we establish connectivity, and making the database accessible to the internet is a terrible idea. In this case, we can configure KDA VPC connectivity, which will allow us to specify a VPC and a private subnet that we want KDA to have access to. KDA will then deploy an elastic network interface into this subnet to communicate with other resources like a database. ENIs are deployed and visible once we start our KDA Flink application. We can further control access to the database by having KDA ENIs belong to the security group, `kda-sec-group`. Then, in the case of the database security group, we allow traffic originating from `kda-sec-group`.

> **VPC connectivity for KDA**
> VPC connectivity is only available for KDA Flink applications. It is not an option for KDA SQL applications.

Monitoring KDA applications

CloudWatch is a service used to monitor applications in AWS. In addition to CloudWatch, we can also use the Flink dashboard when we use KDA for Flink CloudWatch groups metrics in what's known as a namespace, and for KDA, that namespace is AWS/ KinesisAnalytics. When it comes to KDA Flink applications, we can choose to have KDA emit metrics at the Application, Task, or Operator level. The two most interesting metrics are KPU, the amount of KPUs our application is consuming, and MillisBehindLatest, which tells us how backed up we are (the difference between the timestamp of the record we are processing and the record in the stream under the LATEST position).

For in-depth guidance on how to use CloudWatch with KDA for Flink, please refer to the *Enhanced monitoring and automatic scaling for Apache Flink* blog in the *Further reading* section:

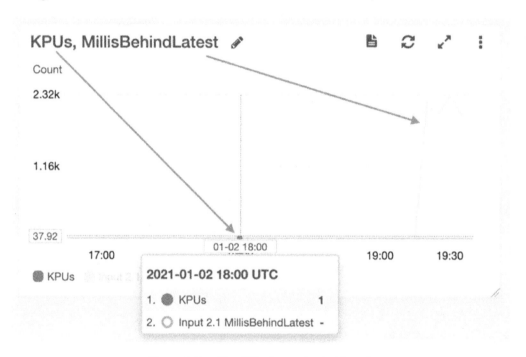

Figure 6.19 – CloudWatch metrics dashboard

Please note that we can also emit our custom metrics into CloudWatch. For example, instead of sending bike station summary data every minute to S3, we could deliver that data to AWS Lambda and then emit it as a customer metric. Using this approach is a convenient way to have our users use data and create their CloudWatch dashboards based on data we emit.

Summary

In this chapter, we learned about the core concepts and capabilities, as well as approaches, regarding common deployment patterns, monitoring and scaling, and the KDA application's security. We built real-time streaming applications using both SQL and Apache Flink.

KDA has many applications, but it's most commonly used for clickstream and big data analytics. When used with other AWS services, it enables us to build sophisticated and scalable solutions. It is easy for those of you with a SQL skillset to translate those and create your KDA SQL applications. On the other hand, if you are coming from a Java or Scala background, using KDA for Flink should be a breeze.

In the next chapter, you will learn to consume and process stream video with **Kinesis Video Streams** (**KVS**). KVS allows us to build applications that stream video from connected devices to use it for other processing, such as **machine learning** (**ML**) or simply for the purposes of playback. As is the case with other Kinesis services, KVS is a managed service, and it scales the underlying infrastructure for us, which enables us to focus on processing video streams.

Further reading

- KDA SQL Developer Guide:
- https://docs.aws.amazon.com/kinesisanalytics/latest/dev/ what-is.html
- KDA Apache Flink Developer Guide:
- https://docs.aws.amazon.com/kinesisanalytics/latest/java/ what-is.html

Blogs

- Extract Transform Load pipeline that also uses KDA:
- https://aws.amazon.com/blogs/big-data/unified-serverless- streaming-etl-architecture-with-amazon-kinesis-data- analytics/
- Deep dive into setting up your autoscaling for KDA Flink: https://aws. amazon.com/blogs/big-data/enhanced-monitoring-and- automatic-scaling-for-apache-flink/
- Similar to the use case we covered in this chapter; NYC Taxi rides:
- https://aws.amazon.com/blogs/big-data/streaming-etl-with- apache-flink-and-amazon-kinesis-data-analytics/

Workshops

- Flink KDA workshop:
- https://streaming-analytics.workshop.aws/flink-on-kda/
- SQL KDA workshop:
- https://real-time-streaming-with-kinesis.workshop.aws/ kda-sql-lab3.html

7
Amazon Kinesis Video Streams

Kinesis Video Streams (KVS) is different than the other Kinesis services you've learned about in the previous chapters. Whereas those services primarily processed independent records in JSON or CSV, KVS is designed to handle **time-encoded data**. When an application needs to support real-time two-way communications or support the ingestion of video from devices, KVS is the best choice.

Amazon KVS is a managed, secure, durable, low-latency service that can scale to support video ingestion from millions of devices for processing, including analytics and machine learning.

Throughout this chapter, we will refer to the real-time functionality as KVS-WebRTC and the ingestion for further processing or storage as KVS. Together, these two capabilities enable you to build systems that support IoT devices and applications for connected homes, enterprise security, connected vehicles, and manufacturing. You want to use KVS when you need computer vision across multiple cameras, and KVS-WebRTC if you want to allow users to access a remote camera.

In this chapter, you will learn about the concepts and capabilities, monitoring and scaling, security, and deployment patterns for real-time communication and data ingestion. We will step through a data streaming solution that will set up real-time access and ingest video data for the SmartCity data system.

The following topics will be covered in this chapter:

- Understanding video fundamentals
- Discovering Amazon KVS WebRTC
- Discovering KVS
- Building video-enabled applications with KVS

Technical requirements

There are a few things that you will need to set up and configure before we start exploring KVS. These are mentioned in the following sections.

AWS account setup

You will need to get an AWS account to run the examples included in this chapter. If you do not have an account already, you can go to `https://aws.amazon.com/getting-started/` to create an account. AWS accounts offer a **Free Tier** (`https://aws.amazon.com/free`).

The AWS **Free Tier** allows you to use many AWS services for free within specified usage limits. Some of the services examples in this chapter are outside of the AWS **Free Tier** and will incur some charges for service usage.

Using a local development environment

You will need a working **AWS CLI v2** environment. You can install the AWS CLI by downloading and running the installer (`https://aws.amazon.com/cli/`) for your environment's operating system. Some of the examples will require that you install the `jq` command-line JSON processor (`https://stedolan.github.io/jq/`).

You will also need **Android Studio** for editing and compiling the sample Android application. You can install it by downloading and running the installer (`https://developer.android.com/studio/index.html`). The VLC media player (`https://www.videolan.org/`) will also be used to display video.

Docker will be used to help stream video data into KVS. If you do not already have Docker installed, you can go to `https://www.docker.com/products/container-runtime#/download`.

Code examples

The code examples in this book are available on GitHub at `https://github.com/PacktPublishing/Streaming-Data-Solutions-with-Amazon-Kinesis`. You will need a Git client to access them (`https://git-scm.com/`).

Now that the technical requirements are out of the way, let's get started by getting a deep understanding of video fundamentals.

Understanding video fundamentals

Even though KVS can handle any form of time-encoded data, its primary use case is for video and audio media. To better understand how to use KVS, we need to cover the basics of video. The two main attributes of a video are its *resolution* and its *bitrate*.

The resolution is the pixel size of the video, normally presented as horizontal x vertical – for example, 1,920 x 1,080 – and its bitrate is the amount of data that's encoded in the video per second, measured in Mbps. In general, the higher the bitrate and the higher the resolution, the higher the quality of the video.

The following diagram shows a high-level overview of how video is captured, compressed using a codec, put into a container, decompressed, and then played:

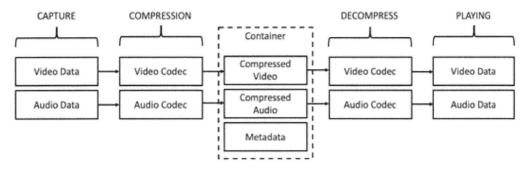

Figure 7.1 – Overview of codecs and containers

Audio and video technology is incredibly complicated, so we'll generally stay at a high level and focus on the aspects that are important to KVS and KVS-WebRTC. First, we will cover containers, and then we will cover codecs since they are how the video data is structured.

Containers

A **container** is a file format that contains multiple data streams and metadata in a single file. It contains the video stream, the audio stream, and metadata, including bitrate, resolution, and codecs. MKV and MP4 are the two containers relevant to KVS. Let's take a further look at each of these containers:

- **MKV**: The **Matroska Multimedia Container** (**MKV**) is an open standard that is designed to contain an unlimited number of audio and video tracks. Its file extension is .mkv. The **KVS Producer and Consumer libraries** send or receive data in MKV format. A fragment in KVS represents a segment of video and it maps directly to the MKV cluster.

- **MP4**: MP4 container (**MPEG-4 Part 14**) is an extension of the **QuickTime file format**, is the most commonly used container, and supports an unlimited number of audio and video tracks. Its file extension is .mp4. MP4 is only supported via the KVS GetClip API call.

Now that we've reviewed the containers that KVS works with, let's dive into how the data that is stored in them is encoded.

Codecs

A **codec** is a standard that describes how to compress and decompress audio and video files. We will be concerned with inter-frame compression codecs, which use multiple frames in a sequence to compress the video. They are based on keyframes, a full frame of the video, and subsequent frames that contain only information that has changed. The goal is to create the highest quality video that plays back smoothly, and there are trade-offs based on computational requirements, file size, and network performance.

There is a large number of codecs for audio and video files, but with regards to KVS and KVS WebRTC, we will only concern ourselves with a few important ones. For video, we will focus on H.264 and VP8, while for audio, we will focus on OPUS, G.711, and AAC:

- **H.264/Advanced Video Coding** (**AVC**): H.264 is the most widely supported video codec and has excellent performance, but it is encumbered by patents.

  H.265/High Efficiency Video Coding (**HEVC**), the successor to H.264, has a compression rate that is twice as good that reduces the file size by 50% for the same quality; however, it requires significantly more processing power to encode and decode and has royalties associated with it.

- **VP8**: VP8 is an open and royalty-free video codec that is mainly used with WebRTC. It has a successor, VP9, that is comparable to H.265.

- **Opus**: Opus is an open audio codec and is used with WebRTC.

- **G.711**: G.711 is a widely supported lowest common denominator codec. It's also unfortunately very inefficient, so it should be used as a last resort.

- **Advanced Audio Coding (AAC)**: AAC is the successor to MP3 and provides higher quality sound at the same bitrate. It is extremely widely supported; however, it is not part of the WebRTC standard.

Now that we've covered the basics of video containers and codecs, let's jump into peer-to-peer streaming with WebRTC.

Discovering Amazon Kinesis video streams WebRTC

Kinesis video streams with WebRTC (KVS WebRTC) is a fully managed service that is a standards-based implementation of the **web real-time communication (WebRTC)** standard. KVS WebRTC provides two-way low-latency live media streaming, enabling the development of video and voice applications.

It is not like any of the streaming technologies discussed in this book. Instead of using producers to send messages to a stream and then using consumers to retrieve them, it creates a peer-to-peer connection that allows you to directly send data from one system to another. This allows applications to get sub-second video playback end to end.

KVS WebRTC provides four core capabilities:

1. **Signaling**, which allows clients to exchange connection metadata.

2. **Peer-to-peer connections** are then established using that connection metadata.

3. **Media** can then be streamed between the clients over the low-latency peer-to-peer connection.

4. **End-to-end encryption** ensures that all of this is done in a secure manner.

The details of how all this happens will be discussed further in the next section.

Core concepts and connection patterns

The WebRTC specification defines lower-level primitives to access media devices (cameras and microphones), to create the direct peering connection between peers, and to send data over a UDP-based data channel. It doesn't define the signaling channel, which is necessary for peers to connect and learn about the network capabilities of each peer. These network capabilities are used to establish the direct peer-to-peer connection.

WebRTC takes advantage of the **IETF protocols – Interactive Connectivity Establishment (ICE)**, **Traversal Using Relays around NAT (TURN)**, and **Session Traversal Utilities for NAT (STUN)** – to understand the client's network capabilities and establish the connection. Since this is a peer-to-peer streaming mechanism, AWS only manages the signaling channels, TURN services, and STUN services. In this section, we will go over the core concepts necessary to understand how WebRTC connections are created and how to use the open source AWS WebRTC SDK in JavaScript to stream video.

WebRTC is strict about the media formats it supports, which can make interoperability difficult. It supports H264 and VP8 for video, and Opus and G.711 for audio, which can cause problems when you're integrating WebRTC with HLS since HLS doesn't support Opus.

Now, let's review how what these components are and how they interact.

Signaling channel

Signaling is the fundamental resource in KVS WebRTC and is what enables applications to establish a peer-to-peer connection. It facilitates a many-to-few model, where one master peer can stream video to up to 10 viewer peers. It is the only AWS resource that needs to be created to enable WebRTC communication, since each signal channel receives its own **AWS Resource Name (ARN)**.

The master peer usually maintains a persistent secure WebSocket connection to the signaling channel. When another client wants to connect to the master, it connects to the signaling channel and sends a **Session Description Protocol (SDP)** offer.

The signaling channel is essential to establishing a peer-to-peer connection because it allows the peers to communicate all the information that they need to connect to each other. Signaling channels are Amazon resources that run in a specific region.

To achieve sub-second latency between clients, it is important to create the signaling channel in a region as close to the users as possible. This is because each signaling channel has a corresponding TURN server in the same region. The TURN server relays packets when a direct peer-to-peer connection between clients cannot be established. The farther a client is from the region, the more latency the client will experience.

Session Traversal Utilities for NAT (STUN)

STUN is a protocol defined in IETF RFC5289 that is used to determine the public IP address and port of a client assigned by NAT. The STUN server returns information about the connectivity of the client. STUN works by having the client send multiple messages and responding with the public IP addresses and ports used by the client. This allows the client to discover what IP address and port NAT is assigning to it. This is a key way to generate ICE candidates.

Traversal Using Relays around NAT (TURN)

TURN is a protocol defined in IETF RFC5766 that allows clients to communicate with each other when NAT prevents the peers from communicating directly. When they cannot establish a peer-to-peer connection, each client connects to the TURN server, and it relays the packets between the peers. Multiple clients can connect to the same relay address. The TURN server is a fallback mechanism so that your application will still work, even when a client's network makes peer-to-peer streaming unviable.

Session Description Protocol (SDP)

SDP is a data format defined in RFC4566 that is used to enable two peers to communicate effectively. It consists of an **SDP offer** and an **SDP answer**. These both contain metadata that describes the multimedia content of the connection that the data passed over, so that the connection can be understood by the peer.

It includes information about the resolution, formats, codecs, and encryption. It also includes connection information as a set of ICE candidates that the peer can use to attempt to establish a connection.

SDP users the offer/answer model:

- **SDP offer**: This is the message that's sent by a client and initiates the peer-to-peer session. It includes media metadata and ICE candidates.

- **SDP answer**: This is the message that's sent by the peer as a response to the SDP offer. It also includes media metadata and ICE candidates.

Interactive Connectivity Establishment (ICE)

ICE is a protocol defined in IETF RFC5245 that facilitates a connection between two clients that are unaware of their own topologies and may be behind one or more NAT gateways. ICE uses STUN, TURN, and the local interfaces to create a set of ICE candidates.

ICE candidate

An ICE candidate is a potential transport address; that is, it is an IP address and port pair. It can include a directly attached network device, a translated address on the public side of a NAT gateway, and the transport address of the TURN server. The following diagram shows the core components necessary to establish a WebRTC connection:

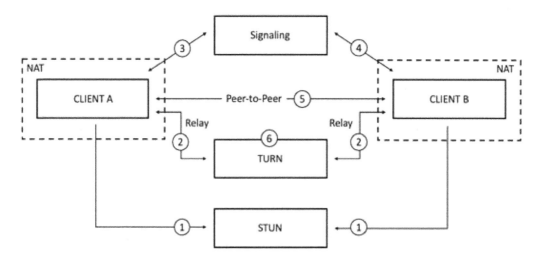

Figure 7.2 – WebRTC architecture and workflow

Each number in the preceding diagram corresponds to one of the following steps:

1. Each client sends multiple requests to the STUN server and creates a list of ICE candidates (IP/port pairs).

2. The clients then connect to the TURN server and get an ICE candidate. This can be used if the clients are unable to establish a direct connection.

3. Client A establishes a connection to the signaling server.

4. Client B connects to the channel to get the SDP offer, and then Client A responds with the SDP answer.

5. Each client now iterates through the ICE candidates, sending STUN requests to each other and keeping track of the successful results. Once they've evaluated all the ICE candidates, they establish a peer-to-peer connection and can stream data.

6. In the case that the clients are unable to successfully create a peer-to-peer connection, they fall back to the TURN relay server's ICE candidate, which was acquired in *Step 2*.

Now that we understand the core concepts of how a peer-to-peer connection is established with WebRTC, let's dive deeper into actually creating a stream and looking at the API calls.

Network Address Translation (NAT)

There are a limited number IPv4 addresses, 2^{32} or 4,294,967,296 to be exact, and while that is a big number, it is not sufficient for the number of devices and networks in the world. IP addresses are divided into public IPs and private IPs. A private IP address will look like `10.*.*.*`, `172.16.*.*` – `172.31.*.*`, or `192.168.*.*`. These addresses are not routable on the internet and use **Network Address Translation (NAT)** to communicate over the internet to public IPs.

When the router receives the packet, it rewrites the from address to the router's public IP and assigns it a port. The NAT router keeps track of the port number in a NAT forwarding table, and when the server responds, it will forward the packet to the appropriate private IP address. Eventually, when IPv6 is fully deployed with its 2^{128} addresses, it will make NAT obsolete as every device will be able to have its own routable address.

Creating a signaling channel

Let's get started by creating a new signaling channel. The console is displayed in the following screenshot. When creating a signaling channel, the only required parameter is the channel name, and it must be unique for the account and region. You can optionally change the default amount of time that the signaling channel will retain undelivered messages, and this can range from 4 seconds to 2 minutes. You should always tag your resources so that you can keep track of your workloads with regards to resource usage and cost:

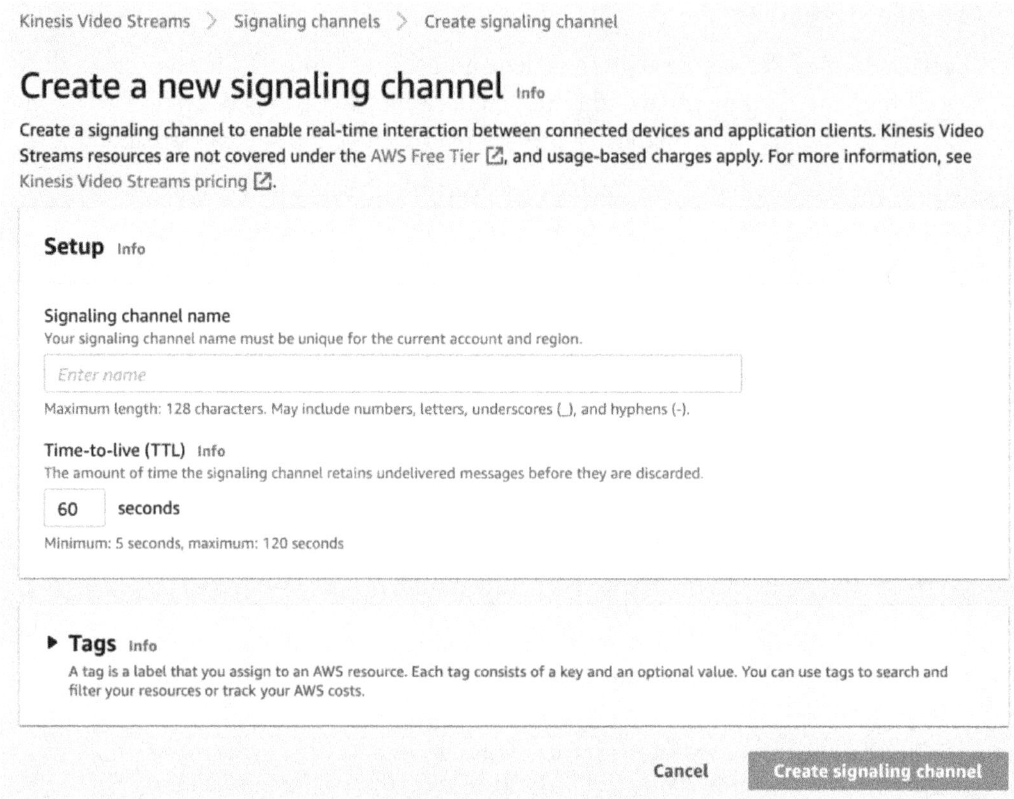

Kinesis Video Streams > Signaling channels > Create signaling channel

Create a new signaling channel Info

Create a signaling channel to enable real-time interaction between connected devices and application clients. Kinesis Video Streams resources are not covered under the AWS Free Tier ☑, and usage-based charges apply. For more information, see Kinesis Video Streams pricing ☑.

Setup Info

Signaling channel name
Your signaling channel name must be unique for the current account and region.

| Enter name |

Maximum length: 128 characters. May include numbers, letters, underscores (_), and hyphens (-).

Time-to-live (TTL) Info
The amount of time the signaling channel retains undelivered messages before they are discarded.

| 60 | seconds |

Minimum: 5 seconds, maximum: 120 seconds

▶ **Tags** Info
A tag is a label that you assign to an AWS resource. Each tag consists of a key and an optional value. You can use tags to search and filter your resources or track your AWS costs.

Cancel   Create signaling channel

Figure 7.3 – Creating a signaling channel

Once you have entered the appropriate information, all that's left to do is click **Create signaling channel**. The console will then redirect you to that signaling channel's page. On this page, you can quickly test the channel by clicking **Webcam demo**; it will connect to the stream from your browser. You can also connect to the stream as a **Viewer** by clicking on **Media playback viewer**, as shown in the following screenshot:

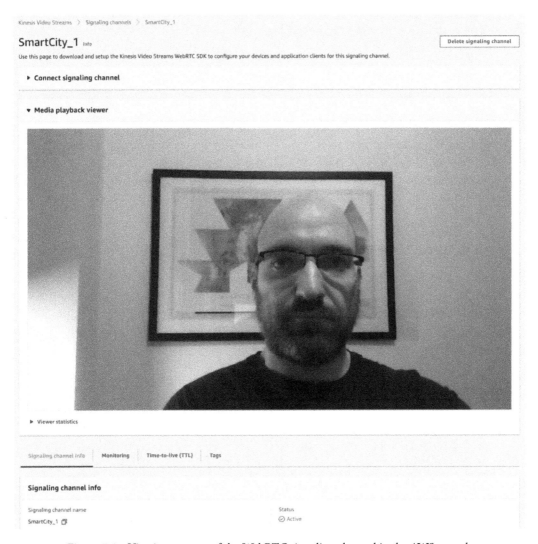

Figure 7.4 – Viewing content of the WebRTC signaling channel in the AWS console

There is a soft limit of 1,000 signaling channels per account per region, and it is important to remember that you are billed based on the number of signaling channels that are active per month. A channel is considered active if a device or application connects to it. You are also charged per signaling message and for TURN streaming minutes.

A signaling channel can also be created using the AWS CLI by specifying its name:

```
aws kinesisvideo create-signaling-channel --channel-name
"myChannel"
```

Now that we've created the channel, let's connect to it and send data.

Establishing a connection

In this section, you will learn how to create a WebRTC connection and receive data using the Amazon KVS WebRTC JavaScript SDK, but first, we'll connect to our signaling channel as both a master and viewer peer using the WebRTC Test Page. Then, we'll go over the SDKS before creating a JavaScript client to connect to the stream going over the individual API calls.

AWS KVS WebRTC Test Page

AWS provides a WebRTC test page, as shown in the following screenshot, that fully exercises KVS WebRTC's functionality. It allows you to connect to the signaling channel as a master or a viewer peer and send audio, data, and video at two different resolutions. It also allows you to force the client through the TURN server or use the STUN/TURN setup we created earlier.

It can be found at `https://awslabs.github.io/amazon-kinesis-video-streams-webrtc-sdk-js/examples/index.html`:

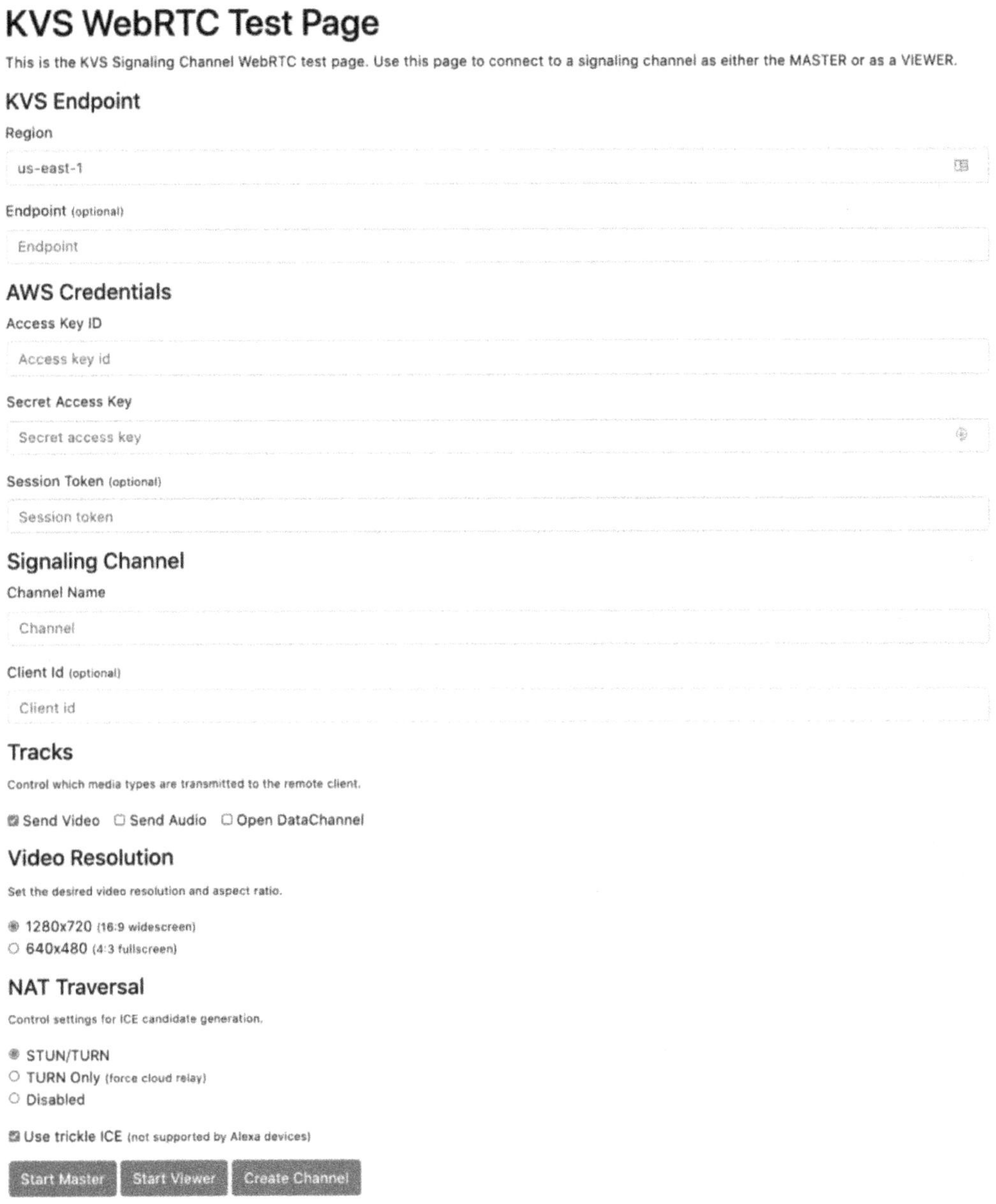

KVS WebRTC Test Page

This is the KVS Signaling Channel WebRTC test page. Use this page to connect to a signaling channel as either the MASTER or as a VIEWER.

KVS Endpoint

Region

> us-east-1

Endpoint (optional)

> Endpoint

AWS Credentials

Access Key ID

> Access key id

Secret Access Key

> Secret access key

Session Token (optional)

> Session token

Signaling Channel

Channel Name

> Channel

Client Id (optional)

> Client id

Tracks

Control which media types are transmitted to the remote client.

☑ Send Video   ☐ Send Audio   ☐ Open DataChannel

Video Resolution

Set the desired video resolution and aspect ratio.

◉ 1280x720 (16:9 widescreen)
○ 640x480 (4:3 fullscreen)

NAT Traversal

Control settings for ICE candidate generation.

◉ STUN/TURN
○ TURN Only (force cloud relay)
○ Disabled

☑ Use trickle ICE (not supported by Alexa devices)

[Start Master] [Start Viewer] [Create Channel]

Figure 7.5 – KVS WebRTC Test Page

You can also run it locally by running the following commands and then visiting the site in your web browser at `http://localhost:3001`:

```
git clone https://github.com/awslabs/amazon-kinesis-video-
streams-webrtc-sdk-js.git
cd amazon-kinesis-video-streams-webrtc-sdk-js/
npm install
npm run develop
```

Now, let's see how we can use the SDKs and API to create our own viewer.

WebRTC SDKs

AWS provides client WebRTC SDKs for Android, iOS, and JavaScript to make it easy to stream live audio and video from one platform to another. These SDKs are different than the traditional AWS SDK and need to be installed separately.

In addition to the client SDKs, AWS provides an open source C SDK for embedded devices, which enables manufacturers to easily integrate audio and video access to their devices using the same standard interfaces found in the client SDKs. It is designed to run on limited hardware with a memory footprint of about 4 MB and is designed for fast connectivity by supporting the **Trickle ICE protocol**, a modification of the ICE protocol described earlier, that connects and starts sending when the first valid candidate is discovered. It supports H.264 and VP8 for video codecs and Opus and G.711 for audio codecs.

Using the JavaScript WebRTC SDK

In this example, we will use the KVS JavaScript WebRTC SDK to build a web that connects as a view to the WebRTC stream:

1. First, create an HTML file called `viewer.html` and include the AWS JavaScript SDK and the KVS JavaScript WebRTC SDK inside it:

    ```
    <script src="https://sdk.amazonaws.com/js/aws-sdk-
    2.585.0.min.js"></script>
    <script src="https://unpkg.com/amazon-kinesis-video-
    streams-webrtc/dist/kvs-webrtc.min.js"></script>
    ```

2. Then, create a Kinesis Video client with the values from a config:

    ```
    const kvs = new AWS.KinesisVideo({
       region: config.region,
       accessKeyId: config.credentials.accessKeyId,
    ```

```
    secretAccessKey: config.credentials.secretAccessKey,
  });
```

3. We can use the client to get the signaling channel's endpoints (WSS and HTTP), where we specify that `Role` is `KVSWebRTC.Role.VIEWER` and that the signaling channels are ARN. The `getSignalingChannelEndpoint` method will return both `HTTPS` and `WSS` endpoints:

```
const endpoint = await kvs.getSignalingChannelEndpoint({
  ChannelARN: config.channelARN,
  SingleMasterChannelEndpointConfiguration: {
    Protocols: ['WSS', 'HTTPS'],
    Role: KVSWebRTC.Role.VIEWER,
  }}).promise();
```

4. Next, we need to get the ICE server configurations. `GetIceServerConfig` can be used to get the TURN servers, but to simplify this example, we'll hard code the STUN server for our region. This is done to instantiate `RTCPeerConnection`, which will be used for WebRTC communication between the two peers:

```
const peerConn = new RTCPeerConnection([
{ urls:
  'stun:stun.kinesisvideo.us-east-1.amazonaws.com:443'
}]);
```

5. The last client we need to create is the client that will actually communicate with the KVS signaling channel:

```
let client = new KVSWebRTC.SignalingClient(config);
```

6. The client has event listeners that need to be set. The first one is executed when the signal channel is open and needs to send an SDP offer to the master. The second is for when the SDP answer is received, while the last is for when ICE candidates are sent from the master:

```
client.on('open', async() => {
  localStream = await navigator.mediaDevices.
getUserMedia(
    {video:{ width: { ideal: 640 },
      height: { ideal: 480 } }, audio:true});
```

```
localStream.getTracks().forEach(track =>
  peerConnection.addTrack(track, localStream));

const offer = await peerConnection.createOffer({
  offerToReceiveAudio: true, offerToReceiveVideo:
true})

await peerConnection.setLocalDescription(offer);
signalClient.sendSdpOffer(peerConnection.
localDescription);
});

signalClient.on('sdpAnswer', async answer => {
await peerConnection.setRemoteDescription(answer)
});

signalClient.on('iceCandidate', candidate => {
peerConnection.addIceCandidate(candidate);
})
```

7. The peer connection will also need an event listener for when tracks are added so that it can play the media:

```
conn.addEventListener('track', event => {
  video.srcObject= event.streams[0]);
});
```

8. Open the client:

```
signalingClient.open();
```

This starts the connection process. When the peer-to-peer connection is established, it will fire the event to play the media stream we set in the preceding callback.

Now that we've learned how to do real-time two-way streaming between devices with KVS WebRTC, let's learn how those same devices can use KVS to ingest media into the AWS cloud for further processing and storage.

Discovering Amazon KVS

KVS is a fully managed service that helps devices stream live video data into AWS for further processing and storage. It is durable and time indexed both when the media is captured by the camera and when it is received on the server. The AWS KVS console can play back the media stream if it's encoded in H.264 format. It can scale to handle millions of devices and it integrates with AWS machine learning resources such as Amazon Rekognition.

There are costs for data ingestion, storage, and consumption. Fortunately, the storage cost is the same cost as S3, so there is no penalty for using Kinesis for long-term storage. It also facilitates video workloads by allowing you to access data through time-based queries. The API also makes it easy to generate HLS streams, Dash streams, and MP4 clips from data in the stream.

KVS is finding use in the surveillance space to store information for retrieval so that it can be automatically analyzed by machine learning algorithms. When latency matters, it is better to use WebRTC as KVS can have seconds of lag. It does not do any transcoding – that is, converting from one encoding to another – but it does do transmuxing, which is repackaging from one container format to another without altering the encoding of the contents, to create HLS streams.

Now, let's start reviewing the key components of KVS.

Key components of KVS

As with the other Kinesis services, there are three main components:

- **Producers**
- **Consumers**
- **Streams**

These components, however, are quite different in KVS. Time-encoded data, such as video, is much more difficult to work with since it is large and produced at a fast rate. The best way to interact with KVS is through the SDK and CLI; writing custom code that interfaces with the raw API is only required for truly unique use cases.

The fundamental construct in KVS for messages is the *fragment*, which represents a segment of video or other time-delimited data. It is a self-contained sequence of frames; that is, no frame in a fragment should have a dependency on a frame in another fragment.

Fragments must have a timecode span of less than 10 seconds; they cannot contain more than 50 MB of data, they must contain at least one frame for each track, and they cannot have more than three tracks. Kinesis takes the following steps when a fragment arrives:

1. Each fragment is automatically assigned a unique number in ascending order.

2. The fragment is joined together with a copy of the media metadata and the Kinesis metadata, which includes the fragment number, the server-side timestamp, and the producer-side timestamp.

3. The chunks are indexed, and the stream is quarriable by the fragment number, the producer timestamp, and the server timestamp.

The process of ingestion and retrieval is shown in the following diagram:

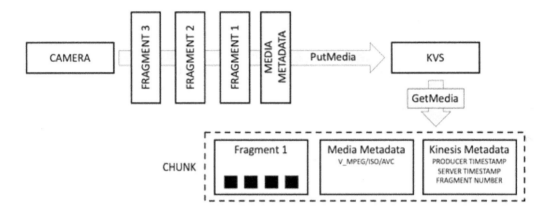

Figure 7.6 – Producing fragments and consuming chunks

Due to the complexity of the PutMedia and GetMedia APIs, we will not be using them directly; we'll be using various SDKs that wrap them.

Stream

The stream is the fundamental AWS resource that ingests, stores, and serves time-encoded data. Each stream can support multiple consumers, but unlike other Kinesis services, each stream in general has only one producer. The maximum data retention period is 10 years.

Kinesis producer

The `PutMedia` API accepts data in MKV container format and can be used to send data in real time or in batches. Since KVS doesn't do transcoding, it will only return what you put in. To take advantage of the higher-level APIs that support playback, the video needs to be encoded in H.264. The API can read media data at a rate of 12.5 MB per second or 100 Mbps.

There is an entire ecosystem of SDKs that enable developers to build applications at the right level of abstraction and get the performance they require. The producer SDK layers are shown in the following diagram:

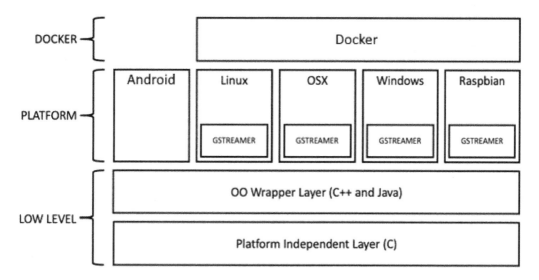

Figure 7.7 – Producer SDK

We'll now quickly review the different SDKs. Later, we will use the Android producer to send data to KVS from an Android phone.

Low-level SDKs

The base of the SDKs is written in a platform-independent manner using the C programming language. This low-level API focuses on state management, buffer management, network management, and video chunking. This is a high-performance, low-level library designed for hardware manufactures to develop custom firmware. It is wrapped and presented in an object-oriented wrapper to provide access in C++ and Java.

Platform SDK

These lower-level functionalities are then packaged into the **GStreamer** plugin, which allows you to use Gstreamer's managed media pipeline. It makes it easy to capture video from a webcam or IoT camera and send it to KVS. The KVS Producer SDK uses a GStreamer sink element, `kvssink`, to send the data to KVS. The Android producer library provides a Java interface that connects to the camera and sends the data to KVS.

Docker images

AWS provides a preconfigured Docker image that is already configured with the GStreamer pipeline to help you get up and running quickly. The Docker image is a private ECR registry, and the instructions for accessing and executing it are located here:

`https://docs.aws.amazon.com/kinesisvideostreams/latest/dg/examples-gstreamer-plugin.html`.

Now that we've covered how data gets into KVS, let's see how we can get it out.

Consuming

There are four main ways to view video in the KVS: **GetMedia**, **MPEG-DASH Streaming URL**, **HLS Streaming URL**, and **GetClip**. Each of these will be discussed further. The **KVS Parser Library** provides a Java wrapper to the GetMedia API. In this section, we'll focus on the `kinesis-video-archived-media` CLI.

The GetClip CLI makes it easy for users to export a video clip for machine learning purposes, as well as for supporting current business processes. For instance, if you have a surveillance camera and you need to send a video clip to the police, it only takes a few keystrokes to retrieve it from the KVS stream.

`GetDashStreamingSessionURL` and `GetHLSStreamingSessionURL` generate URLs that can be used to view the video contents in a web browser or in a media player. Since they are very similar and differ only in their distribution method, we will only cover `GetDashStreamingSessionURL`.

Now, let's see them in action.

GetClip

The GetClip API will download an MP4 file containing the data from the specified time range. In the following command-line example, you can see that we first call `GetDataEndpoint` and specify the stream name and the type of endpoint.

In this case, we need to provide an `api-name` parameter value called `"GET_CLIP"`. The GetClip API requires that the media in the stream be encoded in H.264 or H.265 and that the data retention for the stream be longer than 0.

The `jq` utility is used to extract the endpoint URL from the JSON returned by the `get-data-endpoint` command. `FragmentSelectorType` accepts two timestamps: one for the start of the fragment and one for the end. There is a limit to how big the MP4 file can be; the clip will only contain the first 100 MB or first 200 fragments from the starting timestamp:

```
STREAM_NAME="<STREAM NAME>"
API_NAME="GET_CLIP"
ENDPOINT_JSON=$(aws kinesisvideo get-data-endpoint --stream-name $STREAM_NAME --api-name $API_NAME)
ENDPOINT=$(jq -r '.DataEndpoint' <<< $ENDPOINT_JSON)
FRAGMENT="FragmentSelectorType=SERVER_TIMESTAMP,TimestampRange={StartTimestamp=2021-01-01T05:58:00,EndTimestamp=2021-01-01T05:59:00}"
aws kinesis-video-archived-media get-clip --stream-name $STREAM_NAME --clip-fragment-selector $FRAGMENT --endpoint-url $ENDPOINT myvideo.mp4
```

When the `get-clip` command is executed, it will create a file named `myvideo.mp4` that can then be opened in a media player, such as VLC. Next, we'll learn how to open up the same fragment as a stream.

GetDASHStreamingSessionURL

The `GetDASHStreamingSessionURL` API creates an authenticated URL that includes an encrypted session token so that a media player can steam the data from the KVS stream. Just as with GetClip, we need to get an endpoint. This time, we must specify `api-name` as `GET_DASH_STREAMING_SESSION_URL`. There are three types of playback mode:

- `LIVE` is used to get the latest fragments as they become available.

- `LIVE_REPLAY` is similar to `LIVE`, except that it allows you to specify the start time. For example, you can start the feed from 2 minutes ago and it will be continually updated.

- `ON_DEMAND` allows you to specify the start and end time for a clip and be able to scrub forward and backward in the video.

In this case, we will select `ON_DEMAND` and specify a 1-minute interval:

```
STREAM_NAME="<STREAM NAME>"
API_NAME="GET_DASH_STREAMING_SESSION_URL"
ENDPOINT_JSON=$(aws kinesisvideo get-data-endpoint --stream-
name $STREAM_NAME --api-name $API_NAME)
ENDPOINT=$(jq -r '.DataEndpoint' <<< $ENDPOINT_JSON)
EXPIRES=4000
PLAYBACK_MODE="ON_DEMAND"
FRAGMENT="FragmentSelectorType=SERVER_TIMESTAMP,TimestampRan
ge={StartTimestamp=2021-01-01T05:58:00,EndTimestamp=2021-01-
01T05:59:00}"
aws kinesis-video-archived-media get-dash-streaming-session-
url --stream-name $STREAM_NAME --playback-mode $PLAYBACK_MODE
--expires $EXPIRES --endpoint-url $ENDPOINT --dash-fragment-
selector $FRAGMENT
```

When `get-dash-streaming-session-url` is executed, it returns a JSON object with the following authenticated URL:

```
{
    "DASHStreamingSessionURL": "https://XXXXXXXXX.
kinesisvideo.us-east-1.amazonaws.com/dash/v1/getDASHManifest.
mpd?SessionToken=CiCSKbC-1CylV2GEK6g8VRdo9HBWNbANgq891D63VAAgsh
IQV1S0hbQmlEQM5nr2NFaMoRoZzVImpdI4gvqY4suc5QeqvIDjahO_40qITiIgV
e9cBGFzcsJnLYobfxnvoAk0YQfzpAhfeXe7N2Ji-2w~"
}
```

The DASH stream can then be opened in VLC, which will allow the user to use the slider to scrub the video forward and backward for the given time span.

Now that we've covered how to use the CLI to consume data from the stream, let's create a stream, a producer, and a consumer.

Creating a stream

When creating a stream, all you need is a unique name for the account and region. The main option, as shown in the following screenshot, is to change the data retention configuration from the default of 1 day to up to 10 years:

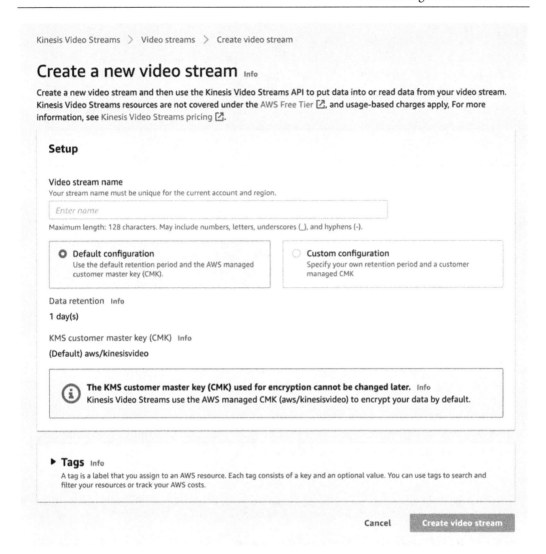

Figure 7.8 – Creating a new video stream

A KVS stream can also be created using the AWS CLI, by specifying its name and retention period. In this example, they are `"myStream"` and `"24"` hours, respectively:

```
aws kinesisvideo create-stream --stream-name "myStream" --data-
retention-in-hours "24"
```

Now that the stream has been configured, it's time to start putting data into it.

Producing

There are a wide variety of KVS Producer SDKs, as we covered earlier *Figure 7.7*, and in this section, we'll focus on the AWS Docker images and the Android SDK. With these Docker images, we'll show you how to use GStreamer to stream video from a static file and live video from an IP camera. For Android, we'll go over the API at a high level so that an Android device can stream data directly to KVS.

Producing with Docker

The AWS Docker container comes preconfigured with GStreamer and the KVS Producer SDK element as a sink. The AWS Docker images are in a private registry, so you will have to authenticate the Docker client with the registry, as shown here:

```
Aws ecr get-login-password –region us-west-2 | docker login –
username AWS –password-stdin 546150905175.dkr.ecr.us-west-2.
amazonaws.com
```

Once you are logged into **Amazon Elastic Container Registry** (**ECR**), the Docker image can be downloaded into your Docker environment with the following command:

```
sudo docker pull 546150905175.dkr.ecr.us-west-2.amazonaws.com/
kinesis-video-producer-sdk-cpp-amazon-linux:latest
```

The following command will launch the Docker image and provide it with access to the local filesystem path, /Users/$USER/data, at /mnt/data. This can be useful if you want to stream a large video file from your system:

```
sudo docker run -v /Users/$USER/data:/mnt/data -it
--network="host" 546150905175.dkr.ecr.us-west-2.amazonaws.com/
kinesis-video-producer-sdk-cpp-amazon-linux /bin/bash
```

Now that we are logged into the Docker environment, we can do a quick test to make sure that GStreamer is configured with KVS. This can easily be tested by running GStreamer with the kvssink command, which should return a list of command options. It will say *"No such element or plugin 'kvssink'"* if it has not been configured correctly:

```
gst-inspect-1.0 kvssink
```

Now that the Docker image is set up, let's stream a file.

Streaming a static file

KVS can accept any time-encoded data, but for us to be able to play the media in the console, it must be in the MKV container, with track 1 encoded with the H.264 codec; track 2 should contain AAC encoded audio. To make sure that a sample file that will play, we'll use the following command to download a test video into our Docker container:

```
wget https://github.com/Matroska-Org/matroska-test-files/blob/
master/test_files/test2.mkv
```

GStreamer commands are long and need to be all one line. In this command, we'll send the `test2.mkv` file we downloaded to the KVS stream that we created earlier; that is, `myStream`. We will also need to set `Access Key Id` and `Secret Access Key` to access KVS and the region where the stream is. It is important to set the region; many users encounter difficulties because it will automatically create the stream in `us-west-2` if one is not provided:

```
STREAMNAME="myStream"
ACCESSKEY="*******************"
SECRETKEY="****************************************"
REGION="us-east-1"

gst-launch-1.0 -v filesrc location="/mnt/mydata/test2.mkv"
! matroskademux name=demux ! queue ! h264parse ! kvssink
name=sink aws-region=$REGION stream-name=$STREAMNAME access-
key=$ACCESSKEY secret-key=$SECRETKEY streaming-type=offline
demux. ! queue ! aacparse ! sink.
```

While this command is executing, you should see a lot of data scrolling across the terminal. This is GStreamer sending the data to KVS. If you launch the **AWS console** and go to **KVS's Media Playback** for `myStream`, you will see the video playing.

Now that we've streamed a static video file, let's see how we can do the same for live video.

Live streaming with RTSP

Internet Protocol (**IP**) cameras are primarily used for surveillance and transmit data over the network using the **Real-Time Streaming Protocol** (**RTSP**). GStreamer makes it easy to access the camera, usually on a local network, and send the data to KVS. For this example, you'll need to have an IP camera and get its URI. Notice that this URI contains a username and password for the stream:

```
STREAMNAME="kvstream"
ACCESSKEY="********************"
SECRETKEY="****************************************"
REGION="us-east-1"
URI="rtsp://username:pass@192.168.1.22/live"
```

```
gst-launch-1.0 rtspsrc location=$URI short-header=TRUE !
rtph264depay ! video/x-h264, format=avc,alignment=au ! kvssink
storage-size=512 aws-region=$REGION stream-name=$STREAMNAME
access-key=$ACCESSKEY secret-key=$SECRETKEY
```

You should now be able to see the live video feed in the KVS console. Now, let's quickly look at the Android SDK.

Producing with Android

Building an Android application takes a significant amount of work. Luckily, the Android Producer Library provides a skeleton that is quite easy to build on. It's available at https://docs.aws.amazon.com/kinesisvideostreams/latest/dg/producer-sdk-android.html. There is some configuration required, but we'll focus on the three main essential actions: creating an instance of KinesisVideoClient, creating an instance of MediaSource, and starting the stream. Let's get started:

1. KinesisVideoClient reads the credentials that have been set in a config file to connect to AWS Cognito. When the application starts up, it will allow the user to log in:

    ```
    KVSlient =. KinesisVideoAndroidClientFactory.
    createKinesisVideoClient(
      getActivity(),
      KinesisVideoDemoApp.KINESIS_VIDEO_REGION,
      KinesisVideoDemoApp.getCredentialsProvider());
    ```

2. Now that we have a client, we need to use the KVS
    `MediaSourceConfiguration` to connect to the camera and set the video
    encoding, as well as other settings.

3. The configuration is then used to create a `MediaSource` instance:

```
mediaSource = (AndroidCameraMediaSource)
   KVSClient.createMediaSource(streamName, configuration);
```

4. Once the media source has been created, it can start to capture data and send it to
    the stream:

```
mediaSource.start();
```

Now that we have data being sent into KVS, we can connect the KVS stream to
Rekognition to detect if any faces in the stream match ones in our collection. Let's see how
that's done.

Integration with Rekognition

Amazon Rekognition is a fully managed service that offers advanced machine learning
models for analyzing images and video. It can be used to detect objects, scenes, text,
inappropriate content, and, in our case, faces. Rekognition can detect faces and provides
highly accurate facial analysis and search capabilities.

In this section, we will assume that Rekognition has already been configured with a
collection of images containing the faces of known vandals, called `"faces"`. Over the
past few months, we have collected images of people who have damaged bike stations,
and now, we want to be alerted if they are detected in any of our KVS streams.

We also had to configure the appropriate IAM role for Rekognition to grant access
to the KVS stream, and then created a **Kinesis data stream** to receive notifications
of face matches.

We will use the AWS CLI to have Rekognition consume the KVS stream by executing the `create-stream-processor` command. This passes in the video stream ARN, the destination data stream ARN, the role ARN for Rekognition to assume, the faces collection, and its name; that is, `kvsprocessor`:

```
aws rekognition create-stream-processor --name kvsprocessor \
  --input '{"KinesisVideoStream":{"Arn":"arn:aws:kinesisvideo
:us-east-1:XXXXXXXXXXX:stream/demo-stream/1609995253290"}}' \
  --stream-processor-output '{"KinesisDataStream":{"Arn":"arn:aw
s:kinesis:us-east-1:XXXXXXXXXXX5:stream/kvs-ml"}}'\
  --role-arn arn:aws:iam::XXXXXXXXXXX:role/test-kvs \
  --settings '{"FaceSearch":{"CollectionId":"faces",
"FaceMatchThreshold":85.5}}' \
```

This stream processor can then be started by calling the `start-stream-processor` command and providing its name, which in this case is `kvsprocessor`:

```
aws rekognition start-stream-processor --name kvsprocessor
```

The stream processor can be stopped by executing the `stop-stream-processor` command and passing in its name:

```
aws rekognition stop-stream-processor --name kvsprocessor
```

At this point, we've created a KVS stream, created producers using Docker and Android that can stream video data into the stream, and set up Rekognition as a consumer to detect faces and send the matches to a Kinesis data stream.

Next, let's learn how to take the functionality we've described in the preceding sections and use it as part of our SmartCity application.

Building video-enabled applications with KVS

Now that we have learned the fundamentals of KVS and KVS-WebRTC, they can be combined to enable video functionality in the SmartCity use case. The architecture shown in the following diagram fully exercises the video capabilities of KVS:

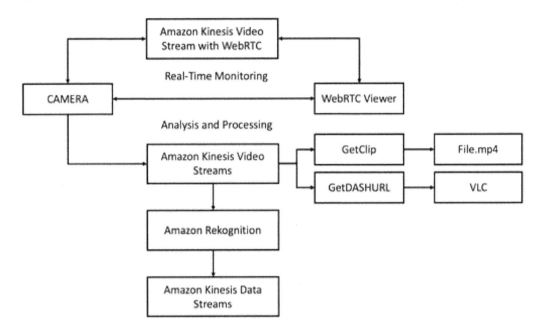

Figure 7.9 – SmartCity monitoring architecture

Throughout this chapter, we have built the component pieces of this architecture. The full solution is available in this book's GitHub repository. The application provides security and situational awareness for the users of the SmartCity bike system. It all starts with a camera pointed at the bike stands and supports the following three capabilities:

- Real-time access to the camera via a browser using WebRTC

- The ability to pull archival clips based on a timeframe using the AWS CLI to get a media file and using the CLI and VLC to view a stream

- Automatic detection of known vandals via facial recognition using Amazon Rekognition, and placing the event into Amazon KDS so that it can be integrated into other systems

By using KVS, we are able to quickly stand up functionality that can scale and securely ingest, store, and distribute video.

Summary

In this chapter, we reviewed the fundamentals of video encoding, how KVS can be used to build systems to process and store video, and how KVS WebRTC can be used for low-latency real-time streaming. We went into detail on how to work with the APIs, and then designed a smart city system that leveraged KVS to add video capabilities to improve monitoring and the security of the bike stations.

This is the last chapter on the Kinesis set of services. In the next chapter, you will learn more about how Kinesis can integrate with other Amazon and third-party services.

Further reading

For more information on the topics that were covered in this chapter, you can refer to the following links:

- Amazon KVS API Reference: `https://docs.aws.amazon.com/kinesisvideostreams/latest/dg/API_Reference.html`

- Amazon KVS Developer Guide: `https://docs.aws.amazon.com/kinesisvideostreams/latest/dg/kinesisvideo-dg.pdf`

- Android Producer Library:

  `https://docs.aws.amazon.com/kinesisvideostreams/latest/dg/producer-sdk-android.html`

- IETF RFC 5766 (TURN), RFC 5389 (STUN), RFC 5245 (ICE):

  `https://www.ietf.org/rfc/rfc5766.txt`, `https://www.ietf.org/rfc/rfc5389.txt`, and `https://www.ietf.org/rfc/rfc5245.txt`, respectively

Section 3: Integrations

In this section, you will gain a better understanding of how the Kinesis services can be integrated with other AWS services and third-party applications.

This section comprises the following chapters:

- *Chapter 8, Kinesis Integrations*

8
Kinesis Integrations

In the previous chapters, we covered the four Kinesis services: **Kinesis Data Streams (KDS)**, **Kinesis Firehose, Kinesis Data Analytics (KDA)**, and **Kinesis Video Streams (KVS)**. When we looked at their core concepts, usage patterns, and examples, each service was shown in isolation or in combination with other Kinesis services. In this chapter, we will explore how the Kinesis family of services integrates with other AWS services to create applications or end-to-end solutions.

We will cover a wide variety of services, including **Amazon Connect, Amazon Aurora, Amazon DynamoDB, Amazon Athena, AWS Glue**, and third-party services such as **Splunk**. This chapter will serve as a good primer on these services, if you are unfamiliar with them. We will start by covering the basics of the services, and then focus on using them in conjunction with Kinesis. This book was written in the middle of the COVID-19 pandemic, and if there is one thing that's clear, it is that technology has made it possible for us to stay connected. Without the use of Amazon Chime, Slack, or GitHub, we would not have been able to complete this book.

We believe that the Amazon Kinesis family of services represents a connecting tissue for other AWS (and non-AWS) services. When used appropriately, the cloud allows us to quickly create new solutions and applications. In this chapter, we will integrate Kinesis with a wide variety of services and create a serverless data lake.

In this chapter, we're going to cover the following main topics:

- Amazon services that can produce data to send to Kinesis
- Amazon services that consume data from Kinesis
- Amazon services that transform Kinesis data
- Third-party integrations with Kinesis

Technical requirements

In this chapter, we will touch upon multiple services and technologies. The core technical requirements are listed in this section. There are numerous Git repositories that you will use for the integrations; we will call those out in their pertinent sections.

AWS account setup

You will need to get an AWS account to run the examples included in this chapter. If you do not have an account already, you can go to `https://aws.amazon.com/getting-started/` to create an account. AWS accounts offer a **Free Tier** (`https://aws.amazon.com/free`).

The AWS **Free Tier** allows you to use many AWS services for free within specified usage limits. Some of the service examples in this chapter are outside the AWS Free Tier and incur some service usage charges.

AWS CLI

You will need the **AWS Command-Line Interface** (**CLI**) to execute the commands for multiple AWS services that will be used throughout this chapter. We recommend that you use AWS CLI v2 as it offers more interactive features.

For Windows, you can download and run the Windows installer here: `https://awscli.amazonaws.com/AWSCLIV2.msi`.

For MacOS, you can download and run the MacOS PKG installer here: `https://awscli.amazonaws.com/AWSCLIV2.pkg`.

Kinesis Data Generator

To create streaming data, we will use **Kinesis Data Generator** (**KDG**). If you haven't set up KDG already, please navigate to `https://awslabs.github.io/amazon-kinesis-data-generator/web/producer.html` and complete the setup portion.

Code examples

The code examples in this chapter are listed throughout multiple GitHub repositories; you will need a Git client to access them (`https://git-scm.com/`).

Amazon services that can produce data to send to Kinesis

In this section, we will cover services that produce data and then utilize Kinesis to deliver that data to its intended location(s). We will learn how to use Kinesis with those services to get faster insight from data. As is the case with any new technology, integration may present some challenges. It's impossible to cover all the possible integration scenarios, so we will focus on some examples where Kinesis integrates with Amazon Connect, DynamoDB, Aurora, and Spark Streaming.

Amazon Connect

One of Amazon's leadership principles is **customer obsession** (`https://www.amazon.jobs/en/principles`). Any company that wants to have satisfied long-term customers, in addition to having great products, requires excellent customer service. Most businesses need some sort of customer contact center, where a customer can call and talk to a customer service agent, to address customer questions or problems.

Amazon Connect is a service that allows us to run a serverless contact center. Using Amazon Connect, we can set up our customer service center in a matter of hours, and our agents can be virtually located anywhere in the world.

More importantly, AWS has designed Amazon Connect so that it can integrate with other platforms and services. If you are thinking, "*that's where the Kinesis comes in,*" you are correct. If we want to track **Connect Agent Events**, we can send those to the desired destination using **Kinesis Data Streams**. The following diagram shows a reference architecture for Amazon Connect data streaming, with the consumers of that data being AWS services or third-party software solutions:

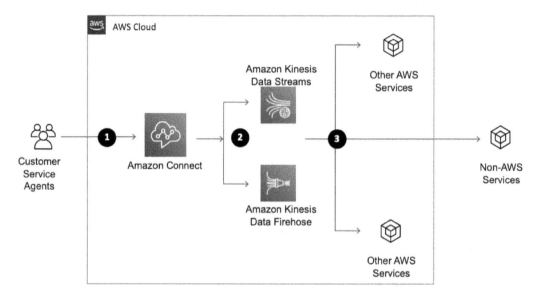

Figure 8.1 – Amazon Connect data streaming flow

One good example of an integration with AWS services would be sending **AWS Connect agent** events to **AWS Redshift** or a **data lake** to perform analysis on how well our agents are doing. AWS Connect generates agent events such as the following (this is a partial list):

- **CONNECTED**: The agent has accepted the contact.
- **MISSED**: The contact was missed by the agent.

As agent events are generated, we can have AWS Connect send those to Kinesis and then deposit them into the data lake. This will allow us to analyze how many missed calls there are, so that we can have additional agents made available and monitor the depth of our customer waiting queue. Similarly, instead of sending records to the data lake, we could send them to third-party systems such as Salesforce or Verint Workforce Management and Optimization.

At the time of writing this book, Amazon Connect doesn't offer support for CloudFormation, so to set up data streaming, we must use the **AWS Console** or **AWS Cloud Development Kit (CDK)**.

> **Amazon Connect with CDK**
>
> To use CDK with Amazon Connect, we need to create a CDK custom resource and then utilize the APIs that are exposed via the *Connect* service. When we use custom resources with CDK, we need to use the Node.js API as a guide.

Let's explore how to set up data streaming with AWS Connect. If you don't have an AWS Connect Instance configured and running, you will need to do that first. Please follow the following guide to complete the Connect instance configuration: `https://docs.aws.amazon.com/connect/latest/adminguide/amazon-connect-instances.html`.

Once you have a Connect instance up and running, navigate to Amazon Connect in the AWS console. You will see your instances on that page. The instance name is a link you can use to get into the configuration; click on it. Click on the **Data streaming** link and then select **Enable data streaming**.

At this point, you can set up either a Kinesis Data Stream or Firehose Stream for **Contact Trace Records**. **Agent Events** can only flow through the Kinesis Stream. We can either select existing streams or create new ones. An example setup for data streaming for Amazon Connect is shown in the following screenshot:

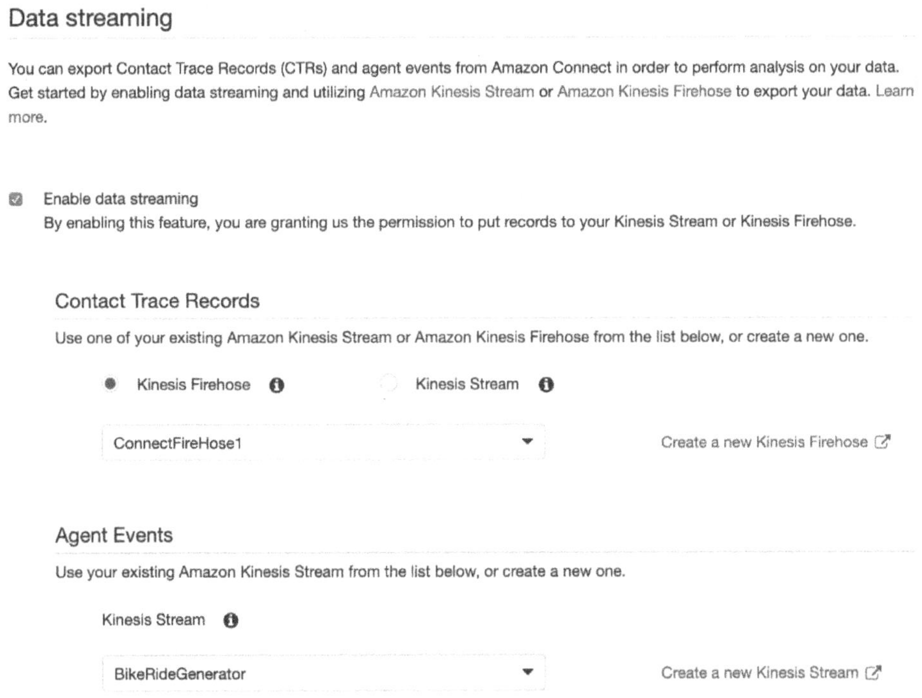

Data streaming

You can export Contact Trace Records (CTRs) and agent events from Amazon Connect in order to perform analysis on your data. Get started by enabling data streaming and utilizing Amazon Kinesis Stream or Amazon Kinesis Firehose to export your data. Learn more.

☑ Enable data streaming
By enabling this feature, you are granting us the permission to put records to your Kinesis Stream or Kinesis Firehose.

Contact Trace Records

Use one of your existing Amazon Kinesis Stream or Amazon Kinesis Firehose from the list below, or create a new one.

● Kinesis Firehose ⓘ   ○ Kinesis Stream ⓘ

| ConnectFireHose1 | ▼ |

Create a new Kinesis Firehose ⬀

Agent Events

Use your existing Amazon Kinesis Stream from the list below, or create a new one.

Kinesis Stream ⓘ

| BikeRideGenerator | ▼ |

Create a new Kinesis Stream ⬀

Figure 8.2 – Streaming data from Amazon Connect

In this section, we learned how to export **Contact Trace Records** (**CTRs**) and agent events from Amazon Connect and then send them to Amazon Kinesis. If you have use cases that require Amazon Connect, then here is a real-world example of how PwC used Kinesis to create unified customer solutions with SalesForce: `https://aws.amazon.com/blogs/apn/intelligent-case-management-using-amazon-connect-and-amazon-kinesis-data-streams/`.

Amazon Aurora database activity

Amazon Aurora is an AWS **Database-as-a-Service** (**DbaaS**) that's offered through a MySQL or PostgreSQL engine. Being a managed service means that we can use the database without doing standard **Database Administrator** (**DBA**) tasks such as setting up actual hardware, establishing related networking and infrastructure, and installing database software. Aurora's most considerable appeal is that it is highly available out-of-the-box, because it replicates data to six storage nodes across multiple availability zones (built into the base price). As Aurora is a managed service, our visibility into the internals of the database's operations is limited, and that's where **Activity Streams** come in.

Aurora database activity streams allow us to extract those *behind the scenes* operations into the Kinesis data stream. Once our Aurora activity is in the Kinesis data stream, we can use it to trigger specific actions and observe usage and database activity. Let's see how we can set this up and get Aurora's activity into Kinesis.

We created the `kinesisbook` database using the Aurora PostgreSQL database with the `db.r5.large` instance. If you aren't familiar with Aurora and need further assistance with creating the database, please follow the following AWS guide: `https://docs.aws.amazon.com/AmazonRDS/latest/AuroraUserGuide/Aurora.CreateInstance.html`.

> **Creating a database will incur a cost**
>
> If you create a database, please be aware that your AWS account will be charged for using that database.

We made the database publicly available (don't do this with your production database unless there is an exact requirement). The following screenshot shows our Aurora PostgreSQL database:

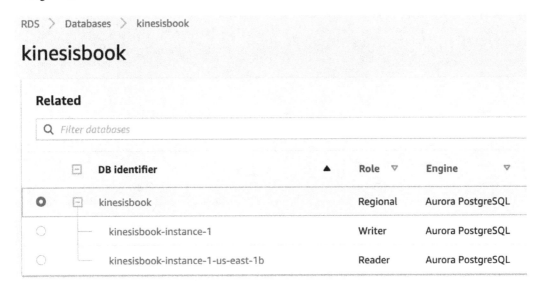

Figure 8.3 – Aurora PostgreSQL database example

Before we start streaming Aurora's activity into Kinesis, we need to create an AWS **Key Management System (KMS)** key. Aurora's activity will be encrypted using the key that we provide. We can initiate sending database activity using the AWS console or CLI.

There are two modes of database activity streaming that are supported: **synchronous** and **asynchronous**. In synchronous mode, the database session blocks until it can write an event to the event stream. If there is an error, the database session continues the process and then creates a second event once the stream has recovered. With synchronous mode, we get the activity stream's accuracy, but that may impact database performance.

In asynchronous mode, the database writes first and returns control. The activity stream event is written separately and then sent. If an error occurs while writing the event to the stream, RDS sends the error itself and not the event. Asynchronous mode is better for database performance, but we may lose some accuracy regarding the activity stream.

To start Aurora streaming from the console, we must select our database cluster, then click on the **Actions** button and select **Start activity stream**. Another way we can do this is by using the CLI, as shown in the following screenshot:

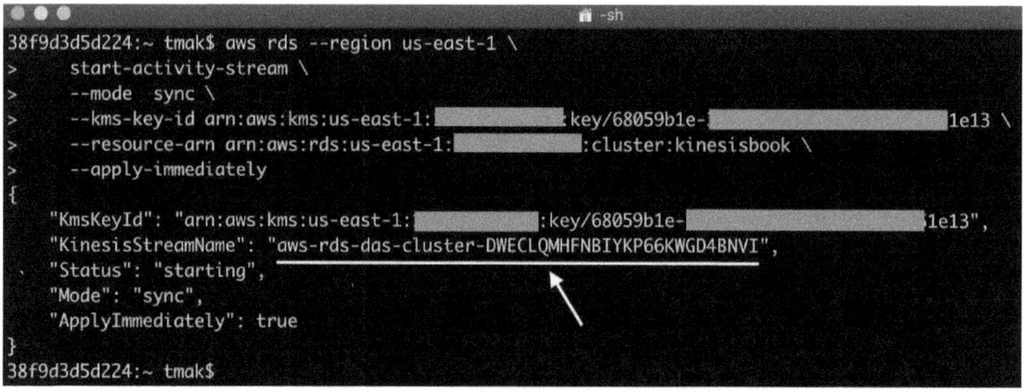

Figure 8.4 – Starting RDS data streaming

Once Aurora streaming is active, we can connect to our database and generate some activity so that data is generated and sent to the Kinesis stream. An example of generating database activity would be creating or altering tables. Once there is some activity in our Aurora database, we can use the CLI to fetch records that Aurora has sent to Kinesis. In the following screenshot, we can see how to retrieve the Kinesis record that was inserted by the Aurora DB seen in Using the GetRecords API section in Chapter 5, Kinesis Firehose:

Figure 8.5 – Example of database activity being retrieved from Kinesis

The Kinesis record we retrieved is `base64` encoded. Using an online `base64` decoding tool (`https://www.base64decode.org/`), we can decode the Kinesis data record. The resulting output of `base64` decoding will look similar to the following:

```
{
"type":"DatabaseActivityMonitoringRecords",
"version":"1.1",
"databaseActivityEvents":"AYADe<ABBREVIATED>/Q=",
"key":"AQIDAHhIKW8loWteYVqlyNhV8cpwWkF6X0PLmiWBsD51+
GYtrAFyxdnoY8TMt7oD8S7n8cl+AAAAfjB8BgkqhkiG9w0BBwagbzBtAgEAMGg
GCSqGSIb3DQEHATAeBglghkgBZQMEAS4wEQQMV2vbuf4HMEouImBtAgEQgDur4d
+efHMtSdcP9czoNUIGCp566cfOuyJkX7kjznliB665iNBXPj9cLsa
7NPH815ev1oIriyVdda4SMg=="}
```

The `databaseActivityEvents` field is encrypted with the KMS key that we specified, and to use it further, we would need to decrypt it. We aren't going to cover the details of decrypting the record here. You can find a full-fledged example in the following GitHub repository: `https://github.com/iann0036/aurora-activity-streams-sechub`.

In this section, we learned how to set up Aurora data streaming and how to fetch generated records from the Kinesis data stream.

DynamoDB activity

In the preceding section, we talked about integrating Kinesis with Aurora. We did this to obtain changes from the Aurora database and then process them as a stream of events using Kinesis. Another top-rated database service is DynamoDB, a fully managed NoSQL database.

DynamoDB is a key-value data store that can automatically scale as our workload grows or shrinks. DynamoDB provides a change data capture feature through **DynamoDB Streams**, which provides us with a time-ordered sequence of row modifications (in DynamoDB, a row is also referred to as an item). Please note that during re:Invent2020, AWS introduced the ability to stream data from DynamoDB directly into Kinesis. Full details can be found here: `https://docs.aws.amazon.com/amazondynamodb/latest/developerguide/kds.html`.

Now, we will explore how DynamoDB streams data into Kinesis. We will start by storing the SmartCity bike station address in DynamoDB, as shown in the following code:

```
{
  "stationId": "100",
  "address": {
    "street": "1 Wall Street",
    "postalCode": "10003",
    "city": "New York",
    "countryCode": "USA"
  },
  "active": "YES"
}
```

We will then create a DynamoDB Stream stream to notify us if any new stations are being added or removed. Whenever we add, modify, or delete (set `"active"` to NO) in the DynamoDB table, we will receive a record in our DynamoDB Stream with rows (items) that were modified.

Unlike with Aurora, we can set up a DynamoDB stream so that it includes the `"before"` and `"after"` information for the modified rows. Another difference between Aurora and DynamoDB streams is that DynamoDB streams are at the **table level**, and in Aurora, they are **database-wide**.

You may be wondering why we are discussing DynamoDB streams; shouldn't they just work like Aurora streams? The fact is that DynamoDB uses its own streaming technology, and although it is similar to Kinesis data streams, DynamoDB streams are not the same as Kinesis streams.

> **Like Kinesis but not Kinesis**
> *"Although these DynamoDB Streams actions are similar to their counterparts in Kinesis Data Streams, they are not 100 percent identical."* AWS documentation:
> `https://docs.aws.amazon.com/amazondynamodb/latest/`
> `developerguide/Streams.KCLAdapter.html`.

If you want to try out DynamoDB streaming, here are the steps:

1. Navigate to the AWS console and then go to DynamoDB.

2. Create a table called `bike-stations`.

3. Once the table has been created, make sure that a stream has been enabled for the table.

4. Using JSON from this section as a template, create a few rows (items).

5. Once you have created a few items, modify some of them by updating items. The activity will trigger DynamoDB to write that data to the DynamoDB stream. To read from the DynamoDB stream, you can use the following code, provided by AWS: `https://docs.aws.amazon.com/amazondynamodb/latest/developerguide/Streams.KCLAdapter.Walkthrough.CompleteProgram.html`.

This section taught us how to set up DynamoDB Streams and then use Amazon Kinesis Adapter to consume data from the stream.

Processing Kinesis data with Apache Spark

"Apache Spark is a unified analytics engine for large-scale data processing."

– `https://spark.apache.org/`

In simple terms, Spark is an improved version of Hadoop MapReduce. The most significant difference is that Spark uses an in-memory engine, so it outperforms MapReduce in several use cases. The key concept with Spark is its immutable **Resilient Distributed Dataset** (**RDD**), which allows Spark to balance its workload across multiple compute nodes (executors) to achieve parallel processing (improved map and reduce functionality).

We can create RDDs out of many sources, such as databases and files such as those stored in S3 or from our Kinesis data stream. Spark also has SQL support, which allows us to perform functions similar to those in Kinesis Data Analytics, such as joining or aggregating data.

We can deploy Spark on EC2, Amazon EMR, or use AWS Glue services to run Spark applications. Spark provides support for multiple programming languages, such as Java, Scala, and Python. It also supports streaming data, so in this section, we are going to learn how to integrate Kinesis and Spark. An example architecture is shown in the following diagram:

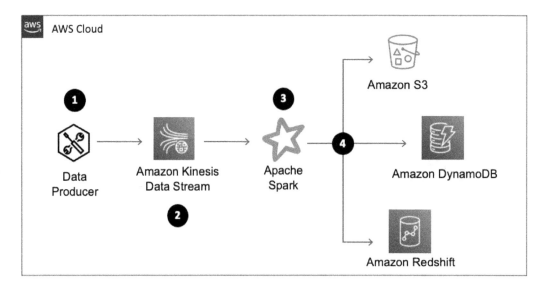

Figure 8.6 – Kinesis as a producer for Apache Spark

To create streaming data, as depicted in preceding diagram under (1), we will use KDG. If you haven't set up KDG already, please navigate to https://awslabs.github. io/amazon-kinesis-data-generator/web/producer.html and complete the setup portion.

> **KDG Setup**
>
> KDG requires you to set up Cognito to create authorized users so that it can put data into the Kinesis data stream in your AWS account.

Once we have configured KDG, we need to create a KDS. We will create a simple stream with one shard named sparky-stream. We can create a stream from the AWS console or using the AWS CLI, as shown here:

```
aws kinesis create-stream \
--stream-name sparky-stream \
--shard-count 1
```

To set up our Spark consumer application **(3)**, we will leverage an existing example that does a word count; we can get the word count code from this repository: `https://spark.apache.org/docs/2.3.0/streaming-kinesis-integration.html`. Once you've navigated to this link, go straight to the *Running the Example* section to set up a Spark consumer application. For this example, we downloaded Spark 2.4.7.

> **Spark Random Data Generator**
>
> Spark can also produce random data and put it into the Kinesis stream. We will not be using it in this example as we have already set up KDG.

Since the Spark application is doing a word count, we will instruct KDG to send Lorem Ipsum lines. Navigate to the KDG console. You will find a link to your personalized KDG console in the CloudFormation output section of the KDG stack.

In KDG, under **Region**, select your region. For the data stream, select **sparky-stream**, and then configure **Template 1** so that it matches the template shown in the following screenshot. Click the **Send Data** button to start sending data to **sparky-stream**:

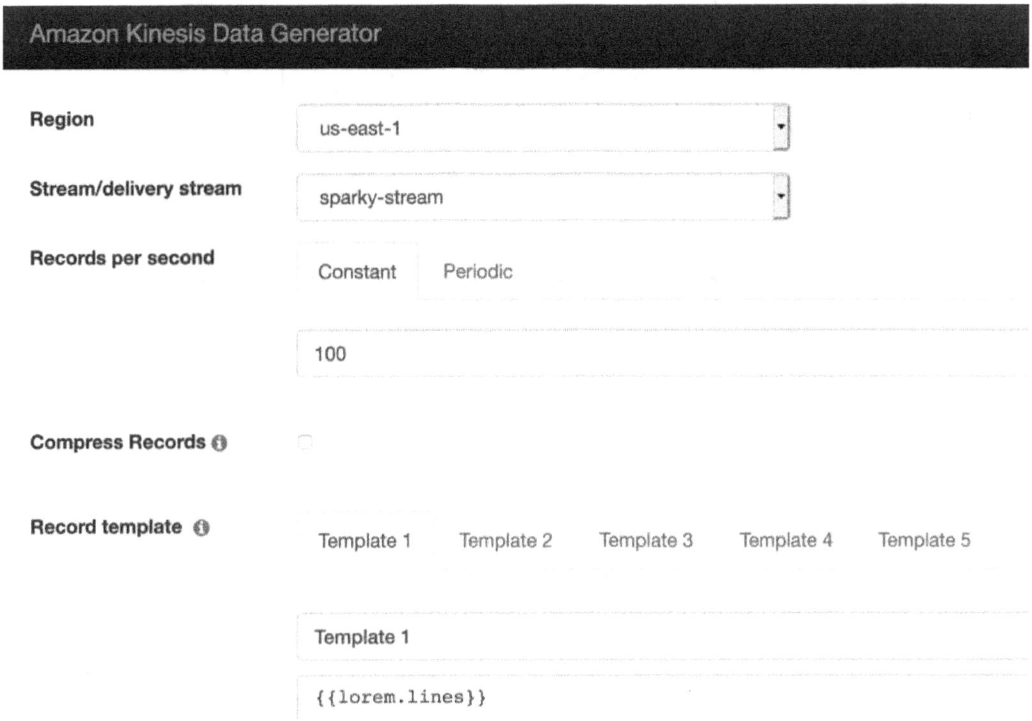

Figure 8.7 – KDG template setup details

Now that KDG is generating data and sending it to **sparky-stream**, we need to consume it. To run the Spark consumer application, navigate to the location where you downloaded Spark and execute the example application. Change the parameters so that they match your environment and configuration, as depicted in following code block:

```
bin/run-example --packages org.apache.spark:spark-streaming-
kinesis-asl_2.11:2.3.0 streaming.KinesisWordCountASL
SparkKinesisTest sparky-stream https://kinesis.us-east-1.
amazonaws.com
```

After our Spark word count application starts, you should see the Spark application outputting word counts, as shown in the following screenshot:

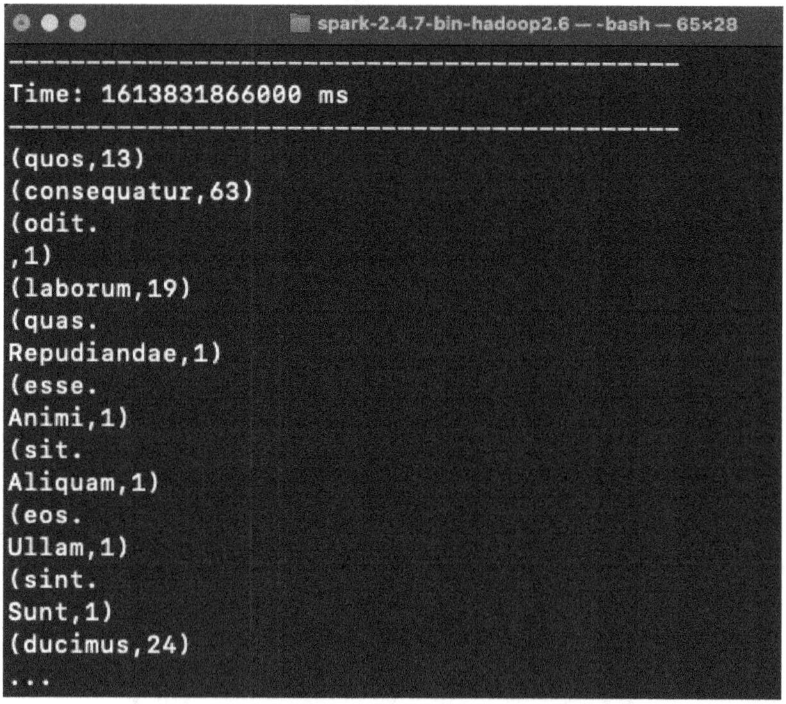

Figure 8.8 – Spark word count application with Kinesis data

In this section, we learned how to configure Spark as a data consumer for the Kinesis data stream. The example that we walked through was simple, but Spark also comes with a collection of algorithms that can help us process graph constructs and do basic machine learning.

Amazon services that consume data from Kinesis

We have spent a lot of time on streaming data, but the question remains: how do we aggregate all that data at scale? This is where **data lakes** come into the picture. The term data lake doesn't describe any single technology or AWS service; it is a pattern that's used to store and analyze massive volumes of mixed data. Using a data lake, we can keep all of our data, be it unstructured, semi-structured, or structured, in a single place for later use.

In this section, we will build a serverless data lake with multiple service integrations. The integration examples in this chapter will follow the persona of the SmartCity AWS technical vendor known as SwipeBike. SwipeBike is responsible for doing the integrations for modernizing SmartCity's bike-sharing capabilities.

Serverless data lake

Why a **serverless data lake**? It's pretty simple. As the SmartCity technical vendor SwipeBike, we have finite resources, and we prefer to focus on what matters to our business (improving our bike service through analytics). Managing servers takes us away from our core focus and diverts precious resources to server maintenance, which doesn't distinguish our SwipeBike from any other bike-sharing service.

Obtaining telemetry and analytics so that we know that our bikes may need a service before they break down, or that any station is running low on bikes, improves our customer's experience and, in turn, pays for our salaries. So, it's a simple choice; instead of managing servers, we will build a fully serverless data lake.

To build our SwipeBike serverless data lake, we will use the following services:

- Kinesis Firehose will stream source data and deposit it into a data lake.
- Amazon S3 will be the data storage repository for our data lake.
- AWS Glue will be used for extractions, transformation, and data processing.
- Amazon Athena will perform searches (SQL queries).

Let's take a look at our overall architecture for the serverless data lake:

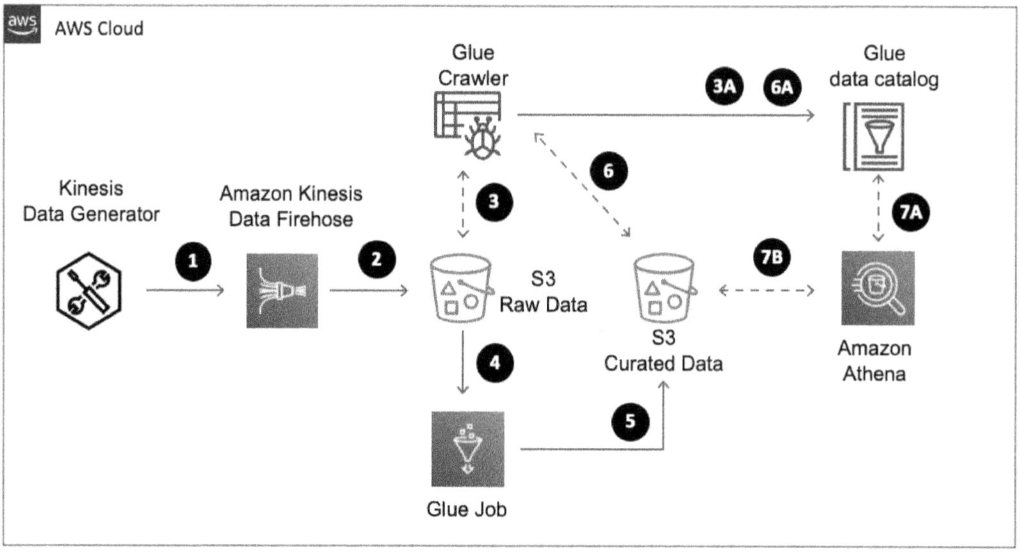

Figure 8.9 – Serverless data lake architecture for SwipeBike

Let's step through the serverless lake architecture and see what's going on here:

1. In this chapter, in the *Processing Kinesis data with Apache Spark* section, we used the KDG tool to send data to Kinesis. It's an easy way to produce some random data and send it over to Firehose, so we will use KDG again and simulate the data producer.

2. We will use **S3** for serverless data lake data storage. S3 is affordable storage for petabytes, and along with it, we get a high availability of 99.99% and a durability of 99.999999999%.

3. We will learn how to use AWS Glue, which is a serverless **Extract Transform Load (ETL)** service that allows us to discover, arrange, and integrate data for analytics. We will use Glue crawlers to create metadata that describes the structure of the data in S3 buckets:

    a) **Glue crawler** will inspect our raw data and create metadata in a **Glue Data Catalog**. A Data Catalog is a **Hive** compatible data store.

4. With Glue, we will also handle data transformations such as relationalizing data and converting it into more optimized formats such as Parquet.

5. The output of our Glue data transformations will be stored in S3 in a `curated` directory. This directory will contain an optimized data format and structure for improved query performance at a lower cost.

6. As with *step 3*, we will use Glue crawlers to extract the metadata from the files stored in the curated directory of the S3 bucket:

   a) Glue crawler will inspect curated data and create metadata in the Glue data catalog.

7. To create our reports and gain insight from our data, we will use Athena by creating SQL queries:

   a) Athena will look up the Glue data catalog to obtain information about the locations of files in S3, their format, and their structure.

   b) Using the information provided by the Glue data catalog (7a), Athena will execute the query.

Creating serverless data storage using S3

Let's start building our serverless data lake.

First, we will create an S3 bucket that will be used as the storage layer. S3 is a **Simple Storage Service** (**Amazon S3**) that focuses on simplicity and robustness. We are using S3 because it is a versatile yet cheap storage option that is protected by 99.999999999% (11 9s) of durability. S3's durability ensures the data is protected in the case of outages or failures.

With S3, there are no servers to manage, and we can scale up storage without having to purchase any additional hardware. We will start by creating an S3 bucket with the `<yourname>-dl-bucket` naming convention. Navigate to your command tool and execute S3's `create-bucket` API, as shown in the following code:

```
aws s3api create-bucket --bucket tarik-dl-bucket --region
us-east-1
```

If you are using an AWS region other than us-east-1, you will need to add `create-bucket` configuration, as shown in following code snippet:

```
aws s3api create-bucket --bucket tarik-dl-bucket2 --region
us-west-2 --create-bucket-configuration LocationConstraint=us-
west-2
```

After you execute `create-bucket`, you will get confirmation that the bucket was created. If you receive an error, it's likely because someone else has created a bucket with the same name. S3 bucket names are global, so there can't be two buckets with the same name. Try adding digits to your name until you get a unique name.

As a next step, we will create a Firehose delivery stream that the KDG data producer will use. Firehose will deliver the data into the S3 bucket's `rawdata` directory. We covered Firehose destination delivery in depth in *Chapter 5, Kinesis Firehose*, so we will skip those details here and jump right into creating a Firehose stream and configuring destination delivery to the S3 bucket RAW directory.

Landing data into S3 using Firehose

Before we can use Firehose to write data to the S3 bucket, we need to create an IAM role with permissions that give Firehose privilege to write, read, and list files in the `<yourname>-dl-bucket` S3 bucket.

Open up the AWS Console, navigate to IAM, and click **Create Role**. When you're prompted to select a trusted entity, select **AWS Service** and then choose **Kinesis** from the available services list. You will be prompted to **Select your use case**. Choose **Kinesis Firehose** and click the **Next: Permissions** button. Click the **Create policy** button, which will open up a new window or tab in your browser, then click the **JSON** tab and copy and paste the policy from the `chapter8/FHSwipeBikeDataLakepolicy.json` GitHub repository (`https://github.com/PacktPublishing/Streaming-Data-Solutions-with-Amazon-Kinesis/tree/main/chapter8/FHSwipeBikeDataLakePolicy.json`).

> **Creating your IAM policy**
>
> Make sure you use the appropriate bucket name and replace **AWS-REGION** and **AWS-ACCOUNT-NUMBER** with your values.

Click **Next: Tags**; you can leave tags blank for now and click the **Next: Review** button. Call your policy `FHSwipeBikeDataLakePolicy`, and then click the **Create policy** button. Go back to the browser window where you had started creating a role and select `FHSwipeBikeDataLakePolicy` (you may need to hit the refresh button for the newly created policy to show up). Click the **Next: Tags** button, then the **Next: Review** button, call the role `FHSwipeBikeDLRole`, and then click the **Create Role** button.

We are now ready to create our Firehose delivery stream. You will need to provide a `cli-input-json` file, which you can download from the Git repository. Download the `fhCreateFile.json` file, modify the parameters accordingly, and save the file locally. Open up your command-line tool and execute the following code:

```
aws firehose create-delivery-stream --delivery-stream-name
dl-delivery-stream --cli-input-json file://fhCreateFile.json
```

If everything worked correctly, you should receive a Firehose delivery stream ARN in the following format: `arn:aws:firehose:[REGION]:[AWS-ACCT-NUM]:deliverystream/dl-delivery-stream`.

AWS CLI trick

If you are like us and can't remember all the CLI options and parameters, `https://awsclibuilder.com/home/services/firehose` can help you.

For the next step, we are going to set up KDG. If you haven't already set up KDG, please navigate to `https://awslabs.github.io/amazon-kinesis-data-generator/web/producer.html` and complete the setup portion.

Using KDG to produce random data

Let's begin!

First, navigate to KDG; a link will be available in the CloudFormation console. Select an appropriate **Region**, then select `dl-delivery-stream` from the delivery stream dropdown. Scroll down to the template section and enter the template. You can download the template from GitHub under *the chapter8 folder*, `kdgTemplate.json`. Click the **Send Data** button to initiate data generation for KDG. After a minute or two or roughly around 10,000 records, click the **Stop Sending Data to Kinesis** button.

At this point, we should have data in our S3 bucket under the `rawdata` directory. Open the AWS console and navigate to `<yourname>-dl-bucket/rawdata`. You should have data files that have been produced by the KDG under the `rawdata` directory that are structured like so: `{rides}/{YEAR}/{MONTH NUMBER}/{DAY NUMBER}/{HOUR NUMBER}`.

While we are still in the S3 console, let's upload the `bikeStations.csv` file (available in the `chapter8` GitHub repository folder). This file contains detailed station information, such as the address of the bike station and its longitude and latitude. We will use this file's information in our Athena SQL queries to join it with information about our bike rentals (KDG-produced data) to produce more rich information for our customers.

Create a new `stations` directory in your S3 bucket; that is, `<yourname>-dl-bucket/rawdata`. Once the directory has been created, upload the `bikeStations.csv` file into the `stations` directory. Your S3 bucket hierarchy should, at this point, look like this:

```
<yourname>-dl-bucket
    rawdata
        rides
        stations
```

We are now ready to inspect our raw data using Glue so that we can catalog it for usage by Athena. Using Glue crawlers, we will go through our bucket's `rawdata` directory and create corresponding metadata in the Glue data catalog.

> **AWS Lake Formation**
>
> You may need to turn off Lake Formation in **Lake Formation Console**, under the **Settings** section. You may need to manage the IAM permissions yourself beyond the scope of this chapter: `https://docs.aws.amazon.com/lake-formation/latest/dg/change-settings.html`.

Using Glue for ETL

Glue crawlers are like forensic inspectors that will look at the data structures in our `rides` and `stations` directories, and then create information about the data structure of those files as if it's a database table. Glue crawlers will enable us to query the data using Athena and deal with changes and additions to schema changes in our raw files. Let's set up a Glue crawler.

In the AWS console, navigate to Glue, click on the **Crawlers** link, and click the **Add crawler** button. Enter the following values when prompted:

1. In the **Crawler name** field, enter `rawdata-crawler`, then click **Next**.

2. Leave the defaults as **Data Stores** and **Crawl all folders** and click **Next**.

3. Select **S3** as the data store, select `<yourname>-dl-bucket/rawdata` as the include path, and then click **Next**.

4. Select **No** for **Add another data store** and click **Next**.

5. Select **Create an IAM role** and give it a name; ours is `AWSGlueServiceRole-GlueSwipeBikeRaw`. Click **Next**.

6. For **Frequency**, select **Run on Demand** and click **Next**.

7. Click **Add Database**; for the database name, enter `swipebike`, click **Create**, and then click **Next**.

8. Finally, click the **Finish** button.

Once `rawdata-crawler` has been created, click the checkbox next to it and click the **Run crawler** button. It will take about 1 to 2 minutes for the crawler to finish.

Let's see what the crawler created. In the Glue console, click on the **Databases** link on the left-hand side menu. Then, click on the `swipebike` database. If the database isn't showing, try hitting the refresh icon in the Glue console. Click on the `swipebike` database and then click on **Tables** in the `swipebike` link; you should see two tables, as shown in the following screenshot:

Figure 8.10 – Glue data catalog for Swipebike

The Glue crawler created an inventory of data in our datastore (S3 bucket). The crawler examined the schema of the data files in our S3 bucket and, using a classifier, inferred the structure of that data; that is, metadata. The crawler then wrote the metadata into the Glue data catalog (the `swipebike` database and its corresponding tables).

We can now try and query the `swipebike` database using Athena. Navigate to the Athena console and select `swipebike` from the database dropdown.

> **Athena setup**
>
> If you are opening up Athena for the first time, you will have to go through the initial setup to configure the S3 bucket so that Athena can output query results: `https://docs.aws.amazon.com/athena/latest/ug/getting-started.html`.

Query data with Athena

We will begin by opening the **New query** tab in Athena and entering the query shown in the following screenshot (you can copy the query from `chapter8/sql/ stationIncome.sql`):

Figure 8.11 – An Athena query to summarize income by station using raw data

Once the query completes, you should be able to see the result. Our query took **1.5 seconds**, and it scanned **5.17 MB** of data. This isn't bad so far; we can query `rawdata` and get results, so why bother with curating data any further? There are several reasons, but the primary ones are as follows:

- We want to expose data to business users so that they can get results swiftly without having a granular understanding of the underlying raw data and its relationships. Queries that use `rawdata` could get gnarly!

- If you expand the `rides` table in Athena, you will notice that the `bikedetail` field is defined as `struct<>`. It's not easily consumed, so we want to transform it into a more functional structure. We are going to use Glue jobs to do this.

- **Security**: We may not want everyone to *swim* all over our data lake, so exposing a subset of data is preferred.

- **Cost**: For the query to find data that matches our search, it has to traverse (scan) the data storage in S3. We scanned 5.17 MBs, but imagine if we had a data lake fully loaded with petabytes of data. This approach can get expensive if we are scanning massive amounts of data (kind of like a cartesian product query in a relational database).

Optimizing a serverless data lake

To curate our data further, we will use Glue jobs. Glue jobs come pre-packaged with several ETL routines, which we can use with minimal configuration. We are going to do two things to produce a curated dataset:

- Create a `station-income` dataset that only contains data users need in Parquet optimized format. Parquet format and removing unused columns should lead to scanning less data; hence, it should be less expensive.

- Relationalize the `bikedetail` field so that values from `struct<>` become their own dataset (table) and are easier to query.

> **Glue – Relationalize**
>
> Athena can relationalize data using **CROSS JOIN UNNEST**, but at some point, that operation will become costly, and relationalizing as part of your ETL pipeline is better: `https://docs.aws.amazon.com/glue/latest/dg/aws-glue-programming-python-samples-legislators.html`.

Curating data in the data lake using Glue jobs

Navigate to the S3 console and create a new directory called `curated` in the `<yourname>-dl-bucket` S3 bucket.

Before we create a Glue job, we will need to modify the IAM role we created for the crawlers (`AWSGlueServiceRole-GlueSwipeBikeRaw`) so that it also has the privilege to write to and delete from S3.

Navigate to IAM, find the relevant role under the **Policies** tab, and click to edit the policy with the same name as the `AWSGlueServiceRole-GlueSwipeBikeRaw` role. We need to add a `curated` bucket to the resources list, as shown in the following code:

```
{
    "Version": "2012-10-17",
    "Statement": [
```

```
        {
            "Effect": "Allow",
            "Action": [
                "s3:GetObject",
                "s3:PutObject",
                "s3:Delete*"
            ],
            "Resource": [
                "arn:aws:s3:::tarik-dl-bucket/rawdata*",
                "arn:aws:s3:::tarik-dl-bucket/curated*"
            ]
        }
    ]
}
```

Navigate back to the Glue console and click the **Jobs** link on the left-hand side. We will create a Glue job script as a template, and then we will edit that script to achieve the two goals we set out. Click the **Add Job** button and call it `SwipeBikeCurateETL`. Select the IAM role from the list of dropdown roles (`AWSGlueServiceRole-GlueSwipeBikeRaw`). We are using the same IAM role that we created while we were setting up the `rawdata-crawler` Glue crawler. Leave the other settings as their defaults and click the **Next** button.

Select the `rides` table as the data source and click the **Next** button. For **transform type**, leave the default as **Change schema** and click the **Next** button. Select **Create tables** in your data target, select **S3** as the data store, format it as **Parquet**, set the target path to `s3://<yourname>-dl-bucket/curated`, and click the **Next** button. Leave the defaults for **Output Schema Definition** as-is and click the **Save job and edit script** button.

From GitHub, download the `chapter8/glue/curationScript.py` Glue script. Replace the `{YOUR-S3-BUCKET}` occurrences with your actual bucket name. This is the same bucket name we have been using thus far. Save the Glue script and run the job. Depending on how much data you created using KDG, the job may take a minute or two to run. Let's walk through some of the pertinent code in the Glue job script.

On line 25, we call Glue's built-in relationalize transformation:

```
25      relationalized = Relationalize.apply(
        frame = ds_rides,
        staging_path = args["TempDir"],
```

```
       name = "rides",
       transformation_ctx = "relationalized")
```

We then proceed to write the relationalized data to the S3 bucket on line 28. Glue will produce two distinct structures: `"rides"` and `"bikeDetail.bikeAttributes"`. If you look into your S3 bucket under the curated directory, you should see these two directories. We will learn how to use these later in this section, when we create Athena queries:

```
28     relationalize_datasink =
           glueContext.write_dynamic_frame.from_options(
               frame = relationalized,
               connection_type = "s3",
               connection_options = {
                 "path": "s3://{S3-PATH}/curated/rides-relat.."},
               format = "json",
               transformation_ctx = "relationalize_datasink"
       )
```

We then proceed to create a summarized version of the income by each station. We loaded the station data into `ds_station_min` on line 31. Then, on line 34, we dropped the columns that we didn't need in the summarized dataset:

```
34     ds_station_min =
           ds_stations.drop_fields(
               ['latitude','longitude']
           ).rename_field(
               'stationid', 'station-st-id'
           )
```

On line 37, we did something similar with the `ds_rides_min` DataFrame. We then joined the two DataFrames on line 43:

```
43     ds_joined = Join.apply(
           ds_station_min, ds_rides_min,
           'station-st-id', 'ride-st-id'
       )
```

Then, on line 47, we exported the income by station data into the `s3://{YOUR-S3-BUCKET}/curated/stationincome` S3 bucket.

Before we can start using data stored under the curated directory, we need to crawl it. Navigate to the Glue console and create a new crawler, as we did for rawdata.

We named our crawler CuratedSwipeBike and set it up to crawl data under the curated directory. The crawler's path is s3://{your-bucket-name}/curated. You can use the same IAM role we have been using thus far: AWSGlueServiceRole-GlueSwipeBikeRaw. You can create a new database for a curated crawler or use the existing database and prefix the table names with c_. We used the existing swipebike database, and we used the c_ prefix for curated tables.

Once you have finished creating the crawler, run it. Once the crawler finishes inspecting the data in the curated directory, you should have three newly created tables in the Glue data catalog (the swipebike database). Let's navigate to the Athena console and see if we have achieved the two desired goals by curating the data.

We will start by examining the station income summary table (ours is named c_stationincome). In Athena, create and run the query, as depicted in the following screenshot (you can get the SQL code from https://github.com/PacktPublishing/Streaming-Data-Solutions-with-Amazon-Kinesis/tree/main/chapter8/sql/stationIncomeCurated.sql):

Figure 8.12 – An Athena query to summarize income by the station using curated data

With the `curated` dataset, the query time dropped to **0.56 seconds**, and the amount of data that was scanned was only **44.15 KB**. When we ran the query that relied on `rawdata`, it took 1.5 seconds for the query to finish, and 5.17 MB of data was scanned. Goal one achieved! It's faster, cheaper, and the query is simpler to create as we are going only after one table.

Now, let's see what happened with the data that was relationalized. With `rawdata`, we had a single table, `rides`, that contained a nested structure for bike details. Now that our Glue job has rationalized the data, we have two tables; in our case, they are `c_rides` and `c_rides_bikedetail_bikeattributes`.

As we examine `c_rides_bikedetail_bikeattributes`, we can see that Glue has kept referential integrity between the two tables. A newly created column named `id` corresponds to the `bikedetail.bikeattributes` column in the `c_rides` table. This looks a lot like a relational database at this point.

Let's put this to the test and see if it was done correctly. Open up any raw files under `rawdata/rides` in S3 (hint: you can use S3 Select to peek into files) and pick one of the records. We selected the following record:

```
{
    "stationId": 130,
    "tripDuration": 131,
    "price": 67,
    "bikeDetail": {
        "bikeNum": "a33492a7-d59f-4484-bb37-7431252d8099",
        "bikeAttributes": [
            {
                "attribName": "color",
                "attribValue": "fuchsia"
            },
            {
                "attribName": "manufacturer",
                "attribValue": "JAMIS"
            },
            {
                "attribName": "bikeType",
                "attribValue": "SIMPLE"
            }
        ]
    }
}
```

Figure 8.13 – Raw record to validate the relationalize function

Let's create an Athena query that will join the two relationalized tables and search for the same record and see if referential integrity is still intact. Navigate to Athena and create a query, as shown in the following screenshot (since the data was randomly generated, we had to narrow down the record using few attributes). You can find the query at `https://github.com/PacktPublishing/Streaming-Data-Solutions-with-Amazon-Kinesis/tree/main/chapter8/sql/relationilizedQuery.sql`:

Figure 8.14 – Athena query using relationalized data

Glue didn't disappoint when it came to referential integrity. We joined the two tables using `c_rides.bikedetail.bikeattribute` and `c_rides_bikedetail_bikeattributes.id`. We validated the values from `rawdata` files that match the relationalized data (split files).

In this section, we learned how to use many services to build a serverless data lake. We used Kinesis Firehose to ingest the data into S3 buckets. From there, we created a data pipeline that ingests raw data. We learned how to use Glue to index the data with crawlers and then transformed and curated the data, which allows our business users to consume it in a performant and frugal manner. Lastly, we used Athena to query the data and gain insights.

In the next section, we are going to learn how to use other AWS services, along with Kinesis, to transform and enhance data.

Amazon services that transform Kinesis data

In this section, we are going to learn about how to use EventBridge to add additional capabilities that aren't present in Kinesis. We will use EventBridge to help us add rule-based routing to our SwipeBike solution.

Routing events with EventBridge

One of the coolest things about AWS services is that they are building blocks. We like to think of AWS services as a set of microservices that enable us to build rapidly, or prototype, working applications. The downside is that with such a large number of services at our disposal, there is an overlap between those services, and often, analysis-paralysis can set in when we have to select a service to use.

> **Two-way door**
>
> The most significant advantage of the cloud is that it doesn't punish us for making a mistake when selecting a service; it's pretty forgiving. Two-way door decisions imply that if we pick the wrong door, we can quickly walk back and go through another door available to us. On the other hand, one-way door decisions are hard to reverse as we can't go back, so a considerable amount of time has to be allocated to deciding when to select the door. An example of a one-way door would be buying brand new servers; there's not much we can do after that. As you adopt the cloud, we encourage you to treat service selection as a two-way door. You are better off picking a service quickly and experiment with your use case, instead of endlessly discussing which service is better!

If you are familiar with **Enterprise Service Bus** (**ESB**) concepts, skip to the next paragraph. Wikipedia describes ESB as follows: "*An enterprise service bus (ESB) implements a communication system between mutually interacting software applications in a service-oriented architecture (SOA).*"

We can think of the postal office (mail service) being an ESB. Each of us can send or receive a postcard, so we are both message producers and message consumers. As consumers or producers, we don't need to know anything about the internals of mail sorting and routing. All we need to do is use a **postal API**, which lets us basically *specify a receiving address* and deposit our letter (message) in the mailbox. From that point on, the postal service takes over and routes and delivers our letter to the recipient. If we want to obtain confirmation that the recipient received our message, that's also possible. We would provide our address and when our letter is delivered, the postal service will send us back delivery confirmation.

Let's see how we can implement some of the ESB principles using Kinesis and EventBridge. Before we get into the solution, let's learn what EventBridge is.

EventBridge is a serverless event bus that allows us to connect applications/services, yet keep them decoupled from each other (two-way door, anybody?). Using EventBridge, we can set up routing rules so that events can be sent to the appropriate service/application to be processed. Why would we want to use Kinesis at all with EventBridge when Kinesis itself can send events? Because Kinesis can't route events.

For example, in our SmartCity bike fleet example, we were ingesting data from each station (our producer simulates 40 bike stations). What if we wanted to send data to those stations? Let's assume the bike docking station is malfunctioning and we need to send it an *unlock code*. If we just drop it into the Kinesis stream, then each station would have to filter its events and discard events intended for other stations; this sounds like a lot of work!

In short, when we use EventBridge with Kinesis, we can route messages/events based on a rule or set of rules. Our architecture looks as follows:

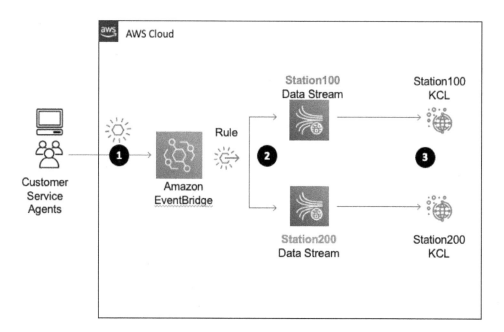

Figure 8.15 – Rule-based architecture with EventBridge and Kinesis

So, let's see how we can do this. Navigate to the AWS console and create two Kinesis data streams, `station100stream` and `station200stream`. These two streams will receive events from EventBridge for their corresponding stations.

The event that we will send to EventBridge has the following structure:

```
[
    {
        "Source": "com.smartbike.maintenance",
        "Detail": "{\"stationId\":\"200\"}",
        "Resources": [
            "unlock-key-34534"
        ],
        "DetailType": "unlockDockingStation",
        "EventBusName": "bike-ride-unlock"
    }
]
```

Navigate to the EventBridge console. Under **Events,** click on **Event busses,** then click the **Create event bus** button. When prompted for the name, enter `bike-ride-unlock`, leave **Resource-based policy** empty, and click the **Create** button. Your console should display a newly created event bus, as shown in the following screenshot:

Figure 8.16 – Custom EventBridge event bus

To route maintenance events to the appropriate bike station Kinesis data stream, we will set up two event rules: `station 100` and `station 200`. Navigate to **Rules** and click the **Create rule** button. Name your event `station100Rule`. Under **Event matching pattern**, select **Custom Pattern**. Under **Event pattern**, enter the pattern shown in the following code:

```
{
    "source":       [ "com.smartbike.maintenance" ],
    "detail-type": [ "unlockDockingStation" ],
    "detail":       { "stationId": [ "100" ] }
}
```

Under **Select event bus**, click on **Custom** or **Partner** event bus, and from the dropdown, select the bike-ride-unlock event bus. Under **Select targets** in the first dropdown, select your first Kinesis stream; that is, station100stream. EventBridge will need IAM privileges to put records into Kinesis and will create the specific role; please leave the defaults as-is. Click the **Create** button.

Repeat rule creation for station200Rule and select station200stream as the corresponding stream. Make sure that your station200Rule for stationId has a value of 200 and not 100.

Once we have created both rules, we should see both rules as **Enabled**, as shown in the following screenshot:

Event bus
Select or enter event bus name

bike-ride-unlock

Rules (2)

Q

	Name	Status
○	station100Rule	⊘ Enabled
○	station200Rule	⊘ Enabled

Figure 8.17 – EventBridge event bus rules summary

Let's see if our rules work correctly. Using the AWS CLI, we will send a few events to the bike-ride-unlock event bus and then fetch the records from two Kinesis data streams.

We will start by creating two files. You can find the sample content under chapter8/eventbridge/sampleEvent.json:

- For the event100.json file, we will set stationId to 100.
- For the event200.json file, will set stationId to 200.

> **The AWS CLI isn't where we set the bus name**
>
> If you haven't named your bus event bike-ride-unlock, then you will have to change the value of EventBusName in both files.

Open your command prompt and navigate to the directory where you saved the two JSON files. Then, execute `put-event` (the following code is for Mac or Unix) for both files. This will put two events into the `bike-ride-unlock` EventBridge bus. EventBridge will respond with an `EventId` for each successful entry as we execute the commands. We are inputting single events, so we should get zero for `FailedEntryCount` and a single `EventID`:

```
aws events put-events --entries file://{filename}.json
```

Once we have input the events into EventBridge, they should be routed to the appropriate Kinesis data stream. The following screenshot shows an example of fetching records from `station100stream`:

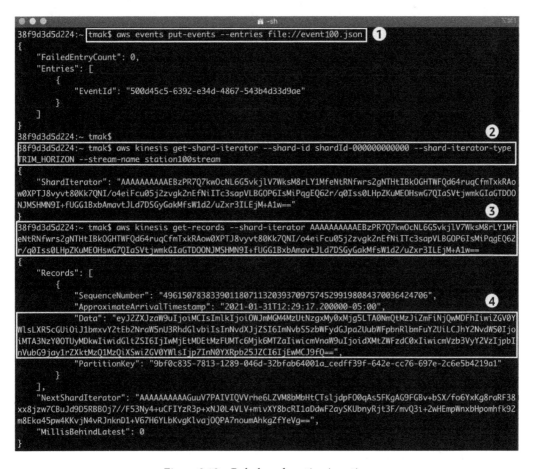

Figure 8.18 – Rule-based routing in action

Once you have gathered data from the Kinesis stream, shown under **(4)** in the previous screenshot, you can go to the online base64 decoder (`https://www.base64decode.org/`) and make sure your data in each of the streams has been routed correctly. You can find the appropriate Kinesis CLI commands here: `https://docs.aws.amazon.com/streams/latest/dev/fundamental-stream.html#get-records`.

In this section, we implemented simple routing using Amazon EventBridge and Kinesis. The key takeaway is that AWS services are like *LEGO* and that we were able to create this solution in approximately 30 minutes. Experiment and fail often!

Third-party integrations with Kinesis

In this section, we are going to learn how to integrate Kinesis with third-party software provider Splunk. Although we are using Splunk to show how we can work around some of the integration intricacies, this approach is applicable to other third-party integrations.

Firehose delivery is possible for generic HTTP endpoints. This enables us to use Firehose, a fully managed service, to send data to HTTP endpoints, and it opens doors for other integration points, including our own applications.

Splunk

If you are not familiar with Splunk, you should still read this section as we will cover some of the nuances of Lambda processing that are applicable, regardless of whether the delivery endpoint is for Splunk or not. We covered Firehose and Splunk integration in depth in *Chapter 5, Kinesis Firehose*, in the *Amazon Kinesis Data Firehose Destinations/Splunk destination* section.

Splunk's website defines the software as follows: "*Splunk makes it simple to collect, analyze, and act upon the untapped value of the big data generated by your technology infrastructure, security systems, and business applications – giving you the insights to drive operational performance and business results.*"

A simplified version would be stating that Splunk is how we make sense of data in logs. While building our SmartCity cloud infrastructure, we have primarily focused on Kinesis services and how to extract the data around our bicycle fleet. But we haven't paid any attention to our overall cloud infrastructure, which includes things such as the following:

- How we analyze if someone is trying to get into our VPC and how to block those IP addresses (flow logs)

- The performance of our EC2 instances or AWS Lambdas (CloudWatch logs)

In this section, we will discuss how to ingest CloudWatch Logs into Kinesis Firehose and deliver those logs to Splunk. Our overall architecture is depicted in the following diagram:

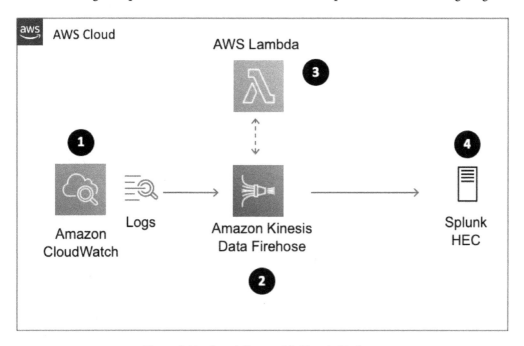

Figure 8.19 – Log delivery with Kinesis Firehose

We use CloudWatch subscriptions **(1)** to send CloudWatch Logs events to the Firehose delivery stream **(2)**. To optimize throughput, CloudWatch will encode the logs to base64 and compressed them into GZIP format. Splunk HEC **(4)** can't accept compressed format, so we will use AWS Lambda **(3)** to decompress the logs before sending them to Splunk HEC.

> **AWS Lambda quota**
>
> Lambda's request invocation has a limit of 6 MB for synchronous and 256 KB asynchronous. This defines how much data can be passed back by AWS Lambda: `https://docts.amazonaws.cn/en_us/lambda/latest/dg/lambda-invocation.html`.

What will inevitably happen is that the amount of compressed data in the Firehose buffer, when uncompressed by Lambda, will exceed the 6 MB quota allowed for invocation. Commonly, GZIP compression is at a 1:9 ratio (1 MB compressed results in 9 MB uncompressed data). At this point, an exception will be thrown by Lambda. Lambda's request invocation quota is not something that we can call AWS to extend for us, so we need an alternative solution. Let's see how we can do that.

AWS offers a **Serverless Application Template** called `kinesis-firehose-cloudwatch-logs-processor` that we can use to work around this issue. We are only going to examine the pertinent code blocks of the solution. You can find the source code for the full solution here: `https://github.com/tmakota/amazon-kinesis-firehose-cloudwatch-logs-processor/blob/master/index.js`.

Open the GitHub link to the code, and let's step through it. The serverless function will be invoked by Firehose and sent a batch of compressed data. In *Chapter 5, Kinesis Firehose*, we discussed how Firehose sends data, so we are assuming you have familiarized yourself with it. The following diagram describes what happens when Kinesis sends compressed data to AWS Lambda, how that data is chunked, and how it is sent back to Kinesis to avoid the 6 MB quota imposed by AWS Lambda:

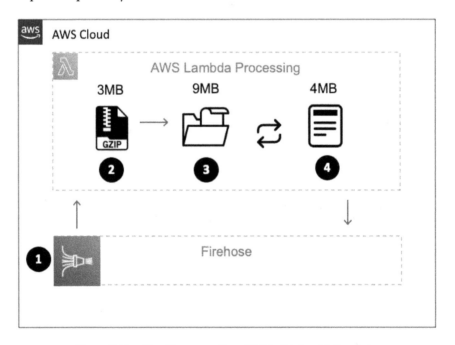

Figure 8.20 – Handling more than 6 MB of data with Lambda

Invocation of the serverless function by Firehose (**2**) starts on line `104` with `exports.handler = (event, context, callback)`. On line `107`, the batch of data that Firehose sent will be decompressed (**3**) with `decompressed = zlib.gunzipSync(buffer)`. If the amount of compressed data being sent by Firehose was, let's say, 3 MB and the compression ratio is 1:3, then the resulting decompressed data would be 9 MB, which is well above Lambda's request quota of 6 MB.

Lines `140` through `148` take decompressed data and compose `recordsToReingest`, which is roughly 4 MBs in size (**4**). Line `153` will invoke the function to send uncompressed data back to Firehose using `putRecords(streamName, recordsToReingest, firehose, resolve, reject, 0, 20)`. You can set up the `maxAttampts` parameter, which is hardcoded as `20`, to be a parameter to the Lambda function.

In turn, the `putRecords` function will send the decompressed data to Firehose by invoking `client.putRecordBatch()` on line `70`. Lines `91` through `100` will handle any retries needed while incrementing `maxAttempts`; this is the code on line `94`; that is, `putRecords(streamName, failed, client, resolve, reject, attemptsMade + 1, maxAttempts)`.

In this section, we learned about ingesting large amounts of compressed data, how to decompress that data using AWS Lambda, and how to work around the AWS Lambda 6 MB request limit using data chunking.

Summary

In this chapter, we learned about the different ways that Kinesis services can work with other AWS services and non-AWS services. We built a few integrations ourselves, which exemplified how easy it is to compose solutions using various services that work with Kinesis.

In addition to what we showed you in this chapter, there are several different ways that Kinesis services can be used. With additional features being added by AWS on an almost daily basis, the only limitation is our creativity. We discussed a two-way door approach for you to adopt as you advance through your AWS cloud journey. AWS services are like LEGO blocks that we can quickly put together, and if we make a mistake, we can quickly take them apart to try again. Embrace two-way doors over analysis paralysis.

We are looking forward to you creating new solutions and letting us know about the unique ways you solved your business problems using Kinesis and AWS Cloud.

Further reading

We covered many different services in this chapter and explained how to integrate them with Kinesis. Covering these topics in-depth would require another book. Please take a look at the following links for further references:

- How to Stream Data from Amazon DynamoDB to Amazon Aurora using AWS Lambda and Amazon Kinesis Firehose:

  ```
  https://aws.amazon.com/blogs/database/how-to-stream-data-
  from-amazon-dynamodb-to-amazon-aurora-using-aws-lambda-
  and-amazon-kinesis-firehose/
  ```

- Top 10 performance tuning tips for Amazon Athena:

  ```
  https://aws.amazon.com/blogs/big-data/top-10-performance-
  tuning-tips-for-amazon-athena/
  ```

- Build a data lake foundation with AWS Glue and Amazon S3:

  ```
  https://aws.amazon.com/blogs/big-data/build-a-data-lake-
  foundation-with-aws-glue-and-amazon-s3/
  ```

Packt.com

Subscribe to our online digital library for full access to over 7,000 books and videos, as well as industry leading tools to help you plan your personal development and advance your career. For more information, please visit our website.

Why subscribe?

- Spend less time learning and more time coding with practical eBooks and Videos from over 4,000 industry professionals
- Improve your learning with Skill Plans built especially for you
- Get a free eBook or video every month
- Fully searchable for easy access to vital information
- Copy and paste, print, and bookmark content

Did you know that Packt offers eBook versions of every book published, with PDF and ePub files available? You can upgrade to the eBook version at packt.com and as a print book customer, you are entitled to a discount on the eBook copy. Get in touch with us at customercare@packtpub.com for more details.

At www.packt.com, you can also read a collection of free technical articles, sign up for a range of free newsletters, and receive exclusive discounts and offers on Packt books and eBooks.

Other Books You May Enjoy

If you enjoyed this book, you may be interested in these other books by Packt:

Mastering Machine Learning on AWS

Dr. Saket S.R. Mengle, Maximo Gurmendez

ISBN: 978-1-78934-979-5

- Manage AI workflows by using AWS cloud to deploy services that feed smart data products
- Use SageMaker services to create recommendation models
- Scale model training and deployment using Apache Spark on EMR
- Understand how to cluster big data through EMR and seamlessly integrate it with SageMaker

- Build deep learning models on AWS using TensorFlow and deploy them as services
- Enhance your apps by combining Apache Spark and Amazon SageMaker

Learn Amazon SageMaker

Julien Simon

ISBN: 978-1-80020-891-9

- Create and automate end-to-end machine learning workflows on Amazon Web Services (AWS)
- Become well-versed with data annotation and preparation techniques
- Use AutoML features to build and train machine learning models with AutoPilot
- Create models using built-in algorithms and frameworks and your own code
- Train computer vision and NLP models using real-world examples
- Cover training techniques for scaling, model optimization, model debugging, and cost optimization
- Automate deployment tasks in a variety of configurations using SDK and several automation tools

Packt is searching for authors like you

If you're interested in becoming an author for Packt, please visit `authors.packtpub.com` and apply today. We have worked with thousands of developers and tech professionals, just like you, to help them share their insight with the global tech community. You can make a general application, apply for a specific hot topic that we are recruiting an author for, or submit your own idea.

Leave a review - let other readers know what you think

Please share your thoughts on this book with others by leaving a review on the site that you bought it from. If you purchased the book from Amazon, please leave us an honest review on this book's Amazon page. This is vital so that other potential readers can see and use your unbiased opinion to make purchasing decisions, we can understand what our customers think about our products, and our authors can see your feedback on the title that they have worked with Packt to create. It will only take a few minutes of your time, but is valuable to other potential customers, our authors, and Packt. Thank you!

Index